THE GREAT HEIST

Democracy's Corrupt Underbelly

BILL MASKE

authorHOUSE®

AuthorHouse™
1663 Liberty Drive
Bloomington, IN 47403
www.authorhouse.com
Phone: 833-262-8899

Published by AuthorHouse 09/21/2023

ISBN: 979-8-8230-1461-8 (sc)
ISBN: 979-8-8230-1460-1 (e)

Library of Congress Control Number: 2023917456

Print information available on the last page.

For all people who seek the truth and pray for
justice in a world where money is God.

For all people who seek the truth and [illegible]

[illegible] justice in a world without [illegible] God.

CONTENTS

PRELUDE

Before the turn of the Twentieth Century, the United States stood poised to ascend to the throne of world economic dominance. The reconstruction period following the Civil War consolidated a nation rich in resources, ingenuity, and opportunity. It also created a governmental and leadership environment of weakness and culpability.

If the weak-kneed leadership of the United States before 1860 gave way to the Civil War, the assassination of Abraham Lincoln, and the weak-kneed administration following the war, gave way to the predatory nature of unbridled capitalism. Who can name the presidents between Lincoln and Theodore Roosevelt? The feeble and ineffective leadership of Andrew Johnson, U.S. Grant, Rutherford B. Hayes, James Garfield, Chester Arthur, Grover Cleveland, Benjamin Harrison, and William McKinley, helped lay the foundation upon which the aristocracy of the United States was built.

A brief review of history reveals that Andrew Johnson, a man of questionable qualifications and disposition, ascended to the presidency upon the assassination of Abraham Lincoln. Johnson faced impeachment charges in 1868 and escaped the impeachment axe by one vote. Grant, a hero of the Civil War possessed leadership timber and served two full terms. However, Grant's administration was involved in a great deal of corruption. In a disputed election, Rutherford B. Hayes ascended to the presidency as a matter of deal-making and power politics. As president, he called the US Army out against striking railroad workers. James Garfield was shot four months into his presidency and died two months later. Chester Arthur, the former collector for the Port of New York, never held an elected office before becoming Garfield's vice president. As the Port of New York collector, Arthur knew and understood the corrupt spoils system all too well. Grover Cleveland, elected to two non-consecutive terms, was a known liar, cheat, and suspected rapist. Benjamin Harrison served as a one-term president between Cleveland's terms. Harrison's weak attempts at reform accomplished little. William McKinley, elected to a second term, was assassinated which gave rise to Theodore Roosevelt in 1901.

Weak leadership in the White House and Congress made it possible for men of greed to lay claim to the public domain. The free enterprise system provided a forum from which men of capital engaged in predatory warfare to establish power and dominance over the entire social fabric of the United States. At the dawn of the twentieth century, the conditions were perfect for launching capitalistic adventurism around the globe. Individual men such as Vanderbilt, Carnegie, Rockefeller, Morgan, and others (The Robber Barons) were on the threshold just awaiting the right time to emerge on the world stage as a new kind of international royalty.

While money has always been a part of the political process in the anointing of the American King, never in the past had it been so prevalent as in the King-making process of 1900. As the Democratic challenger to the almighty McKinley, William Jennings Bryan posed serious concerns for rabid capitalists. As a populist, Bryan cried out for economic justice.

Propagating a fear that only comes with greed as deep as the fiery pits of hell, the bastard capitalists wield their swords of competition for McKinley. Meeting in secret, these despots of industry and Wall Street conspired to ensure their man, a man with the backbone of a worm would remain in the palm of their hand and on the throne of the nation.

In mid-1897, Cornelius Vanderbilt II sent a cable to Rockefeller, Morgan, and Carnegie, the three other members of the Rich Bastards Club. Even though his sins of evil consumption had brought on a stroke in 1896, Vandy (as Cornelius Vanderbilt II was known) fights to protect the family's fortune.

Chapter 1

THE BEGINNING

In a telegram; "GENTLEMEN WE ARE CONFRONTED WITH URGENT BUSINESS. REQUIRES THE UTMOST SECRECY. MEET ME IN MY NEW YORK CITY OFFICE WEDNESDAY OF NEXT." VANDY.

Cornelius Vanderbilt II Is the favorite grandson of Cornelius (Commodore) Vanderbilt. As a result, he inherits wealth beyond all imagination along with control of the New York Central and other railroad lines. He maintains an office at his grandfather's mansion on 5th Avenue in New York City.

Cornelius Vanderbilt II is one of the first of the Robber Barons who doesn't earn his fortune but rather inherits it as a matter of being a fortunate son. The fact he inherits his fortune causes Vanderbilt II to be a bit insecure about his wealth. For this reason, he needs to surround himself with powerful and capable companions.

Entering the 5th Avenue mansion takes away the breath of even the nation's richest men. The Commodore surrounds himself in opulent splendor to satisfy his divinity complex, and to create a true home-field advantage. En route to the library, the two captains of industry and the weasel of Wall Street passed through the picture gallery containing great paintings from around the world. Here, the Commodore has assured himself of his greatness in the company of artistic creations and paintings of heavenly splendor.

Entering the library, the three visitors are greeted by Vanderbilt II as he stands braced against the marble fireplace with its mantle supported by two Greek Women above which sits Persephone, the Greek Goddess of Hades.

"Gentlemen, as you are aware, we all barely escaped the disaster which would have fallen upon this nation in the last election should the Nincompoop of Nebraska gotten hold of the scepter of power," Vanderbilt begins.

Lighting his cigar, Rockefeller declares Bryan's death, "The electorate crucified him on his cross of gold. There shall be no resurrection!"

John D. Rockefeller, Sr. is indeed a self-made millionaire. He was truly in the right place at the right time and made the right decisions. It is difficult to call Rockefeller a visionary, but something led him to see the future of oil. His Standard Oil is the first great business trust in the United States. However, as much as Rockefeller may have seen the future of oil, he will never know the long-range consequences of fossil fuels.

Not to be out bellowed, Morgan demands, "What does that have to do with this meeting? Why is it I have been called away from important business? I do not have time for some social gathering to listen to tirades that will take us nowhere."

J.P. Morgan dominates corporate finance on Wall Street as a banker and financier. Morgan controls immense capital, making it possible for other men to rise to prominence. He controls the flux that welds great industrial corporations and multinational corporations together. His cause and the cause of industrial giants are the same. Morgan understands the importance of governance to the success of business.

With its vaulted ceilings, much like that of a great Gothic Cathedral, the library echoes the powerful voices of these men of rank and privilege.

Not having achieved success through naiveté, Carnegie spouts through his glass of Brandy, "You declare there shall be no resurrection. However, I suggest that like Lazarus, that self-righteous populist could be brought back from the dead."

Andrew Carnegie is not only another self-made millionaire but also an immigrant. Carnegie arrived in the United States as a 12-year-old boy. However, the rags to riches stories are only stories worthy of exaltation, if they result in benefit for the society at large. It is true, that Carnegie gave away a lot of his fortune, but this should not detract from the true nature of Carnegie, which leads to the accumulation and sustaining of his fortune. Carnegie is very much exemplary of the characteristics that earned the infamous industrialists and financiers the name Robber Barons.

Glancing about the opulent library with its great books and crystal chandeliers, the Grandson living off his ancestor's tit feels an even greater than usual inflated sense of importance. "Precisely, Bryan is looking to return from the political grave in all his glory. He is looking to create an army of the Christian poor. He is going to dig deep into the social fabric to mount a crusade against the very thing which makes this country great, our wealth."

"He is an instrument of the devil. My friends are responsible for the greatness of this country, and we cannot allow that greatness to be torn asunder by some Midwestern hick who believes wealth should be shared," Morgan declares as he lights his cigar. Big aromatic cigars are a phallic symbol of dominance and social position. The bigger, the better.

Letting go with a puff of smoke, Rockefeller spouts, "Well I'll be damned if I am going to stand by and allow my wealth to be threatened by some do-gooder."

Sliding back in his chair to admire a first edition copy of Machiavelli's The Prince, Carnegie inquires, "What are we going to do?"

Not to lose control of the conversation, Vandy reveals, "I was recently contacted by Mark Hanna. He asked me to convene this secret meeting. He fears Bryan will appeal to labor, farmers, and the poor in 1900. He wants us to do whatever might be necessary to keep the "Great Commoner" from the Holy Grail. He asks that our deliberations and decisions be kept completely confidential!"

Jumping to his feet, Rockefeller offers a testimonial, "I attended school with Mark Hanna, and he is a man on our side. He believes that wealth belongs to the wealthy as long as he gets his share."

Still standing by the fireplace, Vanderbilt II places his hand in his vest in Napoleonic style, "It is time to unite and leverage our money, power, and influence to see that our will is done. With weak Willy in the White House, we are safe. However, all bets are off should this clod hopper from Nebraska gain the throne. We are the most powerful men in the world, and I have a plan."

Despite an inferiority complex, Vanderbilt never lets down his guard. He has the fortune to protect, and his recent stroke makes the urgency of his mission clear. This is not a time for the faint of heart.

In his brass fashion which allows him to control the men of Wall Street, Morgan demands, "Let's hear this plan of yours."

Vandy removes his hand from his vest becoming animated as never before. "We must do three things to not only secure our power but advance our cause. We must put our differences aside and work together to make this happen. Once the throne remains in the hands of the Republicans under McKinley, we can return to our posture of competition."

William McKinley was elected the 25th president of the United States in 1896. He is a friend of big business. Throughout his political life, he advanced the cause of protective tariffs. Furthermore, McKinley is an unapologetic imperialist. His desire to seize lands held by others to control their natural resources suited the greedy nature of the Robber Barons.

Morgan, holding his cigar in one hand, pours a glass of Brandy. "So, what are the three things?"

Leaving the security of the fireplace and beginning to pace the room, Vanderbilt continues to speak waving his cigar in the air. "First, we must not allow the nation to stand aside in the conflict between Spain and Cuba. Here lies a great opportunity for us to advance McKinley's stature. Second, we must use the conflict in the Caribbean to improve economic conditions even if it involves smoke and mirrors. Third, we must replace that son-of-a-bitch Hobart as Vice President. We need someone more appealing on the ticket."

As a person who has raised great steel structures, Carnegie observes, "You're asking a great deal, Cornelius."

"The Young Commodore is right. We must take matters into our own hands. We cannot allow democracy to be the undoing of our great accomplishments as well as the nation. I shall not surrender my oil empire to some lowlife sodbuster," Rockefeller is convinced a plan is necessary. "Democracy, be damned, capitalism is the name of the game. Let commoners lift themselves out of their pitiful condition, they aren't going to freeload off my oil."

Wearing a grin resembling the Cheshire cat and salivating like Pavlov's dog from under his broad bushy mustache Morgan declares, "There is a great deal of money to be made if Spain's grasp on Cuba can be severed. Success in Cuba's revolution could bring us influence throughout the Caribbean and the Pacific."

"What can we do, involvement by the United States will require an act of Congress. We will need to go to war," declares the man of steel.

"Precisely! What could we possibly do to cause the sentiment of the American people and the United States Congress to enter that war?" says the standard-bearer of oil.

"We need something dramatic, something sensational," proclaims the bull of Wall Street.

Tossing his cigar into the fireplace, Rockefeller wonders aloud, "Can we get Mac to send an American battleship to Havana?"

"That is an interesting idea," Morgan declares while pointing to the vaulted ceiling as if to invoke the approval of God, "The United States has interests in Cuba, and those interests deserve protection. A battleship would be a perfect way to demonstrate our resolve to protect American interests. Surely the public would agree."

"And what if something happened to that battleship?" Rockefeller insinuates.

"I think we have a perfect patsy. We get Mac to send the USS Maine to Havana and boom – "Remember the Maine, to hell with Spain". The Vanderbilt connections with the press will see this splashed on front pages across the nation." The young commodore assures.

"Listen, we have the perfect situation. William Randolph Hearst and his New York Morning Journal are already sensationalizing the conflict between Spain and Cuba. Other publications across the country are getting involved in the same thing. It is the message that controls public opinion, not the other way around," Rockefeller notes.

"Hearst, the Democratic-leaning journalist won't be able to resist. He will play right into our hands," Carnegie shares with a sheepish grin of satisfaction.

"Wall Street would go bullish on a war. We get Mac to win a war, and we get four more years to grow our wealth and solidify our hold on power," Morgan is delighted.

"We get Mac to win a war with Spain; and we need to be prepared to take advantage of the opportunities which will emerge not only in Cuba, but Guam, Puerto Rico, the Philippines, and Hawaii. The avenues of commerce for my steel, Rockefeller oil, and Vanderbilt shipping will flood our coffers as never before," Carnegie is enjoying the idea of being a kingmaker. "Let's stack the deck for Mac."

With his expertise, J.P. Morgan is wondering about the economic side of things, "So what about this prosperity idea?"

We don't need to create real prosperity which might cost us our fortunes. We need to create a semblance of prosperity. A P.T. Barnum type of prosperity," Carnegie suggests.

"Andrew is correct, we need a "snake oil" type of prosperity. Something which makes the people feel better, but it doesn't change things. So, how do we make that happen?" Morgan knows the answer, but he is looking for consensus within the group.

"The Maine and war go hand in hand with a return to prosperity. Everyone knows war is good for business, and if business is good, so is the economy. While we should reap the lion's share, there will certainly be some trickle-down effect for the masses," Vanderbilt boasts to the laughter of the group.

"A nation at war needs more steel and oil as well as railroads to transport all types of goods. When business is good, the banks do well. While we fill our coffers, we can make everyone else feel like they are getting a share. We create an "Era of Good Feeling". When the public feels good, the president reaps the benefit," Morgan smiles at their unity of purpose. Echoing Carnegie, he proclaims, "Let's stack the deck for Mac!"

"So, who do we get to replace Hopeless Hobart, and how do we convince Hanna?" Vanderbilt quickly moves on to the third part of the plan.

"I would suggest we promote Theodore Roosevelt, the President of the New York Board of Police Commissioners. Roosevelt was a power-hungry politician with too many reform and progressive ideas. He may not be now, but he is a dangerous man. We need him out of New York, and where better to bury his ass than in a meaningless office such as Vice President of the United States," Rockefeller notes.

"Your suggestion is intriguing, but I fail to see the relevance of Roosevelt. He holds a rather insignificant position at this time. He is young, so why does he give us concern?" Carnegie is puzzled by the suggestion.

"Roosevelt may be insignificant now, but he is a mover and a shaker. I fear if we don't take control of him, he will eventually seek to control us," Rockefeller responds.

"So, if Roosevelt is perceived to be such a threat, why would we want this fox in the hen house?" Morgan asks. "I understand that Hanna does not like this young progressive, so why would he support such a plan?"

"We must convince Hanna that Roosevelt will be a neutered fox. As Vice President, he will have no power or influence. Remember what John Adams said about the Vice Presidency, "My country has in its wisdom contrived for me the most insignificant office that ever the invention of man contrived or his imagination conceived." Through his political power and influence, Hanna can ensure Roosevelt is out of public sight, and in no position to seek the throne in '04. Roosevelt will have no place to turn. It is perfect for us all," Rockefeller reveals.

"Then Roosevelt it is, we shall show him and the people of New York who is in charge," Vandy says returning to his station by the fireplace. "Our plan is in place gentlemen. Let us lift our glasses in a toast of solemn secrecy as we go about the execution of this plan. In the election of 1900, we shall demonstrate that it is money and not the popular will that determines the course of this nation. Thank you for joining me at my humble abode today."

In unison, they toast, "One nation, of, for, and by our almighty dollar!"

The stage is set for a defining trend in American politics. Many people cast aside collusion and conspiracy as fringe thinking. Yet, it is within the realm of conspiracy that most things happen. The fact of the matter is the worst and most successful conspirators always hide in plain sight.

Chapter 2

THE POWER OF A GUN

Did Vanderbilt, Rockefeller, Morgan, and Carnegie even consider the long-term consequences of their actions? Did their vision include the seismic shift about to occur in U.S. politics due to the rise of the new American aristocracy? Did they even imagine they were about to usher in a new century of American politics in which elections would be managed, manipulated, and won by the dollar rather than the vote? Money might not buy you love, but it sure the hell can buy an election.

These four men of power, sitting like Greek Gods atop the world on 5th Avenue in New York City, plotted to secure their will, not the nations.

As planned by these four conspiring scoundrels, President McKinley sends the USS Maine to the Caribbean as a display of the United States' military prowess. Nearly one hundred years prior, Secretary of State John Quincy Adams drafted what became known as the Monroe Doctrine. Now, in 1898, the United States had the money to enforce the doctrine, especially against a declining power like Spain.

Still, public sentiment in the United States is against the war. This public sentiment doesn't fit into the plan of Vanderbilt, Rockefeller, Morgan, and Carnegie. Something drastic had to happen, and it did on February 15, 1898, in Havana Harbor. A horrific explosion rips a gaping hole in the hull of the USS Maine, sinking the ship, and killing 260 sailors.

When the USS Maine sinks in Havana Harbor from some mysterious explosion, Vanderbilt with his connections to the emerging 4th Estate sees to it that headlines splashed across every major newspaper in the nation read, "Remember the Maine – To Hell with Spain!" Like pawns on a giant chessboard, yellow journalists, with no evidence to support their assertion, work overtime to sensationalize the sinking of this United States Battleship and push public opinion toward war. With the sinking of the USS Maine, the deal has been sealed. War will assure McKinley of a second term.

Using threats and international positioning, the administration of King William rides the issue of the USS Maine sinking like some jockey heading for the finish line. Finally, Spain has had enough and declared war on the United States. A fatal mistake, which necessitates the U.S. to enter the war, and advance the plan hatched in Vanderbilt's unsavory nest.

Fate and destiny are powerful cousins beyond the grasp of human control. Theodore Roosevelt had no idea what the Robber Barons had planned for him, nor did President McKinley. In 1897, McKinley elevated Roosevelt to the assistant secretary of the Navy. When fate brought the war with Spain to the United States in 1898, destiny thrust Roosevelt into action. Joining the cavalry, Teddy Roosevelt led the charge up San Juan Hill which earned him widespread fame for his acts of heroism. Later in 1898, Roosevelt rode his fame into the Governorship of New York State.

By now, the conspiring Robber Barons are nervous and even more determined to see their plan of action carried out.

With war comes the anticipated prosperity. Ironically, Vice President Hobert died of heart disease on November 21, 1899. Hanna, who originally opposed the scheme to replace Hobert with Roosevelt, now accepts the idea of Roosevelt as Hobert's replacement. Hanna continues to dislike the idea of Roosevelt being but one heartbeat from the presidency. Nonetheless, he sees no other option. With the pieces in place, and the election secure, these four conspirators return to the business of profiteering off the land and the people.

On Tuesday, November 6, 1900, William (I'm in their pocket) McKinley gained re-election with Theodore (Rough Rider) Roosevelt as his Vice President. The stage is now set for God to serve up a bit of the unexpected.

On September 6, 1901, just six months after his inauguration, the news emanated forth from the Pan-American Exposition in Buffalo, New York where President McKinley made a speech and explored the newest ideas and contraptions to come forth from the Industrial Age. It is not breaking news. In the early twentieth century, news moved at a snail's pace with events far outdistancing the news. Erroneous news requires ages to retract. By the time any retraction occurs, the erroneous news finds acceptance as fact.

In the Temple of Music, a dramatic crescendo occurs when Leon Czolgosz (anarchist) rushes toward the President's receiving line with a revolver in his right hand wrapped with a handkerchief. Thrusting the revolver into the President's chest . . . "He has been shot! the President has been shot!" comes a cry from a nearby witness. Everyone in the hall doesn't doubt this fact. The shots are loud and the smell of gunpowder quickly fills the hall. The hall goes into pandemonium with men shouting and women screaming. The President has been shot, is he dead?

As the news streams out across telegraph lines connecting the nation like some gigantic spider web, the reports were vague and uncertain. On the morning of September 7, 1901, our four Robber Barons receive a dose of their own medicine, "Extra, Extra, Read all about it. President McKinley has been shot in Buffalo, New York." The lights of capitalism begin to dim, and the future rapidly becomes uncertain for our four conspirators and their friends. Did karma arrive in the form of an assassin's bullet?

While McKinley attended the Pan-American Exposition, Vice-President Roosevelt vacationed in his beloved Adirondack mountains. In the mid-19th Century, the wilderness of the Adirondacks was romanticized and popularized by Henry David Thoreau and Ralph Waldo Emerson. Unintentionally, Thoreau and Emerson's musings about the Adirondacks led to a surge of people from the city to seek refuge and solace in the wild. With the completion of the New York City to Quebec railroad line, people had easy access to the Adirondacks. With timber in demand, deforestation threatens the environmental health of the entire area. Fortunately, in 1894, the state of New York passed Article XIV of the New York State Constitution protecting the Adirondacks as "Forever Wild."

Vacationing in the Adirondacks, Teddy Roosevelt receives word of the assassin's attempt when his butler delivers a telegram, "President shot in the gut while attending Pan-American Exposition in Buffalo. stop. President's condition appears stable. stop. No need for urgency. stop. Will keep you posted on President's condition. stop.

Roosevelt, no fool, and a veteran of combat is aware that anytime a person has been shot in the abdomen, the situation is serious. Rushing from the room with the telegraph still clutched in his fist, Roosevelt spouts in his raspy New York brogue, "Driver have the carriage ready to roll within a moment's notice!"

Thoughts of horror and excitement run through Roosevelt's mind. So sudden, so unexpected the mantle of power can shift, and now his time may have come. He steadies his stature even though his lower lip quivers as it often does when experiencing stress. Entering a room where he has been visiting with a friend, Roosevelt proclaimed, "Those fools, those idiotic fools."

"What causes such an eruption of emotion," his friend inquires.

"The Bastards of Wall Street, who sentenced me to this God-awful position to disrupt my efforts at Business Reform in New York are about to have the tables turned."

"What do you mean," asked his friend.

"The President of the United States has been shot, and I believe the wound to be fatal. The President is alive as of this moment, but the Grim Reaper is knocking at his door."

"Not another assassination? This would be the third time a gun has nullified the democratic election of a president in just 36 years. This is awful news for the Republic. Thank God you are in the wings, and not that, bless his soul, worthless Hobert," his friend responds in agonizing astonishment.

"Mark Hanna and those money-grubbing sons-of-bitches thought they could lock me away while they controlled the levers of power. Well, we shall see about that, we shall see about that."

"You must be careful Theodore, money like power corrupts, and these men have no interest in losing grasp of their money or power," his friend reminds him to be careful.

"My dear friend, the mantle of power is not an easy one, and I am bully-ready to serve as Chief Magistrate for this great nation. I must ask you now to take your leave as I have serious business to tend to."

As the days unfold, the Vice President anxiously awaits further news from Buffalo. Isolated in the Adirondacks, he is not in a position to initiate the consolidation of power. He knows the buzzards of Wall Street and the Robber Barons are working overtime to counteract what he expects to be his rise to the throne. He also knows that any movement on his part before the notification for action could be interpreted as opportunistic and undermine his credibility with the American people. Roosevelt knows the presidency is his should McKinley die. The precedent of ascension has been in place since the rise of John Tyler (His Accidency) upon the death of William Henry Harrison in 1841.

As Roosevelt waits for further news at his vacation cabin in Upper Tahawus, brutal weather sets in making travel unadvisable. Then on September 13, the Vice President received a telegram "The President is critically ill. stop. His condition is grave. stop. Oxygen is being given. stop. No hope. stop."

Upon the reception of this news, Roosevelt sprang into action ordering his driver to bring the carriage around. Bad weather or not, they are setting out on the seven-hour journey to North Creek station where he can catch a train to Buffalo.

Even before leaving the cabin, Roosevelt receives a second telegram, "The President appears to be dying. stop. Members of the cabinet are in Buffalo. stop. You should lose no time coming. stop.

In the pitch of dark near midnight, in weather not fit for man nor beast, Theodore Roosevelt climbs into his carriage for his precarious descent of Mount Marcy, and his rendezvous with destiny. As he cracks the whip to set the carriage in motion, the driver proclaims to his most important passenger, "God be with us, or the nation could be without a President and Vice President."

"Stay the course driver, and do it with the utmost haste," came the response from his passenger of destiny.

With visibility near zero, the driver relies on the horses to know their way. Soon, Roosevelt climbs from the carriage and sets himself alongside the driver so he can give the driver some visibility by holding a lantern.

Slipping, sliding, careening through the wooded and muddy slopes of Mount Marcy, Roosevelt arrives at North Creek station to find a telegram from Secretary of State John Hay. Hay started his public service as a young secretary to Abraham Lincoln. Later he served James Garfield as Assistant Secretary of State, and now as Secretary of State under William McKinley. He experienced the assassination of all three Presidents. Hay's telegram to Roosevelt simply says, "The President died at two-fifteen this morning."

Theodore Roosevelt departs on the train from North Creek to Buffalo knowing he is the President of the United States. Born into a family of affluence, Roosevelt never really coveted money. What he wanted came to him that day in the most unwelcome way, the power of political position. As the train (owned by Vanderbilt) clicked and clacked its way over the ribbon rails of steel (produced by Carnegie) and made its way to Buffalo (powered by Rockefeller Oil), the new President thought long and hard about the future. At forty-two years of age, the youngest person to ever be President, he sets his jaw in preparation for the many battles that lay ahead. The nation needs reform, and by God, he now has the Bully Pulpit from which to make it happen.

Chapter 3

ROOSEVELT THE SCOUNDREL

In Buffalo, six members of a grieving cabinet have decided to hold Roosevelt's Inauguration in the room directly below the dead president.

"It is only fitting the new president be seen as receiving a blessing from King William above," proclaims one cabinet member.

"It is only right that such an imposture as Roosevelt should be required to bow before his fallen King," chimes in another.

Upon his arrival in Buffalo, Roosevelt learns of the arrangement for his inauguration. "I'll be damned if I am going to be inaugurated beneath a corpse. I will not hear of it!" exclaims Roosevelt.

His friend Ansley Wilcox explains, "The cabinet feels adamant that your inauguration in a room below McKinley will provide a sense of transition as if you are being ordained by God."

"Ordained by God my ass," yells Roosevelt. "It would be more like being ordained by a soul descending into Hell. I am sorry, McKinley is dead, but the country is the better for it," registers Roosevelt. "Now make arrangements for my inauguration in a proper place and location."

Wilcox invites Teddy to stay at his home. With most of his family and household in the country, the new president will have a peaceful place to rest. Roosevelt accepted the invitation. He finds his friend's home so much to his liking that he wants the inauguration held in the library. Unlike most inaugurations, Teddy Roosevelt didn't swear on the Bible. He understands the separation of church and state better than most.

Democracy by bullet always tests the mettle of democracy. This was true in ancient Rome, and it is true in the United States. With the death of a president, there are more than enough mixed emotions to go around! The temptation of a power struggle at the moment of a power vacuum is an ever-present danger. Nothing is different this time.

The Robber Barons grieve, knowing their puppet no longer lives at 1600 Pennsylvania Avenue. They are furious that their plan, so well-conceived and executed, was undone by some madman with a pistol. Two bullets and medical incompetence bring down what Robert Burns in his 1785 poem, "To a Mouse" called, "The best-laid Plans of Mice and Men."

On Fifth Avenue, up and down Robbers Row, the word is spread to batten the hatches and prepare for the catastrophe known as Teddy. Morgan weeping fervently at the news of McKinley's death has visions of his own economic decline. To his new friend Charles Schwab, the President of Carnegie Co., he says, "Honorable men such as ourselves are about to fall under undeserved scrutiny. Now is the time to consolidate money and power before this new tyrant seeks to chase the money changers from the temple. Join me to form a great steel company that can withstand the evils of such an anti-capitalist as this boy president."

In other parts of the nation and the world, people of all stations in life recognize the dramatic change which will soon impact the United States and the lives of people everywhere. The assassination provides an opportunity for prophets to arise proclaiming their powers of observation and prognostication. To many, God has reached down and plucked an unworthy and unhealthy fruit from the tree of government. He has replaced it with the fruit of promise and hope.

No one represents the sentiment across the nation better than Secretary of State John Hay. His life experience has left him old, deeply saddened, and yet ever-optimistic. Speaking to a friend, "I scarcely know, from hour to hour, the true source of my tears. I weep for my dead son, my murdered President, and yet, I know Roosevelt's will be a glorious presidency. There are no bounds to the good this young man of unlimited energy and promise can accomplish for our country." Continuing on he says, "Mine has been a long and distinguished career. I am in the twilight of my days, and yet I see the sun rising on the horizon, and it is a bright and glorious sun!"

Upon his arrival in Washington, the most two-faced of all cities in the world, Roosevelt proceeded immediately to the White House to begin the important work ahead. He knows the importance of continuity during a time of crisis, but he also mistrusts most of McKinley's men for their connections to Hanna and the industrialists. He will have to find a way to seize the mantle of power from those who place self-interest above the public good. His most formidable tool, the one which has served him so well thus far in life, cannot be taken from him unless he yields it willingly. As Theodore Roosevelt set forth as the new leader of the United States, he prepared to use the power of his personality to bring change to a wayward nation.

Roosevelt well established his philosophy on power in a letter of January 26th, 1900 to Henry L. Sprague, a dear friend from New York, who had served in the state legislature. In the letter, Roosevelt speaks about some of his accomplishments and says, "Speak softly and carry a big stick; you will go far." Historians often associate this statement with T.R.'s foreign policy. There is no doubt this represents Roosevelt's modus operandi. The Robber Barons know Roosevelt, and they know how he operates. They did not need a statement to prove the case, they knew economic war lay on the horizon, and they began to muster all the weapons available to withstand the assault on their empires. They are not about to allow some pretender, some ninny they placed in the Vice Presidency themselves to lay waste to all their worldly possessions.

No one hates Theodore Roosevelt more than Henry Clay Frick, from which comes the statement, "You're such a Fricken Asshole". Frick is an American financier and industrialist. He takes great pride in being a union buster. Frick rose to become chairman of the Carnegie Steel Company and plays a major role in the formation of U.S. Steel. He is also a founding member of the South Fork Fishing and Hunting Club.

The South Fork Fishing and Hunting Club is comprised of many of the wealthiest business tycoons in Pennsylvania. This group includes

Frick, Andrew Mellon, Andrew Carnegie, Philander Knox, and many others. On May 31, 1889, the earthen dam which holds back the waters of Lake Conemaugh, which belongs to the South Fork Fishing and Hunting Club, gave way flooding Johnstown, Pennsylvania, and killing 2,209 people. Despite incompetent care of the dam by the club, the club members, behind the defense of high-profile lawyers, escape any responsibility. As a result, no legal compensation is paid to the survivors of the flood.

Frick has no love but money and power. He treats his dogs with gentle kindness and his workers with cruel disdain. In a tirade expressed to Andrew Carnegie, a close associate, Frick proclaims, "That bastard, son-of-a-bitch Roosevelt best watch his back. I am not about to tolerate his meddling in business any more than I will tolerate workers thinking they deserve a part of the pie. Worker or president, they can and will be crushed." Frick quickly sits down in a nearby chair, feeling a pain in his back, which frequently visits him ever since he escaped two bullets and four stab wounds when the anarchist Alexander Berkman made an attempt on his life in 1892.

In 1901, the United States arrived at a crossroads. A young president with a steady jaw and a vision for the future assumes the reign of power. At his very core resides courage and a determination to achieve greatness. Theodore Roosevelt brings multitasking to a new level. He does not want to wait, whether it be issues of domestic or international consequence, he knows only one thing – action! Over the next seven years, President Theodore Roosevelt addressed more issues and achieved more results than almost any other President in the history of the United States.

Chapter 4

A MAN OF ACTION

Teddy Roosevelt kept his friends close to his vest. His gregarious personality hides a mistrust for the motives of most men. He knows human nature, and he understands that men, even those pretending to be his friends, might try and use his position for personal or unscrupulous means. Before leaving Buffalo for Washington, the new President holds a cabinet meeting to firm up his government. During this meeting, he sizes up these men who have previously been loyal to William McKinley. To assure the nation of continuity and stability, he seeks and receives their assurance to remain a part of his government. Unfortunately, absent from this meeting are Secretary of State John Hay and Secretary of the Treasury Lyman Gage. Roosevelt feared their departure from public service, not because they were irreplaceable, but because they were a major part of McKinley's Administration.

"Gentlemen, I have asked you to meet this morning to address urgent business before this great nation," Roosevelt begins. "The people have lost a president, and I fear the abandonment of your posts by any of you would cause a loss of faith in the Republic."

"I assure you Mr. President of my loyalty and service to your administration. While I grieve the demise of President McKinley, my love and life belong to my country," exclaims the Secretary of War Elihu Root.

"Secretary Root, the firmness of your position pleases me. What do the rest of you say?" Circling the table like a hot potato, the responses come quickly with each member affirming their intentions to remain as long as the young President needs their service.

President Roosevelt's willingness to maintain McKinley's Cabinet represents the first of what will become a presidency of bold moves. A couple of McKinley's Cabinet members are like having a fox in the hen house.

Attorney General Knox comes from a family of means well associated with Henry Frick and Andrew Mellon. His wife comes from a family of steel. On February 25, 1901, just two months before becoming William McKinley's Attorney General, Knox helped J.P. Morgan and Andrew Carnegie organize U.S. Steel. He represents the least likely of bedfellows for a man hell-bent on becoming the nation's Trust Buster.

As Secretary of the Treasury, Lyman Gage comes from a background in banking and finance. His association with Wall Street runs deep. As Treasury Secretary, he seeks to create flexibility in the currency which allows for a great deal of manipulation. President Roosevelt didn't trust Lyman, but pragmatism led him to keep the Treasury Secretary close at hand. He doesn't want to unsettle the markets at a time when he has his eye on a much bigger prize.

Teddy quickly finds a kindred spirit in his Secretary of War Elihu Root. Root, a product of academia, is the son of Cube and the younger brother of Square, both mathematicians. Elihu originally became a corporate lawyer but found his passion in international affairs of goodwill. He believes wholeheartedly in the rise of nationalism. He wants the United States to be the preeminent world power, but power for good. In a culture of manifest destiny where the Christian God ordained the United States to be an imperial power, Root stands as an exception.

Before making the final move to Washington, D.C., President Roosevelt stopped at his Sagamore Hill home for a couple of days. He knows this might be the last time he will see this place, he loves, for some time. He invites Secretary of War Elihu Root to join him. As Secretary Root steps into Roosevelt's Sagamore office, his eyes take in the furnishings which are a testimony to this man of action. At one end of the room, Elephant tusks form an arch as if suggesting entrance into a world of adventure. The floor is covered with a lion's skin, leopard's skin, and bear's skin. The walls are adorned with the heads of Water

Buffalo, Moose, Big Horned Sheep, and Elk. The walls are covered with endless shelves of books. To the right side of the desk is a large globe. There are portraits of Washington, Jefferson, and Lincoln. As Root takes a seat in the rocking chair opposite the president sitting behind his desk, he is in awe. This is the first opportunity the two have had for a private conversation. President Roosevelt wasted no time getting at it:

"Mr. Secretary, I see you quickly becoming my right hand in the orchestration of government."

"I appreciate that Mr. President."

"Tell me, Elihu, what do you see as things needing to be done as we move forward?"

"May I speak frankly Mr. President?"

"I count on you to always speak frankly Sir. To do otherwise would be a disservice to your country and me as president."

"In this first year of the new century, our nation is worth twenty-five billion dollars more than her nearest rival, Great Britain. The United States has a gross national product of more than twice that of Germany and Russia. We must seize the time, and use this great economic position for national and international good."

"And how do you suggest we make that happen, Mr. Root?"

"At home, the disparity between the insanely and immorally wealthy, and the common people, is a crime against humanity and God. It pains me greatly to say this, but if not for an assassin's bullet, the Robber Barons would have continued to plunder and pillage our natural resources and human resources unchecked. We are on the cusp of a modern Middle Age, in which the Captains of Industry oversee the wealth of our nation, and keep common people subservient to their will and whim."

"So, what now, Mr. Secretary?"

"Now, opportunity knocks. An opportunity to head off the building of private empires whose wealth rivals the wealth of most nations. You, sir, need to lead the charge, as you attempted in New York, to bring these dastardly fellows to the realization that no one is above the law or the good of the nation. Your leadership can assert the principle that business exists to create wealth that improves the lives of all. I believe it is called the common good."

"You inspire me, Mr. Secretary. It is much easier to lead a charge when you have able-bodied people at your side. I am pleased you are such a person. Now, who else might be of service to this cause?"

"As much as Attorney General Knox would seem to be in the back pocket of the Industrialists and financiers, looks are deceiving. As a man who already possesses great means, he now desires great action. I am convinced he will march with us," Secretary Root reveals a keen sense of human nature.

"I am glad to hear this, as I need a strong and determined Attorney General."

Secretary Root continues, "I would make plans to rid your administration of Lyman Gage. He will not support anything which might jeopardize his interest, and such a man at treasury will be the source of great trouble. Furthermore, Gage is more than strange. He believes in the occult, and relies on seers and soothsayers to guide his actions."

"What about Secretary Hay, he has been a loyal public servant since the Presidency of Abraham Lincoln. His knowledge and experience seem indispensable."

"Secretary Hay is a good and honorable man. His life in public service has been of great achievement and great tragedy. I respect him immensely, but he is advancing in age, and this last blow (three Presidents murdered while you are in their service), combined with the recent loss of a son has left him shaken and distraught."

"I understand, but now is not the time to cut this fine man loose. He will be loyal, and he still has much to offer. I must wait until a time when he is ready. At that time, I will offer him a way out," the new president says revealing his compassion beneath the surface of a rough and ready exterior.

"I could not agree more, it is indeed the wisest approach. I know Secretary Hay will work as one mind with you as we pursue the best interest of this nation and the world."

"I recently heard that Mr. Carnegie proclaimed that the nation that makes the cheapest steel has other nations at its feet. While this may be true, I do not intend to conduct the international business of this nation in the same manner as the great trusts. Least of all, I do not intend to heed the advice of men like Carnegie," the president says through gritted teeth.

"I am glad to hear this Mr. President. With more than half the world's cotton, corn, copper, and oil flowing from the bounty of the United States, and one-third of all gold, silver, iron, and steel, the United States must represent itself as smart in business, and benevolent in character."

"Trade is the secret to the prosperity of our people, and we can do nothing greater to become the masters of trade than to see a grand canal built across Central America. I will not be satisfied until such a canal has been accomplished!"

"Yes Mr. President, there is much to be done!"

From the moment he assumed office, Theodore Roosevelt set his sights on busting up the great trusts. As a man of wealth, he understands the lustful desire and greed wealth creates. He understands wealth to be like standing in a room of beautiful women with unblemished skin, flashing eyes, ruby lips, flowing hair, succulent bosoms, and hitherto hips. You just don't want one, you want them all.

He knows the Robber Barons and their great trusts present the greatest threat to a Democratic and free people. How can democracy exist when men can purchase power in the marketplace of ideas? How can freedom and independence exist for people who have no control over their economic future? If freedom is to exist, then economic justice must exist. Freedom is not found in the ability to purchase some things; freedom is found in the ability to advance your economic and social status for yourself as well as your family. The great trusts do not open up avenues of advancement for people. The trusts hold people in check, while they advance their selfish interests.

When Theodore Roosevelt arrived in Washington D.C., he felt "Bully". Convinced that Elihu Root is the right man to serve as his closest confidant and advisor, T.R. (as Roosevelt is known) steps forth from the train with confidence and resolve that things will change. He knows the office he has ascended to is wrought with danger, but he is not about to allow personal fear or anxiety to close him off to a nation so in need of his service. In just over thirty-five years, three Presidents have been murdered, and he did not intend to be the fourth. Even facing these dangers, he demands all security keep a fair distance.

Arriving at the White House, T.R. steps forth and marvels at this citadel of power. Here resided every President since John Adams. Here worthy men turned a great opportunity into a national promise. Here, lesser men squandered opportunity, and weak men allowed corruption to stain and tarnish the nation's very foundation. He has no intention of being one of those lesser or weaker men. And so, he stands as tall as his 5'10" frame will allow, sets his jaw, and crosses the threshold into a world of power and responsibility.

Chapter 5

TROUBLED WATERS

Roosevelt didn't care for what he called the decrepit and cramped quarters of the White House. The offices of the President are intermingled with the living quarters on the second floor. His nature cries out for change, but like all things, renovation takes time. So, taking a deep breath, he set to work in a White House he felt was falling down around him.

As his Attorney General Philander Knox enters the Treaty Room, he finds the President standing in a pensive mood gazing out the south window across the lawn. The President appears deep in thought and doesn't even notice the Attorney General enter the room.

"Mr. President, you wanted to see me."

Whirling about on one foot, his eyes ablaze with the fire of a determined man, Roosevelt proclaims, "Let them eat cake!"

"What is that Mr. President?"

"Marie Antoinette, let them eat cake. The heartless bastards think they are superior to the government and the very people it represents. They have placed themselves like Gods atop Mt. Olympus looking down on the nation as if they rule. They are about to meet their demise," the president exhibits his determination.

"Whom are you talking about?" the attorney general asks a bit perplexed.

"Those insufferable Industrialists, the Robber Barons, the Captains of Industry, or whatever you may want to call them. They are low-life thieves if you ask me. They suckle at the bosom of the nation leaving nothing for anyone else."

"Is it not they who have breathed life into this nation making it the wealthiest in the world?" the attorney general wonders.

"General, they have made themselves the wealthiest in the world, not just this nation. They rape and pillage the natural resources of this nation with no consideration for the people. They subjugate workers to their whim offering only crumbs in return. They are thieves, pirates, and marauders, who plunder the treasure of a nation to satisfy their limitless greed," President Roosevelt's jaw is set during this proclamation.

"But, have they not helped build a prosperous economy?" Attorney General Knox challenges.

"If the economy is defined by the financiers on Wall Street, they have indeed helped create an American Aristocracy. As for the vast majority of this nation, they have left them, and their families scraping and scratching to obtain the very essentials of life."

"Do they not put the people to work?" the attorney general will not relent.

"Knox you fool, you know better than anyone else, that their very credo is, "The commoners be damned." You have consorted with the likes of Carnegie, Frick, and Mellon. You married into steel and helped create the largest steel company in the world. Are you too close to the trees to see the forest?" the president asks while looking over his glasses.

"I see a nation in need of leadership," Knox replies.

Pounding his fist on the table in the middle of the room, T.R. continues, "Well I am determined to provide that leadership come hell or high water. If we do not confront the power being amassed by the Industrialists and Wall Street, if we do not find a way to narrow the gap between the insanely wealthy and the common people, we will face a new American Revolution."

"Sir," is all the attorney general can get out before the president continues.

"For the past decade, this government has sat idly by while the courts have nullified the Sherman Anti-Trust Act. The Sherman Anti-Trust Act is an act of Congress signed in 1890 by President Benjamin Harrison, the grandson of old Tippecanoe himself. How dare the courts oppose the nation in its fight against sinister behavior." There is no doubt about how the president views the aristocracy created by the great industrialists, also known as the Robber Barons.

"Mr. President, it is the role of the courts to interpret the law. It is all a part of the Constitutional balance of power created by our forefathers," the attorney general attempts to explain a process T.R. clearly understands.

"Our forefathers represented an Agrarian Aristocracy of their own, but they sought to create a system of opportunity for all. The emerging industrial wealth of the North was balanced against the agrarian wealth of the South. The idea was to create national prosperity for all. The common good Knox, the common good. The Great Civil War changed the game, the agrarian wealth of the South lay in ruins while the Industrialists perched like Vultures at a feast." Roosevelt sounds sympathetic to the South, but this is not true. The president is a staunch Unionist, but he understands the history and shortcomings of reconstruction. He understands the concept of "To the victor belongs the spoils."

"We can blame Lincoln, and the abolitionists for that," Knox asserts.

"How dare you sully our slain president's name. We can blame greed, Mr. Attorney General. The South's greed would not allow the agrarian aristocracy to remove the chains of slavery. They kept black people subjugated to their will to advance their self-interest. Such a wrong could not go unaddressed. It required a leader of courage and conviction. Thank God for Lincoln and the abolitionists!" President Roosevelt says with fire in his eyes.

"Indeed, a rare and great man," Knox responds realizing Roosevelt is in command of this conversation.

"Now is our time Knox. The common man may not be enslaved, but he is certainly subjugated to the will and whim of the Industrialists. Furthermore, even women and children are being used to advance the greed and sinister nature of these titans of industry. Now is our time to act," Roosevelt reveals his resolve.

"What do you suggest."

"What I first must know above all else, are you with me in busting up trusts as a means of bringing economic justice to the people of this nation," T.R. is direct!

"I serve at the president's pleasure," Knox is not interested in losing his job. He knows that he can better serve his wealthy friends by being part of the administration.

"Then let us get to work. What is your legal opinion of the Sherman Anti-Trust Act?" the president puts Knox to the test.

"I believe it has failed to produce results in the past due to poor presentation. The Sherman Anti-Trust Act does not oppose trusts in and of themselves, but opposes the negative impact trusts have on free enterprise and the economy," the attorney general is a scholarly man.

"Do you believe we need to seek other legislation as a means of busting up trusts? How can we create an economic environment of greater competition?" The president is looking to see if his attorney general is a man of ideas.

"Absolutely not, the Sherman Anti-Trust Act contains all of the legal remedies necessary to deal with the harmful nature of trusts. With diligent preparation and presentation, we should be able to prevail upon the court a successful vote," the attorney general offers his opinion tempered by his past association with the Robber Barons.

"Then let us get to work. I want you to look into the activities of the Northern Securities Company. This is where we shall start," President Roosevelt directs.

In February 1902, Attorney General Knox at the direction of President Theodore Roosevelt filed a suit against the Northern Securities Company under the Sherman Anti-trust Act of 1890. For adversaries, the President has selected E.H. Harriman, James Hill, J.P. Morgan, and John D. Rockefeller. This represents a game of high-stakes poker, the likes never seen before. The big question involving these titans of power is, who holds the ace in the hole?

Learning of the suit only after it has been filed infuriates J.P. Morgan who feels the honorable thing would have been to offer a warning. Ironically, Morgan never offered a warning to his competitors before lowering the boom. He never offered a warning to workers before imposing new working conditions. Isn't this the case, the powerful always want that which they are never willing to do themselves. Irate, Morgan takes his muscle to the White House.

Knowing Morgan is on his way, President Roosevelt braces himself for the indignities to come. While the White House offers a formidable home-court advantage, it does not and cannot rival the elegance and majestic nature of the 5th Avenue Robbers Row Mansions. Roosevelt decided to face Morgan in his office, otherwise known as the cabinet room, where Lincoln signed the Emancipation Proclamation. If anywhere, Morgan will be humbled in such a setting.

Entering the White House, and then the President's office, J.P. Morgan feels anything but humbled. "I will not allow anyone, let alone the President of the United States to treat me like a common criminal," Morgan declares upon entering the room.

"You sir are being treated like a citizen of the United States. No one is above the law! As long as I serve this country as Chief Magistrate, I will use the law as I see best fits the interest of this nation." President Roosevelt is not impressed by Morgan. He has known many scoundrels, and now with the power of the presidency behind him, Roosevelt knows he has the upper hand.

Morgan sensing a formidable foe, steps back, "What, Mr. President, must be done to resolve this issue?"

"There is nothing you can do. Attorney General Knox has filed a suit against Northern Securities Company. It is now a matter to be settled by the courts," Roosevelt plays his hand perfectly.

"You are making a grave mistake. The wheels of economic power are what run this country. Those wheels are well in motion, and they will not be stopped by you or anyone else," In his indignation, Morgan resorts to threats.

"We shall see about that," the president is unimpressed. This is not his first go-around with an extremely oversized ego.

"So, who is next? Are you proposing to take on all the trusts?" Morgan is looking for a revelation.

"Only the ones that have done something wrong will be prosecuted. I assure you of that. You may show yourself out," the president says while flipping his hand towards the door.

Having received nothing from the new president, Morgan at least now knows that Teddy Roosevelt intends to use his office to leverage power against those of great wealth. He departs the White House feeling like the president considers him and his associates little more than highwaymen and bands of robbers. Roosevelt did not say it, but he inferred that the Industrialists and Financiers made their money by exploiting workers. He further insinuated they accumulated massive wealth by looting from the American people. Discouraged by this meeting, Morgan is determined to find another way.

Concerned about this new suit under the auspices of a new president, J.P. Morgan decides to visit his old friend Supreme Court Justice Edward D. White, whom he calls Ned. Attempting to maintain as much discretion as possible, Morgan makes arrangements to meet Justice White at his home near Thibodaux, Louisiana.

"J.P. how the hell are you doing, and what brings you to this neck of the woods?" Justice White inquires as his butler ushers Morgan into his study.

"Ned, we got a real jackass in the White House who seems to think he can push people around," J.P. minces no words. "He is a Maverick! Why that son-of-a-bitch would rather fight than share a good glass of whiskey is beyond me. I know you are aware he is bringing his fight right into my home with this suit against the Northern Securities Company."

"I have seen the suit filed by the attorney general, but I don't see it going too far. Every attempt to regulate trusts under the Sherman Anti-Trust Law has gone down in defeat," Justice White shrugs off Morgan's concern. "I am not sure why you have made a long trip for such a trivial reason. With Knox as the attorney general, he may follow the president's wishes, but he will not make the case."

"Ned, I need you to do everything under your power to see that the court does not look favorably on this president and his anti-trust efforts."

"What is it you think I can do J.P.? I am but one member of the court. I can only assure you that such suits have not found favor with the court. I don't see how this will," the justice responds.

"By God, I know what you can do. I watched carefully as you maneuvered your colleagues away from a majority decision on the E.C.

Knight Company," J.P. is hedging his bet that Justice White can pull strings.

"What do you mean maneuvered? Attorney General Olney bumbled that case from the very beginning. The man was an incompetent buffoon. He had no clue how to apply the Sherman Anti-Trust Act to his case." Justice White is acknowledging that success with the Sherman Anti-Trust Act is about presentation. He seems to be leaving the door open for success with a more competent approach.

"Ned, your family is up to their ass in sugar. A court decision against E.C. Knight would have brought hardship to your family's sugar interests, and you know damn well I am right. Unless you want some Muckraker to get a hold of information that would impugn your integrity, and end your career on the bench, I recommend you take care of Roosevelt and this suit," Morgan is in blackmail mode.

Muckrakers are reform-minded journalists looking to uncover and expose corruption and the evils of corporate monopolies. Muckrakers seek to reveal issues of poverty, unsafe working conditions, child labor, and other ills of the Industrial Revolution. The writings of Muckrakers can be found in all the popular publications of the time. President Theodore Roosevelt even said that "the men with the muck rakes are often indispensable to the well-being of society . . ."

J.P. Morgan's threats have hit a nerve with Justice White. While the justice does not respond, J.P. can see and sense that it is time to go.

"I shall take my leave now," J.P. has made his point and exits quickly.

Dragging on through the court for nearly two years, the Northern Securities suit finally achieved resolve with a 5 to 4 vote in favor of the suit in 1904. J.P. Morgan, John D. Rockefeller, and associates were forced to disband their railroad monopoly through the creation of smaller and more competitive companies. Unfortunately, much like Jell-o, when the trusts are pushed in one direction, they compensate by going in another direction. While power can no longer be consolidated in one company, these titans of business and industry, find ways to fracture a large company into several smaller companies and sell off shares. Ironically, this only tightens their powerful grasp on the market.

Chapter 6

THE SUPERIORITY OF LABOR

The grueling environment for workers at the turn of the century tested the physical and emotional endurance of labor. People consider factories 'sweatshops' where workers labor long and hard hours in working conditions not fit for man or beast. Wages are, what management in this case the Robber Barons, the occupants of Millionaires Row on Fifth Avenue, want it to be. "People should feel damn lucky they have a job," can be frequently heard from the tycoons on Wall Street. By modern standards, the unemployment rate of 4.5% for non-farm employees reflects a healthy economy. However, an average of .17 cents per hour for labor, (and thousands upon thousands of workers made less than that), leaves workers and families clawing to stay economically above ground. The old adage, "Let them pull themselves up by their bootstraps" doesn't fit when many people cannot afford boots.

Stretch a budget? How about surviving on .17 cents an hour when you have to pay .26 cents for a pound of butter and .23 cents for a dozen eggs? But what the hell, butter, and eggs are only three hours of work, and you still have seven hours out of that ten-hour day. Who knows what you can do with the $1.19 earned during the remaining seven hours of the work day? Perhaps you can purchase one of those new-fangled Horseless Carriages at $840.00. This can easily be paid off in 494 working days if there is no interest, and you dedicate every penny to the purchase. But wait, people have to eat, buy clothing, pay rent or a mortgage if lucky, and cover other expenses.

The wage disparity between labor and the Industrialists would make a sober man stager. Most industrialists and financiers are millionaires many times over. Some of them are newly emerging millionaires, and some of them are the fortunate inheritors of old established money. Most millionaires make their money resting on their elbows while smoking large robust Imperial Cigars, and sipping Botella Antigua Cognac Napoleon. The fact of the matter is most of them have well-established Napoleonic complexes. It is worth questioning the value of a Napoleonic complex to a democratic society.

For a common laborer to attain millionaire status at .17 cents per hour, it will take them 1,960 years of hard labor while saving every single penny. With the average life span for a man in 1902 being fifty years, it will take over thirty-nine men a lifetime of work saving every penny of their .17 per hour to accumulate one million dollars.

Theodore Roosevelt ascended to the presidency with an appreciation and respect for the common man and labor. As an outdoorsman, Roosevelt appreciates the rugged life. He feels deep down that pure character comes from facing adversity. He believes that hard-working men and women are honest and honorable people. He knows better about those who occupy places of privilege. He knows that when people feel they are above others, they look down on others, and when you look down on others, it is with a condescending eye.

The young President knows the failure of the Sherman Anti-Trust Act has resulted from bumbling and incompetent administrators as well as the people of privilege sitting on the nation's courts. Why else would the courts use a piece of legislation intended to reel in the Robber Barons as a tool against labor? Up until the positive decision on the Northern Securities Corporation, the courts had used "Sherman" as a means of beating back workers' efforts to organize. Roosevelt understands and respects the courage it takes for workers to stand firm on issues of wages, benefits, and working conditions, especially when all the cards are stacked against them.

"Mr. President"

"Secretary Root, what be the pleasure today."

"Sir, the United Mine Workers on the Anthracite have gone on strike. There are more than 100,000 workers who have walked off the job. I think the situation could become serious," Elihu Root shares.

"How so Mr. Root?" inquires the president.

"The coal being produced now will be the fuel for all of our cities and homes during the winter months. If this strike lasts very long, we have more than a political problem, we have a real human problem," the secretary shares with a sense of impending doom.

"It seems I must talk with my attorney general," the president responds.

"Please do sir, we must develop some options for this situation. This could turn ugly in so many ways," Secretary Root says as he takes his leave.

Aware of the severity of this situation, the President calls for UMW President John Mitchell to join him at the White House.

"Mr. Mitchell, on what grounds do the United Mine Workers in the anthracite coalfields of eastern Pennsylvania go on strike?"

"We strike on the grounds of poor wages, poor working conditions, and long hours. Ten hours down in the mines breathing coal dust in poorly ventilated shafts that could collapse at any moment constitutes a valid and legitimate issue for the workers. Combine that with wages which amount to an infinitesimal fraction of the bounty being raked in by the owners, and you have a crime against society and a sin against God," the union leader proclaims.

"I have long sympathized with labor. I have never felt you get your due, and yet it is important to recognize the importance of capital," the president expresses a weakly held belief in an attempt to flush out the resolve of the union.

"President Lincoln said, "labor is more important than capital. Without labor, you cannot generate capital." The greedy bastards can go to hell. We are fed up with being treated worse than animals," John Mitchell is pissed.

"It is a proverbial question of the chicken and the egg. Yet, it would seem true, once the ball of commerce is rolling that either capital or labor could bring things to a halt. It is for this reason Mr. Mitchell, that you must learn to work together. I shall have a frank conversation with Mr. Baer on behalf of the workers," T.R. is in diplomatic mode.

"Thank you, Mr. President."

After a conversation with Mr. Mitchell, the President wants to have a conversation with his two most trusted confidants, the Secretary of War and the Attorney General. He calls for their immediate attention at the White House.

Upon their arrival, the president eagerly invites them into his study. "Gentlemen, please, come in, come in."

"Good afternoon Mr. President."

"Gentlemen, I recently had a very interesting conversation with UMW President John Mitchell. The Union is lucky to have a man of his caliber representing the working man. The situation is serious. There is never a good time for a strike, but, the working man must stand up for justice. It is a quandary we must address," the president has a soft spot for working people. He served during the Spanish-American War, and he witnessed firsthand the patriotism and gallantry of ordinary Americans ready to sacrifice for their country.

"I would recommend you not validate the union, Mr. President. As you well know, the Supreme Court has not ruled favorably on workers' right to organize," says the attorney general.

"That den of old worn-out thinkers can go to hell. Why the way they rule on issues of race would make you think the North and South were still at war? We need not pay them any more attention than is necessary General. Now let's talk about this coal strike in Pennsylvania. This is a real situation in which the union has justification for its actions," the president is frustrated with how the country has beaten down the very people who have built it up. "The country has suffered enough from worn-out ideas which subjugate the people to the rule of old men. This is a new century crying out for new ideas and a new focus of service to the people. The people are the masses, my friends. Of, for, and by the people seems to have taken a back seat to the self-interest of a few. It is our solemn duty to serve all the people," the president does not suffer fools easily.

"We cannot allow the workers to strike. Their actions jeopardize the good of the country," the attorney general is digging himself a hole from which he may not emerge.

"Hell Mr. President, those workers bust their ass day in and day out to make things work. They receive little compensation and certainly no appreciation. When they strike, the owners are as responsible as the workers. Those son-of-bitches sit in their ivory towers smoking cigars, eating the finest food, served by black servants, and laughing at the indignities they inflict on hard-working men, women, and even children. It is time they got their due," Secretary Root seems to love the idea of screwing over those whom he sees as not only rich but corrupt and entitled.

"I couldn't agree more Mr. Root. The owners have a responsibility to care for their workers, and if they do not do so, the workers should have the right to walk off the job. I did not say this specifically to Mr. Mitchell, but even so, he remained a gentleman in his presentation. The workers in their determination care more about the general populace of the country than any of the entitled bastards of Wall Street. We need to look after our nation, but to me, that involves standing with the working class," T.R. knows he arose to this position of power for a purpose, and he is not about to be negligent in his duties.

"Mr. President, you cannot allow yourself to look biased on this issue. You must take a center position or endanger fracturing the entire industry. I urge you to meet with George Baer, the owner of the Reading and Pennsylvania Railroads, who control the mines, to sound him out and hear his side," The attorney general, while highly qualified, is in deep with the robber barons. Why the president keeps him on is a mystery. Perhaps it is the old adage, "keep your friends close and your enemies closer."

"I intend to do that general, but I know Mr. Baer and a bigger horse's ass would be hard to find. Why I will need to call upon every ounce of self-restraint just to be in the same room as that insolent bastard! But it must be done, and by God, he had better respond as I desire." The president knows that his attorney general may very well be a pipeline to Baer. He is counting on Attorney General Knox to convey to Baer the seriousness and resolve of the president.

George Baer has never been to the White House before. He has never personally met a President before. This doesn't bother him since he lives in an opulent mansion and serves at the pleasure of the House of Morgan. Why will he be humbled in the presence of a President, when he frequently entertains the company of the Emperors of Wall Street? George Baer has never previously met Theodore Roosevelt.

Upon being ushered into the President's office, Baer thinks, "My God, my clerks work in offices of grandeur, and the President works in this old, dingy, congested space".

Entering, the President, "Welcome to the people's house Mr. Baer, I am sure you know the people, so many of them work for you."

"I suppose this pertains to the Anthracite," Baer asks nonchalantly.

"Bully for you sir, I am impressed with your powers of deduction. You must indeed be a very intelligent man. So, tell me, without any bullshit, what is going on that would cause the workers to strike," the president knows the best defense is a good offense.

"This is nothing more than a power play. The workers want to be recognized as a union, and I refuse to recognize or deal with them as an organization," Baer's indignation is obvious.

"Well bully for you, why not just take them out and beat the hell out of them while you are at it? I mean, frankly, they are just beasts of burden. Why lower yourself to recognizing them as important to the success of your business? Seriously, why would you want to sit down and talk with them," the president offers in a sarcastic tone!

"You are correct, that would be the worst of all ideas. The moment I sit and talk with the workers as an organization is the moment, I yield management and control of the company to that organization," Baer reveals his insecurity.

"It would seem to me you currently do not have control. You are headless as a manager. Furthermore, without the respect and loyalty of your workers, you are nothing more than a tyrant, a dictator. Do you know what happens to tyrants Mr. Baer?" T.R. quickly grows weary of a man who understands nothing about leading people.

"Mr. President, you do not understand," Baer makes a grave mistake assuming he is going to lecture the president.

"Oh, what I understand Mr. Baer, is that you said the rights and interests of the laboring man will be protected and cared for—not by the labor union, but by the Christian men to whom God in his infinite wisdom has given the control of the property interests of the country. Your arrogance is astounding."

"My statement has been taken completely out of context."

"Do you believe God has ordained you and all your associates of great wealth with control of the property interests of the country? And if so Mr. Baer, do you consider your workers among those property interests? Something sinister seems to be at hand here Mr. Baer," T.R. is incredibly upset with his visitor.

"Mr. President."

"No, you Mr. Baer. You are responsible for this looming crisis, and I expect it will be you who finds the solution. After all, God seems to be on your side, and I am sure God will not fail you in this time of need. Butler, please show Mr. Baer out," The president's jaw is set, and the fire in his eyes represents a man of resolve and determination.

Theodore Roosevelt became the first President to get involved in a labor dispute. As a man of action and a leader of the highest caliber, it is not in Roosevelt's nature to sit by and allow things to run their course. When he looks in the mirror, he sees a catalyst of change, with the position and power to effect change and create a new world. A world that he defines as "The Square Deal."

At one point during the strike, Roosevelt locks Mitchell and Baer in a room and threatens to leave them there until they arrive at a solution. He formed a commission to investigate the conditions of workers and make recommendations for a solution. He has the Secretary of War put the armed forces on alert. The president is determined, if necessary, to take over the mines and produce the coal required to survive the winter.

While all three of the president's actions move the process toward a solution, it is the commission that makes it happen. Management continues to refuse to recognize the union, so the commission creates a six-man arbitration board made up of equal numbers of labor and management. While the workers are demanding an eight-hour day, the commission suggests a reduction in work hours be approached in steps, and so, they arrive at an agreement on a nine-hour workday. While the workers want a twenty percent wage increase, the commission recommends a ten percent increase. With the solution splitting the difference between labor and management, labor went back to work on October 23, 1902 feeling vindicated by the direct involvement of the federal government and President Roosevelt.

Chapter 7

A GRAND VISION

Theodore Roosevelt adhered to the quote from Shakespeare's As You Like It, Act II Scene VII:

"All the world's a stage,
And all the men and women are merely players:
They have their exits and their entrances;
And one man in his time plays many parts. . ."

To Roosevelt, the world represents the greatest stage, and he desires to be the most formidable player on the stage. Before Internationalism was clearly defined, Roosevelt defined it for himself. The continental United States is settled, and forty-five of the nation's lower forty-eight states have joined the Union. It will only be time before Oklahoma, New Mexico, and Arizona become states.

The President despises the power-grabbing nature of the Robber Barons. He sees their elitist and arrogant attitude combined with a total disdain for the common people as not only contradictory to the principles of the United States but dangerous to its very existence. Yet, he views the productivity of the United States as a source of great power that can be wielded around the globe.

Theodore Roosevelt understood world commerce, and he knew U.S. dominance depended upon the ability of U.S. merchants to get their goods to world markets. Already, U.S. goods such as Ingersoll alarm clocks, Gillette razors, Vaseline tonic, Arrow shirts, Quaker Oats, California Figs, and Maxwell House coffee swamp the British market. U.S. innovations such as the Otis elevator and Edison Lightbulb are in common use. An ironic fact is, that the United States ships beer to Germany, pottery to Bohemia, and oranges to Valencia.

Roosevelt faced a double-edged sword. At home, he battles the industrialists to create a fair economic environment for all people. On the world stage, he strives to increase U.S. dominance which fills the coffers of Wall Street and 5th Avenue with foreign capital which creates an even greater disparity between the wealthy and working-class people.

Not since Thomas Jefferson has a president possessed a vision as grand and determined as Theodore Roosevelt. Where Jefferson saw a continental nation, T.R. saw the world.

"Greetings Gentlemen," the president welcomes his cabinet.

"Mr. President," the group says in near unison.

"I wish to discuss with the full cabinet the matter of a canal across Central America. As you are aware, the French abandoned their project across the isthmus controlled by Columbia. The French had the right idea, but perhaps not the right location. Furthermore, they allowed their project to become bogged down in inefficiency and corruption. A project of this magnitude is always susceptible to incompetence and mismanagement."

"Mr. President, it has been suggested that Nicaragua provides the best location and opportunity for a canal," Secretary of State Hay informs the president.

"That may be true Mr. Hay, but that recommendation served as a ruse to force the hand of the French. As is often the case with the French, they were going nowhere with their project. Something needed to be done," Secretary of War Root reminds.

"You may be right Mr. Root, but the idea of a Nicaraguan route has gained wide acceptance in the House and Senate. You now have a U.S. Congress mired down in the idea that the only viable route is through Nicaragua," Secretary of Interior Hitchcock notes.

"I understand the legal and political implications of the situation, Mr. Hitchcock, but the fact of the matter is the French have abandoned a project in the works which seems to be the shortest and best route for an isthmus," proclaims Secretary Root.

"Gentlemen, it matters not what is or has been, but what will be. We are here to discuss the resolution of the United States to take up this project and achieve success," the president reminds his cabinet.

"I wish it were that easy Mr. President, but there is a formidable advocate for a Nicaraguan route in the Senate who must be dealt with," Attorney General Knox acknowledges the powerful influence of Senator Morgan of Alabama.

"I take it you are talking about the not-so-honorable John Tyler Morgan. How in God's name do former Confederates continue to exercise power in a union they so adamantly opposed? Along with that, what the hell is it about the name Morgan that continues to be a burr under my saddle?" The president stands slamming his fist down on the table. "By God, we have work to do, and we have no time for obstructionists."

"Mr. Morgan is hell-bent on the Nicaraguan route primarily due to his prejudices against the people of Columbia, and in particular those inhabiting the area of the French isthmus. He feels they are nothing more than ignorant Baboons unworthy of any association with a civilized country," injects the secretary of state.

"Mr. Hay is correct. Why he looks more favorably on the people of Nicaragua is a mystery, but Senator John Tyler Morgan is the most insufferable bigot in the United States Government. That damn Alabaman is still fighting the Civil War as a Grand Dragon in the Ku Klux Klan. He has devoted decades trying to find a way to deport Negroes from this country. We cannot allow him to impede a grand design for a Canal between the Atlantic and Pacific," Secretary Root shares the disgust of the entire cabinet.

"So true Mr. Root the only thing admirable about his service to this country is his determination to build a canal across Central America. We must find a way to make his support beneficial to our plan," the attorney general says as he leans on the table holding his chin in folded hands.

"So, Gentlemen, we must use that determination to our advantage.

Who do we have in the Senate agreeable with the French route for a canal?" the president asks.

"Mr. President, Senator Hanna is the only person with the clout to help us make this happen," offers Secretary of the Treasury Shaw.

"That damn Hanna, he finds a way to make his presence felt in just about every instance. The problem with Hanna is his close association with the butchers of Wall Street. Is there not a good and honest man we can turn to for assistance with this dilemma? Everywhere we turn it seems like we must get in bed with Satan's workhorses," the president pleads.

"Good and honest has nothing to do with finding the best man Mr. President. Hanna has a real interest in seeing the best route established at the earliest possible date. He is beholden to the country's aristocracy, and he knows the Isthmus provides that very route. The success of the canal would be a real feather in his hat, and most of all, money in the bank," the secretary of treasury says with a side nod of his head.

"So true Knox, but that self-interest is in direct conflict with my plans to reel in the Industrialists and financiers of Wall Street in creating an economic system that offers a square deal to the American people. Hell, Hanna won't even offer his commitment to my re-election in '04," the president reveals common knowledge. Politicians are always looking ahead, and it is difficult to scratch the back of someone who will not scratch yours.

"Politics makes strange bedfellows. The enemy of my enemy is my friend, and in this case, we need to get Senator Hanna on board with our plan to offset any power plays by Morgan," Secretary of Root is being pragmatic.

"You speak the truth, Mr. Root. I must see Senator Hanna immediately. There is no time to waste. Thank you for your service gentlemen," the president dismisses the cabinet meeting.

Sitting in his office, President Roosevelt is mumbling over his disgust for little men with power. If not the self-absorbed Captains of Industry and the weasels of Wall Street, he has to deal with elected officials such as Senator John Tyler Morgan and Senator Mark Hanna. Democracy indeed makes strange bedfellows of those who seek to represent. He knows that his big stick needs to be used often to keep the wolves at bay.

He thinks to himself; I am the President of the United States, and I will be damn if anyone of wealth or position is going to wrestle the mantle of authority from my hands. I shall serve the best interest of the people, and the nation even if it becomes my undoing.

His silence and contemplation are broken, "Good Afternoon Mr. President. Did you wish to see me?" Mark Hanna has an arrogant tone to his voice as he struts all puffed up into the president's study.

"Senator Hanna, how good of you to come right over," the president says knowing the Senator had best be prompt in his appearance. "We have a bully big issue to wrangle, and I trust you will be of help," T.R. adds stroking his famous mustache.

"I will do whatever I can Mr. President," Senator Hanna responds. Hanna is no fool when it comes to the political game. Passive-aggressive is an art he has honed over the years.

"I understand you support the United States acquiring the Isthmus project currently held by the French. Is that a correct assessment Senator," President Roosevelt gets right to the point.

"I do, such an accomplishment under the control of the United States Government would establish our nation as the captain of capital and commerce around the globe. Our coffers will fill quickly with foreign currency. What a wonderful prospect," The Senator's comment does little to hide his personal agenda.

"Mr. Hanna, I fear you, and I see this infusion of capital much differently." When the president sets his jaw with a stern stare, he is in a don't screw with me mode.

"I pray, what do you mean Mr. President," Playing dumb is the wrong choice for Hanna.

"The benefits to be gained from the accomplishment of this grand project must serve to increase prosperity for all, not just a few. I know you do not agree with me on my actions against the Captains of Industry on behalf of workers. But believe me when I tell you, I will in no way allow the canal project to become a windfall for a few. It must serve to enhance the economic conditions of the United States and all its people. There is no room in this project for shenanigans of a self-serving nature. Do you understand me?" the president says while clenching his fist.

Teddy Roosevelt used to be a boxer in an earlier day. The sight of his massive hand clenched as if preparing for fisticuffs is impressive.

"I understand your sentiment Mr. President, but I also know you thirst to establish the United States as a dominant force around the world. A canal to the Pacific under the control of the United States would create a sphere of influence for the United States in the Eastern Hemisphere. You can't do this alone Sir. You need the help of those you have chosen to oppose, and if they help, they will demand their due. Think about that Mr. President," Hanna has a history of speaking truth to power, and in this case, he is right. Roosevelt can't pull this one off alone.

"It is important! Control of the trade routes is paramount to the control of commerce. The control of commerce means the control of world markets. As we control the markets, we expand our sphere of influence, and therefore the American Empire. I must admit, you stand on rather solid ground Senator," The president must acknowledge that he can't go it alone.

"So, you and I are not that much different. Without your so-called Robber Barons, there is little productivity. Without productivity, our position on the world stage is of little significance," Hanna feels like he is in the driver's seat.

"You are wrong on that matter Senator. You and I are very different. While I understand and believe in the importance of productivity, I also believe the productivity of a nation needs to equally benefit both labor and capital. What I am working for is a more equitable distribution of the wealth generated by that productivity. To me this is not negotiable!" the president is quick to draw a distinct line in the sand regarding the economic well-being of the nation.

"We must agree to disagree, Mr. President. While I do support the building of a canal in the same location as the French, I am fearful my sentiments are in a minority with the Senate. I may be of little help on this issue." Even if Hanna could be of big help on this issue, he is too far into deep pockets to succumb to Roosevelt's position.

"And what do you see as our biggest challenge?" the president asks.

"Senator Morgan of Alabama is a pigheaded obstinate self-righteous bastard. He allies members in favor of Nicaragua using his prejudicial lies. He is a dark and sinister man. We may disagree on many things Mr. President, but I think we both agree that former confederates who have failed to reform to a more enlightened way of thinking have no business serving in the United States Congress. Morgan is nothing more than a confederate serving in the United States Senate. His identity disgraces us all," With these words, Hanna finds favor with the president. Roosevelt had no time for make-believe unionists.

"So why do you favor the French location, Mr. Hanna? Is it purely economic?" the president is looking to restart their conversation and perhaps for an alliance as unholy as it might be.

"Mr. President, an Isthmus of one hundred and sixty miles in Nicaragua is ludicrous when an Isthmus of fifty miles is already partially dug and available in Columbian territory. It seems like a simple matter of deduction," Senator Hanna keeps it simple.

"Senator, I need you to make that sale. Put aside all the other crap, and focus on the logical and sensible nature of the argument. Put all your energies into it, Senator. Muster all in your power to make blind men see. With the French abandonment of their project, we must strike while the iron is hot. The entire future of this nation and our position in the world is at stake. We can argue the details later," The president knows Senator Mark Hanna remains his best bet to push through the Isthmus in Columbian territory.

"It seems we are bedfellows on this issue, Mr. President. I shall do all in my power to make this happen. Good day sir," Hanna takes his leave.

Senator Mark Hanna diligently prepares a presentation for the United States Senate which makes clear the benefits of an Isthmus through the French route versus the route through Nicaragua previously favored by the Senate. His brilliant presentation along with a well-orchestrated campaign in power politics brings the majority of the Senate to the President's view. It is unknown, the role played by the great industrialists and financiers, but it is no secret Hanna works for them on the side. Mark Hanna likes to appear altruistic, and after all, that is the goal of a politician. But, at the core, Hanna is as self-serving as the Robber Barons and Wolves of Wall Street. The Isthmus through Columbia offers the best hope for a canal, and a canal offers great prospects for incredible wealth.

President Roosevelt along with his Secretary of State John Hay and Secretary of War Elihu Root negotiated the purchase of the canal project from the French. At the same time, they negotiated a treaty with the Columbian Government to assume control of the French project and the land including and around the Isthmus. Under Mark Hanna's direction, the United States Senate approved this agreement. However, the Columbian Senate refused to ratify this treaty. The United States is now confronted with a preverbal rock and a hard place.

For years, Panamanian rebels had been fighting to throw off the Columbian shackles of oppression. President Roosevelt now turned to his Secretary of State and War to help guide him and the nation through the shoals inherent in these dangerous waters.

"Mr. Root and Mr. Hay, we now have a U.S. Senate agreeable to our canal plans. Unfortunately, we have a Columbian Senate blocking our treaty agreement," Roosevelt is meeting with his Secretary of State and War in his private office.

"Mr. President, there are Panamanian rebels in the hills surrounding the canal zone who have been fighting for independence from Columbia for several years. Perhaps they offer us a resolution to our dilemma?" Secretary Root offers.

"What are you suggesting Mr. Root?" The president is no amateur to intrigue. Theodore Roosevelt believed in Manifest Destiny. He believes in the exceptionalism of the United States. He is anxious to take the lead in advancing the United States as a world power.

"We could let the rebels know that should they declare independence from Columbia, we would use our naval might to assure Columbia would be unable to retaliate. However, in return for our support, they must be willing to negotiate a favorable canal zone agreement. With Columbia out of the way, we can move forward with our plans," The Secretary of War explains.

"This seems like a dangerous type of Gun Boat Diplomacy Mr. Root. What if it fails?" John Hay has seen it all, and he knows there is never a sure thing. He wants to know what the contingency might be should the plan be unsuccessful.

"Failure cannot be an option, Mr. Hay. However, you do make a valid point. How do you respond?" T.R. is mediating this exchange.

"Mr. President, Columbia may be in a position to keep the rebels at bay, however, they are in no position to challenge a U.S. Battleship. In this case, it is all a matter of muscle. No one will come to Columbia's rescue. This will truly be a one-and-done," Secretary Root is confident his idea will be successful.

"Fine Mr. Root, but what about public perception?" Secretary Hay continues to play the Devil's advocate.

"It will all be over so quickly the public will hardly have time to take notice. Besides, the public expects no less from a great nation. I urge you to proceed. Communicate with the Panamanian rebels, and allow me to dispatch a battleship to the region," Secretary Root sees no reason to delay. The United States holds all the cards, and it is time to ante up.

"The Monroe Doctrine would support our actions should it involve a foreign nation transgressing in the Western Hemisphere, but I am not sure we have the authority to act unilaterally. We may be setting an undesirable precedent," Hay continues to press the issue.

"Precedents always start somewhere Mr. Hay. I believe we are about to set our own precedent. There is a certain destiny at play, and we are very much on the cusp of an American Empire. For us to turn away from such an incredible opportunity would be a disservice to a nation of such lofty ideals and goals. I do not want to be the president who had the canal in my grasp and allowed it to slip away. The canal is not only an incredible idea, it is an engineering marvel. Nothing like it has ever been accomplished in the history of the world. For the United States to achieve such a feat puts us above all other nations. How can you still question this?" President Roosevelt wanted to hear it all. He does not want any stone unturned when it comes to this decision. For this reason, he continues to foster debate.

"This is a dangerous precedent. We must take care to not become the very thing to other people which we despised in the British Empire. What we are doing is a form of colonialism. While I understand and believe in the importance of a canal, it all seems a bit hypocritical," Hay has about run his course on this issue.

"Mr. Hay, modern history is running through the very spot upon which we stand. We can either allow that current to pass us by, or we can seek to use the power of the current to carry us and our nation onto greatness. There are always risks. But a risk not taken is an opportunity missed. We must not shy away from our destiny. Secretary Root has offered us a reasonable plan for success. It is time for us to step up to the plate," the president is bringing closure to this topic.

John Hay served as the most decisive leader of all time. Abraham Lincoln entertained great debate on the many decisions he made, but when it was decision time, it belonged to Lincoln. Hay understood this more than anyone, and he admired Roosevelt for his Lincolnesque approach to decision-making.

"Mr. Hay, cable the Panamanian rebels to see if they are agreeable to favorable terms on the canal zone in return for our naval intervention. Mr. Root, identify the battleship that is most capable and in closest proximity to canal zone waters for providing a successful blockade."

"As you wish Mr. President."

On November 3, 1903, the Panamanian Rebels declared their independence from Columbia. The United States dispatches the USS Nashville to canal zone waters and successfully impedes any interference from Columbia. Less than four months later, the new Panamanian government gave the United States control of the Panama Canal Zone in return for the $10 million agreed upon in the Hay-Bunau-Varilla Treaty of November 18, 1903.

Chapter 8

IT BELONGS TO THE PEOPLE

As a young man, Theodore Roosevelt ascended to the Presidency with a wealth of life experience invaluable to serving the nation. As a child of privilege, he has seen firsthand the impact of unbridled greed on his community, state, and nation. As a soldier, he witnessed the brutality of war, and the struggles facing emerging nations. But no experience impacted his soul and spirit like his experience in the American West.

As an outdoorsman, Roosevelt's love of wildlife and nature grows far beyond the desire to hunt, fish, and camp under the stars. He develops a vision of conservation that emerges from his experience with the unrestricted hunting of species into extinction, the exploitation of nature for wealth, and a total disregard for the future of the nation.

With his inauguration after the assassination of President William McKinley, Roosevelt found himself confronted with issues of great importance. However, despite all the other issues, conservation remains on his mind and close to his heart. T.R. witnessed firsthand the relentless rush to make big money from the professional hunter's slaughter of wild game. He has seen the massive herds of bison, so important to the survival of Native American people, extinguished due to hunting, overgrazing, and disease. He knows the demand for beef in the east caused ranchers to allow their herds to skin the land in a manner that destroyed its ability to revitalize. He knows the Robber Barons, Industrialists, Financiers, and emerging companies have unrestricted access to the nation's natural resources including forests, water, oil, coal, minerals, and land to be sold or used for personal profit.

He now occupies the Bully Pulpit with the key to the future in his hands.

Walking his dog, Jack the Terrier, on the White House lawn under a deep blue cloudless sky, the President enjoys the fresh air and openness of the restrictive White House Compound. He privately calls it his splendid little prison. Since he cannot take the White House to the great outdoors, the President seeks to bring the great outdoors to the White House. He maintains a menagerie of animals such as Jonathan Edwards the Bear, Bill the Lizard, Josiah the Badger, Eli Yale the Blue Macaw, and Algonquin the Pony on the White House grounds.

As he walks, the President contemplates how the very city that serves as the federal capital was once a great swamp. As he considers the impact of human activity on nature, he encounters the American forester Gifford Pinchot, who has arrived for a visit.

"Good morning Mr. President."

"Good morning Mr. Pinchot! What brings you to the White House?"

"I have impatiently waited for a man of your experience and interest in our natural resources to become the Chief Magistrate. My wife has told me patience is a virtue, but I find nothing virtuous in what is happening to our natural resources."

"Walk with me, Mr. Pinchot. Come see some of the pets we maintain here on the White House grounds."

As Gifford Pinchot's eyes peer with astonishment at the wild animals, his thick brown mustache twitches with delight. We indeed have a President who loves and appreciates the importance of the outdoors, he thinks to himself. "Mr. President, this is impressive, and to think you have a name for every one of them."

"I believe you are right, Mr. Pinchot, I have become rather fond of each one."

"Mr. President, the Industrial Revolution, and looting capitalists are decimating our forests and pillaging the nation of natural resources which should belong to all the people."

"You are correct, Mr. Pinchot. In the past, we have elevated the right of the individual to a position where the individual can put the future of the Republic in jeopardy for his own personal profit. In fact, over the last half of the nineteenth century, there has been a good deal of demand for unrestricted individualism. I too believe in the importance of the individual. However, I also believe wholeheartedly in the common good. At no time, should the right of an individual supersede what is best for all! The time has come for a change."

"Papa, look what I have captured on the lawn," exclaims a wide-eyed Quentin Roosevelt as he runs toward the President and Mr. Pinchot carrying a small box.

"Well, let us have a look," his father says while taking a knee for a good look.

Dropping the box to the ground, the lid snaps off, and four snakes slither into the grass. "Look Papa, won't they be a great addition to our pets?" the young boy proclaims.

Gifford Pinchot is not usually squeamish, but he is not a big fan of snakes. As the creatures extend themselves out across the lawn, Pinchot quickly moves to stay out of their path.

"Quinton, pick those snakes up immediately and return them to the box. Go let them loose where you found them. They need to return to their home," the president knows his wife would not care to have snakes as part of their collection of pets.

"But Papa!"

"No buts son, we do not need four snakes occupying the White House. Now do as you are told."

With that Quinton quickly gathers up his four escapees and returns them to their dungeon at the bottom of the box. Affixing the lid, he scampers off to appeal to his mother.

"Mr. President, greedy individuals are commandeering our natural resources for their gain. This rush to wealth at the expense of our national treasures could lead to the destruction of the Nation's future. I urge you to act sir before it is too late," Gifford Pinchot exudes the passion of someone with prophetic vision.

"I have been giving this much thought, and I will be meeting with my Secretary of Interior Ethan Allen Hitchcock at the earliest possible convenience. You know that Mr. Hitchcock is the Grand-Nephew of our patriot Ethan Allen of the Green Mountain Boys. He has every bit the spirit and fortitude of his grand-uncle. I expect your forewarnings will resonate with his love of this land," the president assures his visitor.

"I am glad to hear this Mr. President. We need to be proactive on this issue," Pinchot is feeling like his visit has found a friend in President Roosevelt.

"I will also include my new Secretary of the Treasury Leslie Shaw. Shaw is a former Governor of Iowa from Denison in the western part of the state. He will not only bring monetary knowledge but an understanding of the Great Plains to the table. As you well know, Iowa represents the first extension of this nation west of the Mississippi," the president reminds Pinchot.

Pinchot's expertise is in forestry. He is a practical man with passion and a belief in a controlled and scientific approach to the use of the country's natural resources, in particular the forests. Pinchot understands that the natural bounty of the nation plays an important role in the creation of a society of benefit for all. Proper management is the key. Management under the direction and close eye of the government.

"Thank you, Mr. President. I am at your service should it be needed. I bid you good day." Gifford Pinchot turns to leave the presence of what he considers to be a great man.

Theodore Roosevelt knows that the wealthy are a wretched bunch of self-serving misers with only contempt for anything and anyone who might obstruct their path to the nation's riches. He has already made enemies with the Eastern aristocracy who see him as a traitor to his people. He knows that turning his focus to the West will only create great rancor for his presidency within the ranks of the elite seeking to exploit the great natural resources beyond the Missouri River.

While the eastern Robber Barons seek to extend their monopolistic enterprises to the west, the west gives rise to its own men of great wealth through cattle, forestry, coal, oil, gold, and silver. Great cities are rising up around the natural resources of various regions, and amid these cities can be found an aristocracy of power. Whether East or West, power based on wealth is blind to anything but increased wealth and power. As in the East, the cities of the West are filled with common people struggling to make a living off the scraps tossed from the tables of the rich.

Roosevelt was sitting in his office reading Penhallow's Indian Wars when his Secretary of Interior and Treasury arrived for a meeting. After ushering Hitchcock and Shaw to the Cabinet Room, his secretary informs the president of their arrival. Upon his entrance into the room, the President finds Hitchcock and Shaw huddled examining the huge map of the United States which hangs on the wall.

"Thank you for joining me this afternoon Gentlemen!" the president says in his deep and authoritative voice.

"We serve at your pleasure Mr. President," the men respond in unison.

"It is amazing, isn't it? In just over one hundred and twenty-five years we have gone from a British Colony to a nation that expands the entire North American Continent. Some call it Manifest Destiny, but I prefer to think of it as human ingenuity. The conquering and settlement of this great continent were accomplished by hundreds of thousands of common people seeking to create a better life for themselves and their families. It has not been an easy journey. It has been a journey of unbelievable courage and sacrifice," the president proclaims.

"It is truly an amazing feat Mr. President," Secretary Shaw agrees.

"Did you know that the Indians, what some people call Native Americans, feel inseparably connected to all things of nature? They never take but what they need in an effort to maintain harmony with the world. Under the Indians, all life is sacred and treated in such a manner. As we moved west with our thundering horde, we found the land inhabited by Indian tribes in the same condition as it had for hundreds of years. It is a strange feeling to think about what we have done to land held so sacred by different people and cultures. Do you not share this feeling?" The president puts the question to his Secretary of Treasury and Interior.

"Yes sir!" they respond as expected.

"Mr. Hitchcock, you are to be commended for your honorable treatment of the Indians. They have never had such a good friend in our government. For years, our government has treated the Indians with disdain. We have felt it appropriate to lie and cheat these people to take their land and have our way. The history of Indian Affairs is shameful, and yet, you have worked diligently to restore trust and honor to our dealings with these people," the president is appreciative of Secretary Hitchcock's efforts.

"Thank you, Mr. President!" Secretary Hitchcock is truly honored to receive his president's accolades.

"Gentlemen, we have moved the Indians onto reservations. We have settled the lands which once belonged to their people. We have crisscrossed the nation with railroads. We have built cities, and we have formed forty-five states on a continent that will one day soon boast forty-eight states. In the decades since the Civil War, we have created a nation of immigrants from every European nation in the world. We have created a nation made up of Negros brought unwillingly to this continent and the descendants of these men and women. We have forged a mighty railroad on the back of Orientals who have called this land their home. We are a nation of immigrants from all corners of the world. It is not an easy prospect to have so many people from so many cultures inhabiting the same land, the same nation, under the same rule of law. Some believe we should be a melting pot, but I do not see it that way. Once on an African Safari, I observed many different animals, all with different habits and characteristics, inhabiting the same land. I did not see a melting pot; I saw a harmony of life. Now, in the animal kingdom, life can be rather brutal and harsh. However, in the kingdom of human beings, there must exist harmony. It is not only possible, but it is also essential," the president leaves little to the imagination. He has a core belief.

"As someone from the heart of this nation, I confess it is an unbelievable achievement. You speak with great vision and wisdom Mr. President," Mr. Shaw affirms.

"The achievement is truly amazing Mr. Shaw, but I cannot help but wonder if it is progress. As a people and a nation, we have settled this continent with random abandon. The Industrial Revolution has provided tools of wonder that allow men to harvest vast resources from above and below the ground. As a result, our natural resources, living and inert are being stripped from our world at an alarming and unconscionable rate for the personal gain of a few at the expense of many workers. While our settlement and progress can be good for all people, why are we allowing a few to gain so much for themselves, at the expense of the many?" the president challenges his guests.

"You speak the truth Mr. President, but such is the price of progress. We are a nation of eighty-two million people. Those who possess the capital to render the resources of the land beneficial for the advancement of society are doing a service to the nation," Secretary Shaw plays the devil's advocate on the subject.

"Progress for who Mr. Shaw? It appears to me some are reaping great wealth while the vast majority of people struggle from day to day, and many in our inner cities live in squalor. Is this what we call progress?" the president is not taking the bait.

"It is the kind of progress which if given time will make money available to more and more people. As the rich get richer, they will create more and more jobs. Like a stream flowing from a lake, the higher the lake level, the more water which flows downstream. Such is the way of a free economy," Secretary Shaw sounds Hamiltonian.

"Your analogy makes sense Mr. Shaw, but what happens when those upstream build a damn to keep more water for themselves and allow less to flow downstream? At that point, there must be intervention," the president responds.

"What is your point, Mr. President?" Secretary Shaw knows the president likes to be challenged. Theodore Roosevelt does not shy away from a good debate. In fact, the president welcomes a spirited debate.

"We need a plan, and I expect your help. The natural resources of this nation are being plundered by those who command the mechanisms of capital with little benefit for those who labor. Furthermore, this plundering is being done at a terrible cost to our natural resources. Our timbers are being depleted at an alarming rate, entire mountainsides are disappearing in the search for gold, silver, and coal, our wild animal population is being decimated by commercial hunters or the loss of natural habitat, our freshwater streams are being polluted, and the natural beauty of this country is being destroyed. In a few short decades, we have taken the land so cared for by the Indians for centuries, and treated it with reckless abandon," we need a conscientious approach to stewardship for this land we call home.

"What is it you want from us?" his secretaries ask.

"In the past, this government has turned over natural resources to be sold or used for personal profit. This system has led to a concentration of resources in private hands which have shown little regard for stewardship. This can no longer continue. The fate of our natural resources must not be directed by the whims of individuals, but rather by the common and united determination of the people as represented by their government. We must take control of public lands before it is too late," the president wants action.

Continuing the President says, "We need regulation and oversight of the public domain. We cannot allow our natural resources to be exhausted and destroyed. I want you Mr. Hitchcock and Mr. Shaw to return to me with a plan. Before you return, I want your plan carefully screened by the Attorney General."

"We shall do as you wish Mr. President."

During a speaking tour in 1903, President Roosevelt interrupted his tour for two weeks of camping in Yellowstone National Park. Following this camping expedition, he visits the Grand Canyon where he pleads:

"In the Grand Canyon, Arizona has a natural wonder which is in kind unparalleled throughout the rest of the world. I want to ask you to keep this great wonder of nature as it now is. I hope you will not have a building of any kind, not a summer cottage, a hotel, or anything else, to mar the wonderful grandeur, the sublimity, the great loneliness, and the beauty of the canyon. Leave it as it is. You cannot improve on it. The ages have been at work on it, and man can only mar it," the president is in a love affair with nature.

As the president engages his tour of the West, the conservationist and head of the Sierra Club John Muir invites him to spend a few nights in Yosemite.

"Mr. Muir, I cannot voice the depth of my appreciation for this invitation to share time and space with you," the president says upon arriving at Yosemite.

"Mr. President, I did not invite you to spend time and space with me but to commune with the beauty of nature as found here in Yosemite. I plead with you to listen carefully to the voice of God as witnessed in the wind, the sounds of all living things, and the beauty of creation. This is without a doubt a sacred place," Muir is a priest of nature. He does not speak unless his soul is moved.

After a few days in the park under the guidance of John Muir, Theodore Roosevelt was captivated by the power of nature and this national place of grandeur. He has never matter-of-factly looked at civilization, but now he sees and understands nature as the sacred cathedral of all humanity.

John Muir, knowing his unique time with the president says, "Yosemite is a national park Mr. President, but there are parts of it which are vulnerable to the wanton acts of man. There are valuable natural resources that if unprotected could fall victim to the greed of men with no vision or understanding of the sacredness of nature. I urge you Mr. President to use your power to make Yosemite Valley a part of the larger national park. Protect it from greed!"

The President leaves Yosemite awed by the beauty of this park. After sleeping under the stars surrounded by huge mountains, lush forests, and rugged cliffs, Roosevelt says, "It is like lying in a great solemn cathedral, far vaster and more beautiful than any built by the hand of man."

President Roosevelt returned to Washington more determined than ever to protect the natural resources of the United States. He knows if left in the hands of capitalists and opportunists, the great natural wonders and resources of the nation will be squandered and lost forever. Calling his cabinet members together, Roosevelt told them of his determination to declare as much land as possible under the safeguard and regulation of the public domain. Roosevelt knew that if they missed this opportunity, all of the geographic beauty that defines the character of this nation would be lost to the unbridled greed of man.

"Mr. President, without sounding contrary to your determination, I must remind you that the declaration of a National Park requires the consent of Congress," the attorney general reminds.

"I am aware of this Mr. Attorney General, and therefore, we are going to seek from the United States Congress the authority to create

National Monuments. We shall call this bill the "Act for the Preservation of American Antiquities," Roosevelt declares.

"Is there sufficient support for such legislation Mr. President," Secretary Hitchcock asks hoping the answer is affirmative.

"As you know Mr. Hitchcock, Iowa Congressman John Lacey who chairs the House Committee on Public Lands is gravely concerned about the issue of "Pot Hunters," the president says.

"Pot Hunters Mr. President?" Secretary Root wonders.

"Yes Mr. Root, it seems there are profiteers, thieves, pirates so to speak who prey on American antiquities as a means of profit. Pot Hunters refer to those who invade ancient Indian sites of the southwest and make way with ancient artifacts, pots so to speak. It seems when it comes to money, there is no such thing as honor or integrity. In actuality, it is blatant thievery. Pot Hunters, Grave Robbers, Profiteers, and those who take advantage of any kind of assistance program are nothing more than scum acting in a sinister manner for their own personal good at the public expense." the president reveals his disdain for those who play fast and loose with the public domain.

"How can we be of help?"

"Well, if the Attorney General will please correct me, if necessary, the Act for the Preservation of American Antiquities could be a bill with far-ranging implications allowing the President's discretion in the creation of National Monuments. After all, what is the difference between a thief making way with a pot made by an ancient Indian tribe, and stones made by the hand of God?" the president inquires.

"I do believe you have come up with a grand idea. A national monument could be more than a particular location to encompass a large tract of land under the auspices of the federal government," Secretary Hitchcock suggests.

"Well said, Mr. Hitchcock. It will be like a three-pronged attack. I shall use my powers to declare National Parks, increase the number of National Forests, and proclaim National Monuments. All of which will reduce the impact of those who would rape the land for profit," the president is feeling the power of opportunity is upon him.

"Mr. Hitchcock, you and Attorney General Knox are to work with Congressman Lacey in moving this legislation through Congress. Gentlemen, we are about to reclaim the very essence of this country for the people and future generations."

Chapter 9

SINISTER CABAL

Meanwhile, twenty-five miles north of New York City, at the highest point in Pocantico Hills, on J.D. Rockefeller's Kykuit Estate, his mansion offers an incredible vista of the Hudson River at Tappan Zee. From the mansion which is near Tarrytown and the legendary town of Sleepy Hollow, a person can see the New York City skyline. On this particular day, J.P. Morgan is paying a visit to his friend John D. Rockefeller. Upon entering the estate, it is something to behold. There are statues, fountains, pavilions, and gardens among the beautiful pitch pine, Appalachian oak, hickory, chestnut oak, maple, and a variety of conifers. Opulence is the reason to be wealthy. To be able to claim dominion over the greatest pleasures in life. Morgan's car is met at the front of the house by the butler a tall dignified man who well knows his social position and what the great house serves.

"Good afternoon Mr. Morgan."

"Good afternoon, James, it is a marvelous day indeed," J.P. says as he exits the car and is ushered to the front door.

"I trust you had a comfortable drive from the city?" James asks as he leads the way.

"The damn roads are quite bumpy. However, I marvel at how these contraptions move so quickly. Truly ingenious, a real modern marvel," J.P. is traveling in one of his many cars. Today, he arrives in a bright red Packard Model F with plush black leather upholstery. While the Model F runs on the same 12-horsepower single-cylinder engine as the Model C, it is the first to feature artillery-style wood spoke wheels and the three-speed selective sliding gear manual transmission. J.P. Morgan loves his cars, and he loves this one in particular. When visiting Rockefeller, it is best to come in style. "Is Mr. Rockefeller prepared to meet?"

"He is in the library awaiting your arrival," the butler informs J.P.

Crossing the threshold to the Mansion, Morgan is struck by the incredible chandelier, the large oval opening to the second floor, and the great expanse with the cascading staircase. On the floor is a large colorfully designed Persian carpet, with the walls covered with portraits of the Rockefeller family. There is a marble fireplace, a grand piano, and walnut furnishings throughout the room. The room reflects the home of American royalty.

"Well then, let us not dally, time is money," Morgan has never been one for small talk.

However, as he passes through the rest of the mansion on the way to the library, Morgan is surprised at the sad state of affairs. The structure seems quite disorganized. The ceilings are much lower than anticipated, and the windows are rather small. Morgan is a bit puzzled by what may have happened here. After all, John D. Rockefeller is the wealthiest man in the world. Certainly, he can do much better than this.

Morgan is not impressed with Kykuit Estate. He once visited Rockefeller's Estate in Cleveland and considered it more glorious than all the great palaces of Europe. But then again, that is exactly the point. In 1776, Americans cast off the yoke of British and European dominance only to evolve into a nation that seeks to emulate the very thing from which it originally desired separation. The Robber Barons perceive themselves as great American nobility granted by God the position to which they have arrived. It is their destiny to enjoy the finest things in life and to live in splendor.

As he enters the library, he doesn't notice the gentleman sitting behind the high-backed chair. He is enthralled by the volumes upon volumes of books old and new, all more than likely original first editions. A brilliantly burning fire in the ornate fireplace makes the lighting in the room dance from floor to ceiling and from wall to wall. Few things impress Morgan as he claims his title as part of America's aristocracy, but Rockefeller does know how to build a Library. Then he notices the plume of smoke rising from a chair, and the butler announces, "Mr. Rockefeller, Mr. J.P. Morgan has arrived."

J.D. Rockefeller stands and turns to see Morgan just inside the doorway. "J.P. how are you, my good fellow? Come in and have a seat, we must discuss some things of great importance."

"J.D. it is always good to see you. You certainly have a marvelous estate and an incredible mansion," Morgan announces not revealing his true feelings about the things he has seen.

"Don't be polite J.P., I am extremely disappointed in this estate. The location could not be better. I have a view that allows me to monitor every ship of commerce going up and down the Hudson. Yet, I allowed my son's involvement which led to multiple architects and this horror of a structure. If not for the library and view, I would not spend time here."

Morgan takes his place in a high-back chair alongside Rockefeller. Long before the development of psycho-babble and group theory, men of wealth and success knew that if you were going to collaborate, you sit side by side, whereas if you were going to negotiate, you sit opposite each other. The intentions of this meeting are purely collaborative, if not conspiratorial.

"J.P., since the death of our beloved stooge McKinley, that ninny Roosevelt has done nothing but try to wreak havoc with our empires. Who does this guy think he is? The Roosevelts themselves are a well-to-do family. Why on God's Earth would this son of privilege turn against his own?"

"This is true, J.D. I share your anxiety. However, we have outlived more than one President, and we shall outlive this one. He may be young and privileged, but we have the upper hand in all matters, and regardless of his efforts to undercut our power and position, he will fall short in every way. We J.D. are the captains of our fate, not the president!" Morgan says assuredly.

"How rude of me J.P., can I interest you in a glass of Brandy and a very fine Imperial cigar?"

"Yes, you can J.D., I am a bit parched from the ride, and I never turn down a good cigar."

"And how was the ride J.P.?

"I must say the invention of these automobiles has made travel much more enjoyable. We must do something to improve the condition of the roads, but as for speed, who would have ever dreamed of such a contraption to carry people with such speed from one place to another?"

"Yes, and I hear a man named Ford is attempting to mass-produce automobiles. It is said he wants to make these contraptions affordable to the common man. Should he be successful, I envision a new boom for everyone from finance to steel to oil. Let us toast to his success," Rockefeller has a gleam in his eye.

Morgan and Rockefeller once more settle into their seats sipping their glass of brandy and puffing heavily on their cigars, all of which cost more than what ten men make in an average day.

"So, what is our answer to this ignoramus they call "The Trust Buster?" J.D. poses the question to his guest."

"Are you familiar with the saying "Be careful what you ask for?" Morgan responds.

"I do believe I have heard that one before, what of it?" Rockefeller inquires.

"Mr. Roosevelt broke up Northern Securities thinking he was going to spread the wealth and create a climate of increased competition and he may have done that to a degree. But he did not foresee how Northern Securities would be broken up nor did he anticipate the result," Morgan makes a point.

"Go on J.P. you have my interest," Rockefeller leans forward to the edge of his chair.

"As Northern Securities splintered into several smaller companies, I maneuvered to maintain a majority stock holding in all of the newly formed companies. In essence, they are all still mine," Morgan gives out a laugh.

"Brilliant J.P., but what about the competition and most importantly your fortune," J.D. Rockefeller's only concern is how Roosevelt's activity impacts their wealth.

"As companies all under my control, we have subtly created a competitive ruse which appears to be competitive but in actuality, we are manipulating other factors of business which results in more revenue than ever before," Morgan reveals. "It is the best of both worlds. We create a competitive field, and, we control the field of competition.

Offering a deep sinister laugh, Morgan proclaims, "I am making more money now than ever!"

"Why this is great news, and it is something we must share with our associates to ensure they too rise above the infernal meddling of this cowboy President. Your news makes the brandy even taste sweeter," Rockefeller falls back in his chair.

"This is all well and good, J.D., but we must prepare ourselves for anything that might come our way. When you control an empire, you must always know it is under siege. We can't let down our guard," Morgan says in earnest.

"What do you suggest?" J.P. "Do you have a plan?" Rockefeller is back on the edge of his seat.

"We must communicate with Attorney General Knox and Treasury Secretary Shaw. These men serve the President, but they are wealthy men who have long been subservient to money. We must work to keep them in our camp. With friends inside the tent, we can ensure that they are working for us," Morgan introduces the clandestine nature of his thinking.

"J.D. there is word slipping out of Washington that Roosevelt is broadening his push for reforms to loosen our grip on production and commerce," Morgan continues.

"It is said he is not only seeking to legislate reforms on business but seeking to regulate business indirectly through the confiscation of lands as public domain."

"We have something at our disposal no other man can muster Mr. Morgan. We have a legion of the best-educated and most qualified lawyers anywhere in the world. Let Roosevelt's government try and regulate our business. It is like a game of chess. With every move he makes, we can and will make a countermove. They can legislate until they are blue in the face, and we will still find a legal remedy for the affliction," Rockefeller has picked up on Morgan's power play.

"This will take a great deal of money," Morgan recognizes the obvious.

"Like the man who maintains a private arsenal in the event his property is ever threatened, we maintain an arsenal of wealth. Yes, fighting such a war will cost us, but we have prevailed before, and we will do so again. We may lose a battle, but by God, we will not lose the war," Rockefeller declares.

"What about the lands he is threatening to take out of production?" Morgan is fishing for ideas.

"The west is new. The president cannot take control of all the land. There is plenty of wealth to be had. We just need to capitalize on what is available now and position ourselves for the future. We will not see it J.P., but our children's, children's, children will see the day when even the protected lands must be opened up for production. When that day comes, our descendants will be there as a result of the things we do today," Rockefeller has always been a man of vision.

"Are you acquainted with Mr. Pinchot, whom President Roosevelt is going to name as the Chairman of a newly formed Forestry Department," J.P. inquires.

"I am not," J.D. leans forward on his chair and exhales a plume of cigar smoke.

"There are people in my organization who know Mr. Pinchot. They say he is amiable to control access to the nation's natural resources, even those which may lay within protected areas. He is a man we need on our side," Morgan pitches this angle.

"The measure of a man is not what he is amiable to but what he does when in a position of action. Look at politicians. They are the most two-faced bastards you will ever confront. Their approach is like a man wanting to lay with a beautiful woman. He tells her what she wants to hear as an act of seduction. Then, he has his way with her," Rockefeller is familiar with the art of manipulation.

"We must prepare Mr. Rockefeller. A firestorm of governmental interference is upon us. As Ben Franklin said, "If we do not hang together, we shall surely hang separately," Morgan is speaking metaphorically, but he is seriously concerned about the signs of the times. Teddy Roosevelt is a young stallion looking to make his mark, and the old guard of money does not like what it fears may lay on the horizon.

"Mr. Morgan, you are in a position to bring us all together. I urge you to communicate with Carnegie, Frisk, Gould, and Mellon about the urgency of our situation. Ask each man to send a legal team to a meeting where a plan can be hatched to counteract the conduct of this President,"

Rockefeller appeals to Morgan's vanity in motivating him to take the lead in hatching a plan. Rockefeller is cagy enough to grease the skids and insulate himself from any trouble that may emerge.

"What about Osgood in Colorado, his interests in coal and iron are at risk. And what about Gates in Texas?" J.P. wants to build allies for the task ahead.

"Let the word go forth like a great spider's web. Ask them to send the best legal minds they have to meet secretly at a location you should determine. Convey the seriousness of the situation. We must be prepared to respond to the threat at hand," J.D. is giving J.P. responsibility, and with it comes the authority to act. J.P.'s ego is stoked, and he is ready to act.

"I agree J.D., I shall return to New York immediately and put my men on this task. I shall now take my leave and wish you a most enjoyable day," J.P. Morgan is a powerful man in his own right, but powerful men have big egos that need to be stroked. Morgan likes to be in charge, and when he feels in charge of powerful men, he is anxious for action.

Chapter 10

A PAIN IN THE ASS

From the time he assumed the throne, Theodore Roosevelt sought to consolidate his power through progressive action agreeable to the people of the United States. Mark Hanna, the kingmaker of the Republican Party, will not bestow upon Roosevelt the blessing of a second term. Hanna recognizes Roosevelt is a very young man. Despite his youth, Roosevelt went so far as to proclaim he would not seek the Presidency beyond a second term. This is a proclamation Roosevelt later came to regret.

TR knows that being a successful politician requires the skills of a high-wire act. Political success requires maintaining a balance between opposing forces in order to avoid a fall from grace. It is the curse of every politician, but in a democracy, unlimited power does not exist. The Presidency does not lose the bond that restricts action, but in many ways requires an escape artist's talent while shackled to many points of view.

Teddy Roosevelt wanted to reign in the Robber Barons, and he knew this would meet popular approval. He also knows if he plays too rough, the Robber Barons have the means by which they can make life difficult for him. The wealthy have a tight hold on the economy, and a weak and faltering economy will not be good for his prospects of being elected in his own right.

After ascending to the office of Chief Magistrate, Roosevelt desired to be elected by the people in 1904. No President before Roosevelt, who had ascended the Presidency upon the death of his predecessor, has succeeded in being elected to the office. James Polk defeated John Tyler in 1844 after Tyler ascended to the Presidency upon the death of William Henry Harrison. Millard Fillmore rose to the rank of President upon the death of Zachary Taylor but failed to gain election against Franklin Pierce in 1852. Abe Lincoln's Vice President Andrew Johnson failed to gain election in 1868. In 1884, Chester Arthur who assumed the Presidency upon the assassination of James Garfield failed to be elected in his own right. Roosevelt doesn't want history to place him among such a group of losers.

Even in the areas of labor, conservation, and foreign affairs, Roosevelt had to walk softly with his big stick. Moving too far to the left with his progressive agenda will piss off the conservatives in his party. He needed a united Republican Party for the election of 1904. While he leans progressive in his views and desire for action, the President knows the party bosses rely on and look favorable to big money. If he moves too far, too fast, he will be pushed to his political demise by the power brokers within his party. So, Roosevelt not only walks softly, but he walks with care.

Conducting the nation's business and charting his political future, presents a mosaic that often blurs the lines between public service and self-interest. How can he serve if he doesn't hold office? For Roosevelt to hold office meant getting the nomination and winning the election. Democracy is very seldom about the people. Democracy is about power and those in positions of power with the ability to impact and manipulate events for their purpose. In an election, the people simply get to choose between candidates the power brokers ordain to run. In many cases, the deck gets stacked to ensure a particular result. Democracy is smoke and mirrors, it is snake oil sold from the back of a wagon, it is a placebo for self-government. The real decision-makers hide behind a curtain of wealth and power.

During his first term, Roosevelt placed people loyal to him in positions of party influence. Despite that, he constantly deals with the ever-arrogant, self-absorbed Senator and Party Leader Mark Hanna. Roosevelt hates to grovel, especially to a man like Mark Hanna. Hanna doesn't hide his disdain for the president. He hates seeing Roosevelt in the presidential chair. If not for a gunman, T.R. would have remained in political obscurity.

Shortly after the New Year 1904, Roosevelt called Hanna to the White House to discuss the upcoming Republican Convention. Even though the convention is still several months away, Roosevelt needs Hanna's endorsement for the nomination.

Roosevelt meets with Hanna in his Presidential Office in the newly constructed (1902) West Wing of the White House. President Roosevelt felt the presidential offices on the second floor of the White House had seen their day. The president needs a new home court for meetings and dealing with people like Mark Hanna. Roosevelt kept his office simple with a desk, a rocking chair behind the desk, a rocking chair in front of the desk, a fireplace, a large globe, a couch to the left of his desk, and a picture of a young Abraham Lincoln hanging above the fireplace mantle. To one side of the room, pocket doors opened to the cabinet room. While simple in furnishing, the room exudes the power and determination of the man who sits behind the desk.

Directing Senator Hanna to have a seat in the rocking chair directly in front of him, President Roosevelt gets down to business.

"Mr. Hanna, I have served as President now for the past two and a half years while you have failed to stand with me as the leader of the Republican Party. As president, I am the presumptive nominee for the election of 1904. The time has come for us to either stand together or prepare for battle."

"Mr. President, I should be sitting here with President McKinley charting the course for the future. I can almost assure you if that were the case, you would not be part of that discussion," the senator lets his arrogance come forward immediately.

"I did not fire the gun on that fateful day. I did not ask to be tossed into the storm. I assumed this office with dignity, and I have executed my duties faithfully, loyally, and in good conscience. You can talk all you want about what might have been, but I am here, and it is me with whom you must deal," the president sits back in his chair with arms crossed and a stern look on his face.

"As President, you have caused waves where the water would have best been left still. As a result, there is concern that if given a second term, you will act against the interests of important men, and therefore the best interests of the country," Hanna has always been in the back pocket of the Robber Barons.

"I am president, and I do believe in a progressive agenda. Change must occur to secure the future of this nation. My actions are not against the industrialists or capitalists. My actions are to secure a future for industry and capital while improving the lives of the common people. In case you have been sleeping, working people are only getting the scraps from the table of the rich. The rich have their power, it is time for the working man to have a champion at the helm of government," Roosevelt does not shy away from the task at hand.

"And yet you go at it wielding a broad blade which threatens these great men, and the empires they have built with their very hands," Hanna is a master of bullshit.

"Let's not exaggerate Mr. Hanna, I am also a man of wealth. Like many of the men living on Millionaire's Row in cities across this country, I had the good fortune to be born into money. Acquiring fortunes by birth is hardly building an empire with your own hands."

"Mr. President, regardless of how they have acquired their wealth, these are the leaders of finance and progress in this country. You treat these people as evil elitists. You threaten their very livelihood with increased regulations. You supported the Ekins Act which questions the ethical practices of corporations and railroads. You stood with the coal mine workers against the industry. You even went so far as to threaten the use of federal troops," Senator Hanna does not yield easily.

"I do not hold ill will toward the honest earning of money, but I have a real concern for those who hoard money. I do not respect nor will I support the accumulation of wealth on the backs of common people who see so little for their hard labor. You, senator, are a part of the political machines controlled by these people of great wealth. These machines bestow power upon people of their like mind. When they have enough, they want more. They are predatory creatures with an unquenchable thirst for money and power. It is the role of the government to act in the best interest of the people. In this case, the common people need a government to protect them from the selfish advancement of the wealthy," the president makes his position clear. If he is elected, his second term will be a progressive march forward.

"But it is their money, should they not be allowed to do with it as they wish?" Hanna has no interest in the progressive movement.

"How can we proclaim to be a great nation, when there are people who live in obscene poverty, while others who make money off their labor build palatial mansions on estates rivaling the royal families of Europe? I believe our nation represents something better. We stand against the royal families and aristocracy of Europe. Why in God's name would we want to institute a different version of such a system? We are supposed to be a democracy of the people. It seems to me we are rapidly moving toward an oligarchy of the rich," President Roosevelt is firm in his position, but he just as well be talking to a rock.

"The fact is Mr. President without the support of these captains of industry, it will make your election much more difficult. It is for this reason I have withheld my endorsement. I want to support a winner," Hanna acts as if he still holds the best hand.

"I recognize the truth of your assessment. As you will recognize Mr. Hanna, I have toned down my attack on big business in the last year. I still believe in reform, but I also recognize the futility of tilting at windmills. Help me win a second term, and I will turn my attention to foreign policy. Certainly, enhancing this country's position in the world will be good for everyone," the president is attempting to give Hanna something he can hang his hat on.

"I take you at your word Mr. President, and I will share this with others of my same persuasion. As of right now, I need to ponder our conversation before I can offer you my assurance," Hanna knows that denying Roosevelt the nomination will be difficult.

Mark Hanna leaves the White House still very much concerned about Roosevelt as the nominee. Hanna does not like TR, and he cannot quite clear the hurdle of doubt in his mind regarding Roosevelt's sincerity. He agrees economic fairness needs to be pursued, but he fears Roosevelt will use an ax rather than a scalpel in his second term. He also agrees with the need to establish the United States as a world power, but he is uncertain Roosevelt is the person to make this happen. Yet, the

President has great popularity with the people, and if he is nominated, it is not too difficult to see his election.

Secretly, Senator Hanna wants to replace Theodore Roosevelt as the Republican standard-bearer in 1904. He knows his wealthy friends will rally to his side should he decide to challenge the president. However, he has reservations about his ability to win the election. There is a progressive movement afoot across the United States, and he fears the Democrats might nominate William Randolph Hearst, the purveyor of Yellow Journalism. Only a Republican progressive stands a chance against someone like Hearst.

Roosevelt doesn't trust Hanna. As a man of money, Hanna has too many self-interests to conjure up the objectivity needed to understand the president's perspective. Yet, Roosevelt knew his future depended upon gaining Mark Hanna's support. Without his support, the Republican Convention will become a battleground that will divide the party and give the White House to the Democrats. Something needs to be done, he cannot allow the hourglass to run out on his future.

Theodore Roosevelt grew to trust Elihu Root more than any other advisor. As his Secretary of War, Root, and the President spend a great deal of time together daily. Root, who resigned as Secretary of War in January 1904, continues to maintain a close relationship with the president. When it comes time to relax, the President prefers Root's company over that of almost anyone else. So, the President decides to seek Elihu Root's advice over a glass of whiskey and perhaps a cigar.

"My dear friend, I am in a quandary."

"I suspect you are Mr. President. It seems to be your nature."

"I want to pose to you a very confidential question, and I need your most honest response," the president leans forward to ensure they are not overheard.

"My confidence and honesty are always yours," Root assures.

"Mark Hanna is an insufferable pain in the ass. He holds his position as Party Leader over my head like some weight about to be dropped. I am a bit uncertain about how to best deal with this millstone," the president reveals.

"Hanna has been consolidating power for many years. He sees you as a young whippersnapper unworthy of the position you hold. He is threatened by your success and popularity. Nothing is more dangerous to the holder, and threatening to adversaries than popularity. The power elite threatened by you could stop you from getting the nomination. They know that if you are nominated, that would most assuredly gain your election. It is a double-edged sword," Root shares as he shakes his head in disgust.

"He refuses to endorse my candidacy for President in 1904. I met with him yesterday, and he remains elusive on the subject," the president says as a matter of fact.

"He knows if nominated, you will win Mr. President. However, the scum bag has an allegiance to the Robber Barons on Murders Row. Remember he is cut from the same cloth. He sees money as the rightful way to power. To top it off, he still considers himself the rightful heir to McKinley," the secretary acknowledges the power of self-interest.

"But we must bring reform to business and industry, or we will become nothing more than a modern version of Medieval Europe. What kind of future is that for this nation? I have no desire to be associated with such a calamitous approach. I shall fight the dirty bastards to the bitter end, if necessary," The president has always been a determined man.

"Mr. President, Mark Hanna is not opposed to reform. He is opposed to action and reform which might undo the aristocracy of this country. He and his rich cronies are concerned you will pillage and burn everything they hold dear. Mark Hanna would be amiable to a much more subtle approach to reform," Root is not defending Hanna. In truth, he detests the man as much as the president does. However, Root knows the reality of power, and he knows the youthful president scares the old guard.

"So, what do you suggest be done Elihu?" the president is interested in his friend's advice.

"How set are you on keeping Secretary of Treasury Shaw?" Root asks.

"Why do you ask?" the president perks up with interest.

"Mark Hanna and Leslie Shaw are of the same persuasion. Bring Hanna into the tent Mr. President and make him part of the act. Tell Hanna you will make him Secretary of Treasury in a second term. Make him a grand gesture," Root knows the political game well.

"What if he refuses such an overture?" the president wonders.

"That would be all the better for you. By offering him the position of Secretary of the Treasury if elected, you are sending him a signal regarding your willingness to restrain your approach to big money. What could be more sincere?" Root offers with a sinister smile.

"And what if he accepts my offer? Then what, Mr. Root?" The president sees the danger of such a move.

"Then you remove Shaw and anoint Hanna. If Hanna is loyal to his service to you, then all is well. If not, off comes his head. Those you appoint, serve at the pleasure of the president. Once elected, if Hanna becomes a liability to your agenda, you make his time in office a short one," Root is determined in his advice.

"Bully for you, Mr. Root. I believe we have a plan. Are you willing to float this idea to Mr. Hanna on my behalf?" The president knows the best way to achieve this plan is by using his friend as a backchannel.

"It would be my privilege. I bid you a good day Mr. President," Root has a mission.

In taking his leave from the White House, Secretary Root makes his way to Senator Hanna's office. Upon arriving, Elihu Root finds the Senator reading the newspaper in his office.

"Anything of interest in the paper today, Senator?" Root says upon arriving at the doorway to the Senator's office.

"What do you think of this young man Henry Ford?" Hanna can sense the rise of another industrialist.

"I have heard he wants to make the automobile affordable to all Americans. That would be an astonishing feat," Root acknowledges.

"Well, it says in the paper he just set a new land speed record of 91.37 miles per hour with an automobile. Why the man must be insane to travel that fast? He must have a death wish," Hanna is impressed.

"That is indeed a great speed. Can you imagine how far people could travel in one day at a fraction of that speed?" Truly amazing Root adds. "These are certainly interesting times Mr. Hanna."

"What can I do for you, Secretary Root."

"I just came from the president, and he asked me to convey to you his interest to make you his Secretary of the Treasury should he gain election to a term of his own," Elihu Root wastes no time getting to the point.

"I don't know quite what to say, that is a generous offer," the Senator is genuinely taken back by Root's announcement.

"Please don't feel the necessity to respond immediately. The president understands these decisions take time. He would also ask you to keep this offer secret, so as not to create a stir within the current government," Root's request should go without saying, but securing Hanna's word is important.

"The word is mum, and thank you, Mr. Root!" Hanna is a bit dumbfounded and rubs his head.

Walking down the steps of the Senate Office Building, Elihu Root feels confident in the success of his mission. He saw how Hanna's eyes brightened at the prospect of such an offer. His usually gruff disposition had turned rather pleasant upon receipt of this news. Perhaps he will come around.

Elihu Root knows that Hanna had turned down a cabinet offer from President McKinley. At that time, Hanna was concerned about the backlash regarding his close ties to the president. A cabinet appointment would look too much like a payoff. But this is different. Hanna's disdain for Roosevelt is no secret. For Roosevelt to offer him a post, and for him to accept will bring with it no claims of impropriety. This is a genuine opportunity that Mark Hanna might not be able to turn down.

Mark Hanna is stunned. Why would the President want to make him Secretary of the Treasury unless he truly intends to tone down his attacks on the industrialists and Wall Street? As Secretary of the Treasury, he will be in a position to safeguard against government interference which will be unduly harmful to business. Hanna sits straight in his chair with an ego puffed as big as a balloon. He lights a large cigar to match his inflated sense of importance. All these years jockeying for power, and now in the face of his greatest adversary, he has prevailed for himself and his friends. Taking a deep draw off the cigar and exhaling ever so slowly, Hanna thinks to himself, "Perhaps it is time to endorse Theodore Roosevelt as the Republican nominee for President!"

The next day, word reaches the White House of Hanna's endorsement.

Roosevelt beams at how his plan has reaped such quick results. He can now turn his attention to the campaign.

On February 15, 1904, only a couple of weeks after giving Roosevelt his endorsement, Mark Hanna died. Shocked, and certainly sorry about any man's death, Teddy Roosevelt breathes a sigh of relief. He now finds himself free from the constraints that were Mark Hanna. He knows the nomination will be his uncontested, and a term in his own right looks promising.

At the Democratic Convention, the democrats turned away the candidacy of progressive William Randolph Hearst for a little-known conservative judge Alton B. Parker of New York. While President Roosevelt didn't need it, Parker's nomination is seen as a gift.

Theodore Roosevelt campaigned hard across the country. Surprisingly, before his death, Hanna divulged Roosevelt's offer of Secretary of Treasury to his friend John D. Rockefeller. Rockefeller saw this as a change in Roosevelt's approach to business and led the way with his associates in donating millions to Roosevelt's election. Even with his election assured, Theodore Roosevelt saw the benefit of purchasing a bloc of votes through the issuing of pensions. Leaving nothing to chance, Roosevelt issued an executive order during the campaign providing pensions for all veterans between the ages of sixty-two and sixty-seven. It is called the power of incumbency.

On November 8, 1904, Theodore Roosevelt won the Presidency over Democratic challenger Alton B. Parker. Once the Democrats nominated Parker, the election was never in doubt. As a candidate, Parker's political stance carried little weight with the voters. He represented an unknown commodity to the American people, while Teddy Roosevelt enjoyed immense popularity. In what might be called a landslide, Theodore Roosevelt obtained a presidential term in his own right. T.R. became the first person to inherit the presidency and go on to win a term of his own.

Chapter 11

SAGE FOR THE AGES

With the Presidency of Theodore Roosevelt, a break in the clouds that covered the country since 1865 brought the sunlight of hope to a nation in despair. Even in a state of despair, people carry on doing the things that need to be done. People endure the unavoidable struggles and strife of life as a matter of survival. On the surface, a sugar-coated society looks rich in promise and hope, but digging deeper reveals a society in which little progress is made for common people. Theodore Roosevelt represents someone who wants to break through that sugar-coating and allow more people to reach the surface.

The story of Theodore Roosevelt is the story of a fighter. A man who attempts to land blow after blow upon the head and body of the nation's elite to bring them to their knees, and remove their grasp on the economic soul of the nation.

While Roosevelt did not utter these words until 1910, they echo the very essence of the man.

"It is not the critic who counts; not the man who points out how the strong man stumbles, or where the doer of deeds could have done them better. The credit belongs to the man who is actually in the arena, whose face is marred by dust and sweat and blood; who strives valiantly; who errs, who comes short again and again, because there is no effort without error and shortcoming; but who does actually strive to do the deeds; who knows great enthusiasms, the great devotions; who spends himself in a worthy cause; who at the best knows, in the end, the triumph of high achievement, and who at the worst, if he fails, at least fails while daring greatly, so that his place shall never be with those cold and timid souls who neither know victory nor defeat."

During Roosevelt's tenure as president, the American Aristocracy faced its first real challenge from an American President. Of course, there had been political players and even a president or two who labored to bring economic justice to American society. The problem has always been in the mental and emotional strength of the man. A champion must be soundly grounded in philosophy, idealism, and strength of character. Following the death of Abraham Lincoln, the American political system failed to produce such a man. With Roosevelt, the aristocracy experiences what happens when the right man, seizes the mantle of power, with the disposition and determination to act. These are challenging times for people of substance. Not because it diminishes their opulent lifestyle, but because it puts in jeopardy the perpetuation of their empire.

Rich men are like a disease, they seek to become pervasive in their impact on society and human life. Just as diseases develop the ability to mutate and adapt to new medicines, rich men learn to develop ways of circumventing the manacles of society. If history is the story of the struggles and triumphs of the downtrodden, it is equally the story of the oppressive nature that the rich impose on society. The lessons learned by the Robber Barons at the dawn of the twentieth century are just the beginning of lessons that will shape the course of American politics throughout the century.

Shortly after the turn of the year in 1905, President Roosevelt and his old friend Secretary of State John Hay were enjoying a conversation in the newly completed West Wing. The Secretary of State has fallen into ill health recently, and the President is concerned.

"Mr. Hay, you have been in the service of your country for a long and distinguished career. Your service has been indispensable to your country. I have considered it an honor to have you by my side as Secretary of State," Roosevelt knows the sacrifices Hay has made throughout his distinguished career.

"Thank you, Mr. President. I had the good fortune of starting my service to the country at the young age of twenty-two with President Lincoln."

"What an honor it must have been to know and work alongside such a great man as Abraham Lincoln," the president is a bit in awe at the thought of being in the presence of someone who not only knew President Lincoln but served as a close confidant and advisor.

"With your pardon Sir, I consider it to have been the greatest blessing of my life to have known firsthand the character and constitution of such a person as Abraham Lincoln," John Hay knows that Teddy Roosevelt is Lincolnesque in nature.

"No pardon needed Mr. Hay. Abraham Lincoln stands alongside George Washington in the pantheon of American heroes and leaders. I can only vaguely imagine the burden he carried during those tumultuous years of struggle," Roosevelt's humility is exactly what gives him the potential to be such a great leader.

"While it has been my honor to serve, I grieve at the thought that this nation, so conceived in liberty, has been the incubator of such violence as that which brought an end to President Lincoln, Garfield, and McKinley all during my time of service," the president can hear the sorrow in Hay's voice.

"Yes indeed, Mr. Hay, a sad state of affairs in any nation, let alone one based on the rule of law," Roosevelt responds. "Mr. Hay, what were President Lincoln's thoughts about the Negro and labor unions?"

"Mr. Lincoln possessed an extraordinary gift of vision. Without his perception of the future, I do not believe Abraham Lincoln could have physically, mentally, or emotionally endured the Civil War. A part of this vision included reconstruction following the war," John Hay begins.

"So, what did he reveal through conversation and writing about the future of the Negro," the president is looking for a vision himself.

"He doubted the ability of white people to ever remove themselves from a discriminatory hatred for a people of such difference. He felt that white folk, no matter their social standing, would always seek to keep the Negro subservient in one way or another. He saw the challenge to require a gargantuan effort, and he was determined to face that challenge straight on," Secretary of Hay reveals.

"He must have had a plan?" the president asks.

"He did, after the dust had settled on the Civil War and the Union restored, Lincoln wanted to carve out an area in the west for a Negro state. He hoped to do this along with gaining the Negro the right to vote before he left office," Hay notes.

"What might have been, is now reserved as a question for the history books. Surely, President Lincoln could see that the idea of a negro state was not very practical. Simply look at how the nation has failed to deal with the Indians. Reservations and broken promises make for awful bedfellows. Unfortunately, we shall never know what might have come of Lincoln's leadership. What we do know is reconstruction has been a miserable failure. The North and South remain as divided as ever on the existence and future of the negro," President Roosevelt wishes he could find an easy path to resolving the issue of equality.

"I fear you are right Mr. President," Hay is in a contemplating mood.

"What about labor Mr. Hay? What did Lincoln think about labor?" T.R. is again looking for guidance.

"I have never forgotten President Lincoln's sentiments about labor. President Lincoln spoke of labor often with such fierce conviction. His secretary Nicolay printed his quote on labor and placed it on his private desk. It said, "Labor is prior to and independent of capital. Capital is only the fruit of labor, and could never have existed if labor had not first existed. Labor is the superior of capital and deserves much the higher consideration," John Hay shares.

"Truly words of wisdom Mr. Hay. You and I are not men of capital, we are men of labor. We know firsthand the toil required to keep a government going just as it is the toil of labor that turns the wheels of industry. We have our work cut out for us. The men of wealth shudder at the thought of power in the hands of labor," The president acknowledges.

"Mr. President, not since President Lincoln has a person occupied this office with the character and courage needed to face up to and deal directly with the great challenges which face this nation. The nation is truly fortunate for your arrival. May God protect you!" Secretary Hay is concerned for the safety of such a promising leader.

"I take it you find my stance in contempt of trusts, and my support of unions agreeable?" the president asks.

"While you do not generally seek my deliberation on matters

of domestic importance, I must tell you I find your approach most refreshing. The dunderheads living in their mansions, and seeking to control and manipulate the economy need a good thrashing. I believe in your own words, I should say "Bully good job," the secretary nods in approval.

"It only seems right that should a dragon appear on the scene, there must also appear a worthy dragon slayer. It also seems only right that if capital is given the right to organize, then labor should have an equal and corresponding right. Surely, fair is fair," Roosevelt declares.

"In the election, you called for the Square Deal, not an obtuse deal," Mr. Hay says with a chuckle.

The President does not know how to chuckle and therefore shares a hearty good laugh at which he says, "It has been a most pleasurable evening Mr. Hay. I have a couple of letters I must write before I retire, so I must take my leave."

"Good night Mr. President."

Theodore Roosevelt's boldest move on civil rights came shortly after becoming president when he invited Booker T. Washington to dine with him at the White House. This act of inclusion so outraged news publications across the country that Roosevelt never offered such an invitation again. While he speaks out in such a manner as to make clear his feelings against segregation, he does little to advance the civil rights of Negroes or other people of a non-white persuasion.

Roosevelt's pronouncement of the Square Deal frequently finds him between a rock and a hard place. He believes trusts must be reined in to support an economic system in which all people have an opportunity to participate and benefit. The economic system he inherited as President greatly favors people of capital over people of labor. And yet, like Lincoln, he believes in the supremacy of labor. However, a square deal is a square deal, so how can he reign in the abusive actions of capital while allowing carte blanche to labor?

After his election, Roosevelt began to speak out even more fervently against the evils of big money at the expense of labor. It begins to unfold like some medieval play in which a good king battles the greedy lords of the manor on behalf of the oppressed and struggling serfs.

Significant progress occurred with the passage of the Employers

Liability Act of 1906 only to be struck down by the United States Supreme Court on January 6, 1907, on the basis that it violated state's rights.

After receiving news that the Supreme Court struck down the Employers Liability Act, President Roosevelt prepared to meet several members of his cabinet in the Cabinet Room adjacent to his office. The large rectangular Cabinet Room in the newly constructed West Wing of the White House requires a great deal of artificial lighting due to a lack of windows. The President has a high-back chair at the end of the cabinet table around which are many cushioned chairs. The room has a solid wood floor and a rather high ceiling. On the walls, the President has paintings of his favorite scenes of the West. He also has a painting of Washington and Lincoln along one wall. Off to one side of the table is a large marble fireplace. On the fireplace mantle are reminders of the president's exploits in the Spanish-American War and his time as a cowboy in the Dakotas.

As the door to the room opens, Secretary of the Treasury Cortelyou, Secretary of Labor Straus, and Attorney General Bonaparte arrive for the meeting.

"Good morning gentlemen, please take a seat at the table," the president invites.

"Good morning, Mr. President," the men say in unison.

"I have been fuming for some time regarding the Supreme Court's incompetent handling of the Employers Liability Act. Chief Justice Fuller has no more understanding of the social dynamics at work in this case than a drunk cowboy herding calves. What the hell happened?" the president is speaking to his attorney general.

"The court felt the law impeded upon state's rights," the attorney general unwisely proclaimed.

"Good God, I understand that Mr. Bonaparte. Do you think I am daft? It is your job as my attorney general to prevail upon the court on the necessity to extend federal jurisdiction. It is not your job to kowtow to the court. They are a body of legal minds. It is your job to prevail upon their better judgment. I expected better Mr. Attorney General," the president makes his displeasure clear.

"If I might interject Mr. President, I realize I am new to my position in Treasury, but the railroads continue to hold a tight reign over the economy. This law was not in their interest, and they mustered significant leverage in this case," Secretary Cortelyou states.

"Mr. Secretary, are you saying that the railroad titans possess more power and leverage than the United States Government? I find this unacceptable. Gentlemen, we are engaged in a war to save this nation from a rising criminal class. We are confronted with criminals of great wealth. Yes, they are indeed criminals. When they conduct themselves as if they are above the law, they are nothing more than criminals. They can't be allowed to engage in their predatory practices at the expense of the general populace. Do you understand?" President Roosevelt is commanding as if he is leading the charge up San Juan Hill.

"We are hamstrung by the fact we must work within the law, and the Robber Barons are free to use the law to find ways to work where no law exists. It is a game of chess in which our every move creates a counter-move of opposition. When you add purchased politicians and judicial appointees to the equation, it becomes a very steep climb," says Secretary of Labor Straus.

"Gentlemen, I was not elected, nor were you appointed to find excuses for why we cannot prevail. It is our job to defend the best interests of the people we serve. We do not serve stock gamblers who fleece the public out of millions of dollars with their phantom property. We do not serve the Industrial Barons or the masters of Wall Street. We do not serve the railroads, oil, steel, copper, coal, silver, or gold. We serve the people to whom this nation rightly belongs. We serve the people who work and toil to make a living by the sweat of their brow every day," the president declares.

"But working people do not have the power," Attorney General Bonaparte indicates.

"Mr. Bonaparte, working people are the power. It is the working people who advanced us into office. If we do not achieve success in establishing a balance between capital and labor in which there is fairness in wages, benefits, and working conditions, the working class should revolt. If we do not fight and act to bring fairness to those who break their backs to make a living, there should and will be a revolution. It is our sacred duty under the auspices of the United States Constitution to act for the common good to establish domestic tranquility. We have much work to do, and we must let the wealthy know, we have the power," the president is determined, and he expects his cabinet to be determined as well.

"What must we do Mr. President? We serve at your pleasure," the Secretary of the Treasury inquires.

"In my last message to Congress, I demanded action on inheritance and income taxes, national incorporation of interstate businesses, greater federal power over railroad rates, compulsory investigation of major labor disputes, and wider application of the eight-hour day. It is your job to ensure my message leads to action. I expect nothing less," the president reveals.

"Where do we start?" the three cabinet members are seeking direction.

"Mr. Cortelyou, I need you to be the lead lobbyist for an inheritance and income tax law that will see to it that the wealthy pay their fair share as a member of this nation. I want loopholes closed tight as a drum. Mr. Straus, I need you to push hard for increased federal control over all matters of interstate commerce. Start with a re-write of the Employers Liability Act which will survive any challenge in any court. Attorney General Bonaparte, you move legislation through Congress that will improve the conditions for workers all across this country. I also want you to strengthen the Sherman Act. While we recognize the legitimacy of beneficial combinations, we must continue our pursuit to break up those combinations which are harmful to workers and a free enterprise economy," the president leaves no doubt about what he wants to be accomplished.

"These will not be easy tasks to achieve. We will face great opposition in every quarter as we pursue such reforms. The wealthy will unite and pool their resources to put pressure on the legislative and judicial branches of government," the Secretary of Labor Straus points out.

"Mr. Straus, these are not easy times. These new conditions make it necessary to shackle cunning as in the past we have shackled force. We must muster all our resources. We must outsmart those who would stand in our way. We must rally public sentiment to a fevered pitch if necessary. Let it be clear, that the very heart and soul of this nation hang in the balance. Unless we are willing to accept a nation ruled by the few, we must prevail," Theodore Roosevelt possesses the disposition of a warrior preparing for battle.

"As you wish Mr. President," the three men prepare to exit the room.

"Gentlemen, do not let slip from your mind this fact: The vast individual and corporate fortunes, the vast combinations of capital, which have marked the development of our industrial system, create new conditions. These new conditions necessitate a change from the old attitude of the State and Nation regarding the rules regulating the acquisition and untrammeled business use of property," President Roosevelt is proclaiming a paradigm shift.

As the old Rough Rider begins his crusade toward the end of his term in 1909, he is in for one hell of a rough ride. As a product of eastern seaboard privilege and old money, Theodore Roosevelt is considered a traitor by his own class. While not the first American leader to do so, he is the first American President to do so with such guile and determination.

The wealthy are devoted to their wealth. They perceive their position in society as one and the same as the future of the nation. They are not about to give ground at their own expense, or at the expense of their descendants. They are creating generational wealth akin to the nobility of the old world. They will resort to whatever it takes to bring this President to his knees. Roosevelt may control some levers of government, but they control the levers of power. With this president, they are engaged in a learning curve of how to legally and effectively use their money to wield and maintain power. One of their instruments of power is found in the First Amendment to the Constitution of the United States.

By owning and controlling the news media which amounts to print publications, they control the message. The First Amendment provides them with the power of free speech. Under the cover of the First Amendment, they implement a strategy dating back to colonial times. With a flourish of publications to an increasingly literate public, they seek to control the message and portray the president as an out-of-control tyrant.

Implementing a well-orchestrated attack aimed at the character assassination of the president, the wealthy criminal class buys off the news syndications to malign the president's character. The news portrays

Roosevelt as an alcoholic president, a man prone to the use of Opium. They claim his decrees and messages are the product of a madman, a person gone insane and delusional with power. They say Roosevelt is hell-bent on destroying the very fabric of the United States economy. Surely, the president will bring the entire nation to ruin.

The wealthy criminal class extends their purchasing of influence beyond the scoop of politicians, including academicians. Presidents of some of the nation's foremost universities (those reserved for the children of the privileged class) proclaim President Roosevelt to be incapable of leading the nation.

Roosevelt stood firm in the face of such personal assault. His resolve only becomes greater with every attempt to discredit him. The only salve that tempers the salvos as he nears the end of his second term is the promise, he made upon election to not seek another term. As his term approaches twilight, he regrets making such a promise but feels honor-bound to keep it. He finds his saving grace in his old friend and Secretary of War William Howard Taft. In 1908, with President Roosevelt's help, Taft became the Republican Candidate for President. Roosevelt felt confident that Taft would continue to fight for the things he held so dear.

Chapter 12

THE CHOSEN ONE

Theodore Roosevelt's foreign policy found favor with most sectors of the American public. The wealthy cheer on the Panama Canal, the Roosevelt Corollary to the Monroe Doctrine, and the rising presence of U.S. Naval might around the world. The Captains of Industry understand that American influence around the globe means access to valuable resources, as well as, increased markets for American manufactured goods. Like a good pirate, nothing escapes the eye of the capitalist when it comes to profiteering.

The general public supported Roosevelt's gunboat diplomacy. The concept of gunboat diplomacy is simple. Display military supremacy around the world to gain influence and power. The use of force is not required when other nations can see that resistance would be futile.

In the early 20th Century, the concept of Manifest Destiny ran deep through the veins of Americans as a Christian principle and a matter of national honor. The emergence of the Chautauqua, a traveling cultural festival offers Americans across the country an opportunity to experience the arts as well as dynamic speakers. Russell Conwell, a Baptist Minister is one of those notable speakers. His themes on American exceptionalism are a staple of the Chautauqua circuit. Conwell's bluster fuels the idea that the good is destined to be rich, and the poor are not to be pitied, because their plight results from sin. He transfers this notion between rich and poor to the natural destiny of the United States to dominate a less deserving world. In less than one hundred years, the United States evolved from a fledgling nation to a nation seeking an empire.

As Roosevelt's Secretary of War, William Howard Taft held a good position from which to seek the Presidency. As history closes in on 1908, Roosevelt and Taft spend a great deal of time together discussing politics. Roosevelt didn't feel the White House was a suitable place for such political conversations so he traveled to his Sagamore Hill home to prepare for a transfer of power.

Roosevelt loved to entertain guests in his spacious office/library with its huge Persian carpet, two magnificent Elk heads with incredible antlers, and beautiful wood furnishings. This room offers any guest a peek at the inner sanctum of the nation's leading outdoorsman. On the wall just next to the door of this great room hangs the Nobel Peace Prize President Roosevelt won for his work in resolving the Russo-Japanese War in 1905. The president takes great pride in this award which reflects his willingness to take risks for the greater good. Roosevelt always offered a visiting Secretary Taft a spacious high-backed chair to accommodate his large three-hundred-pound frame.

"Would you like a cup of tea, Mr. Secretary?"

"I would prefer a glass of whiskey, Mr. President, however since it is early in the day, tea sounds fine," responds William Howard Taft in a robust manner.

"It is always a pleasure to have you here William," the president is sincere. Roosevelt and Taft developed a deep and trusting friendship.

"It is always a pleasure to be here. I feel like I am somewhere west of the Mississippi rather than Oyster Bay. Your furnishings create a most inspiring setting. You certainly experienced the western frontier," As a good friend, Taft knows how to stroke T.R.'s ego.

"William, the Republican Convention convenes in Chicago in less than a month. Our party will soon choose its candidate for president. How are you feeling about your chances for the nomination?" the president asks his friend.

"As you know Mr. President there are several notable and highly qualified men wanting that nomination. The general feeling is whoever gains the nomination will probably be the next President based on the popularity of your policies. I would certainly like to be the man to fill your shoes. While no one could match the outstanding leadership you have provided, I certainly feel up to the challenge," Taft knows he will need his friend's support.

"I appreciate those thoughts, Mr. Secretary. The Presidency has been a Bully good time. My unexpected rise to power, combined with my election in 1904, allowed me to pursue a vision for this country I had never dreamt possible. I am hoping my predecessor will continue to pursue this vision," Roosevelt is thinking about his legacy.

"Are you certain you will not seek the nomination yourself? You know another term is within your grasp," Taft wants assurance that the president will not change his mind.

"I am a man of my word, and while I find the prospect most tempting, the nation does not need a president who fails to keep his word. As I have previously proclaimed, I will not pursue nor will I accept the nomination," the president says definitively.

"I understand your silence on the matter of our party's nominee Mr. President, but at some time you need to make a proclamation of support," Secretary Taft wants the president's endorsement. He knows Roosevelt holds the keys to the citadel of power.

"William, I am in a most precarious position. My Vice-President, two former cabinet members, three Senators, a Governor, and a former Speaker of the House have all thrown their hats into the infernal ring of contention. For me to proclaim my support at such an early date would look as if the whole thing were rigged. Of course, that is assuming the convention would follow my lead," the president knows the convention will certainly look to him for guidance.

"You know, Mr. President, the convention is going to look to you to choose a successor. It will be you who determines the nominee." Sitting in Roosevelt's office/library, William Howard Taft in no uncertain terms is trying to obtain the president's nod of support.

"Let me speak frankly Mr. Secretary. Mr. Cannon of Illinois is too old. Vice President Fairbanks does not possess the backbone for this office. I am not certain why I selected him for Vice President. Why if I were to be shot, the damn fool would become President. Maybe my judgment isn't all that good," the president says tongue in cheek.

"And what of the other candidates?" Taft is liking what he has heard so far.

"I have never cared for Foraker of Ohio, and Senator Knox, along with former Treasury Secretary Shaw, is just too close to the battles that must be waged with the trusts and money changers. You know those corrupt bastards on Wall Street will try to game the system. Nothing would please them more than to have a candidate from each party in their pocket. I can't allow that to happen!" Roosevelt is determined to keep the fox out of the hen house.

"That seems to narrow the field, Mr. President. I have not heard you disqualify myself," Taft gets right to the point.

"You are not disqualified, William. I greatly favor you over Governor Hughes and Senator LaFollette. Your work as Governor of the Philippines represented a judicious man of great administrative talent and conviction. I selected you for Secretary of War, because of your commitment to our prestige around the world, and your commitment to fair play for all people," Roosevelt says without committing.

"Hughes and LaFollette enjoy great popularity within the party. They too are very talented and capable men. Either would make a fine nominee and president." Taft wants the nomination, but if it is lost, he wants to lose to men who are worthy and up to the task.

"Yes, they do. That is exactly why I must be patient in offering my endorsement. A rush to judgment on my part could be interpreted as a coronation rather than a nomination. Such carelessness could backfire. It could split the party and throw the election to the Democrats. In that case, we would all lose, especially, the American people. I like you William, but we must be smart in how we proceed," the president is a very smart political operator.

"I understand completely Mr. President. However, if you are going to endorse my candidacy, I would appreciate you do so at your earliest convenience. You know all too well that your nod is going to determine the candidate," Taft is anxious. There is nothing worse than uncertainty.

"William, we are good friends. I have the utmost confidence that you are the best qualified and capable of all the candidates. I trust a Taft Administration will reflect the continuation of the work of this past nearly seven years," T.R. wants assurance from Taft.

"Mr. President, I admire more than I can express your vision for this country. You have been a champion for the people. You have taken on the Goliaths of wealth, Wall Street, and industry in pursuit of economic fairness for all people. You have protected millions of acres of land for the people of this nation and posterity. You have made this nation a major player on the world stage. What is there that a president would not want to continue and build upon?" Taft is all but saying where do I sign the contract of assurance.

"Very well, then it is done. You can trust that at what I believe is the most appropriate time, I will throw my support behind you as our party's candidate for President. This is a bully good thing!" the president says with his big toothy smile.

Before the Republican Convention at the Chicago Coliseum on June 16, 1908, President Roosevelt threw his unequivocal support behind William Howard Taft as the party's Presidential nominee. As a result, the convention took but one ballot to nominate Taft with seven hundred and two votes out of a possible nine hundred and eighty. Taft's closest challenger Philander Knox received but sixty-eight votes.

In the campaign of 1908, Republican Taft faced off with Democrat William Jennings Bryan. To beat the Republicans at their own game, the Democrats are hoping, Bryan who was the progressive candidate in 1896 and 1900, will find his third time to be a charm. On November 3, 1908, William Howard Taft was elected President of the United States with three hundred and twenty-one electoral votes to one hundred and sixty-two. Taft won by more than one million popular votes. The electoral map displays a country very divided. Bryan wins the old South and a couple of Western states. Taft takes everything above the Mason-Dixon Line and just about everything in the West.

On March 4, 1909, William Howard Taft took the oath of office from Chief Justice Melville Fuller. As so many times before, the peaceful transition of power occurs. Theodore Roosevelt departed Washington D.C. confident the only difference in Washington was the man occupying the White House. The Industrialists and Lions of Wall Street breathe a sigh of relief to see Roosevelt ride off into the sunset. Nobody can possibly know the Herculean struggle which lay ahead.

Chapter 13

MISPLACED DESTINY

Most people today have been raised and educated on the notion that anyone can grow up to become President of the United States. In some ways, there is truth to this notion, but not without making friends and selling your soul to those with great wealth. In most cases, there is nothing common about the American Presidency. A close examination reveals it to be a part of the American Aristocracy and in some cases a matter of heredity.

William Howard Taft is no exception to the rule. Taft grew up in a very affluent family. While his father seems to be a self-made man, his success ensures William Howard and his brothers have easy access to the best society has to offer. His father Alphonso Taft served as President U.S. Grant's Secretary of War, and later Attorney General. Alphonso established a firm family (hereditary) foothold in American politics which even continues to this day.

William Howard Taft assumed the Presidency following a man of incredible magnetism. Theodore Roosevelt believed the reigns of state were for wielding on behalf of the American people. The big stick, and the bully pulpit, are ready for the next master of the White House. Roosevelt set precedent after precedent as an executive of courage and action. Now the torch is passed to Taft.

Taft's heart doesn't belong to the executive branch of government. True, he displayed extraordinary skills and ability as the Governor of the Philippines. But, the desire to be President rests with his wife Helen

(Nellie) Herron Taft. Nellie is the daughter of Cincinnati Judge John Williamson Herron, a law partner of Rutherford B. Hayes. Ever since visiting the White House while Hayes was President, Nellie has wanted to be First Lady. William Howard Taft actually wanted to be Chief Justice of the Supreme Court. His passion rests with a judicial life. He feels his greatest contributions to the public good can occur from the bench, not the bully pulpit.

From the outset, Taft doesn't know what to do. He doesn't harbor political instincts, and he views everything from the perspective of a jurist. He befuddled Roosevelt into believing he would conduct himself in a manner consistent with his predecessor. Roosevelt tossed his support to Taft for this very reason. Now, at center stage, he hesitates. Where Roosevelt is a man of action, who only worries about the legal consequences later; Taft can't bring himself to look at things in this manner. Actions must be preceded by legal consideration, and nothing else matters.

Roosevelt sought Taft's assurance that he would maintain his cabinet as a means of continuity. While never making such a bold promise, Taft didn't give Roosevelt any reason to question his intentions.

Not only did Roosevelt believe Taft would act in concert with his work, but so did progressive Republicans all across the country. They count on Taft to move forward in creating a just and fair economic environment. They count on Taft to be dedicated to the principles of conservation. They count on Taft to follow Roosevelt's lead in foreign policy.

One week before Taft's Inauguration on March 4, 1909, Henry Frick, the most despicable of all the looter elite, invites Carnegie, Morgan, and Rockefeller to his mansion on 4th Avenue in New York City. Frick makes his fortune worming and weaseling his way around the great industrialists and financiers of the day. His parasitic maneuvering allows him to fill his coffers with millions, by doing the things his bosses prefer not to do. Frick is not beyond the use of intimidation of every type. He could care less about the impact of his actions on any man or his family. Frick is a brute, a mean and nasty brute. His disdain for workers is only overshadowed by his contempt for the government. He respects nothing and no one. His ostentatious nature leads him to desire the best and most of everything. He wants everyone to witness his greatness, and so he builds himself a mansion, a show palace, much like the wealthy do today.

Upon entering Frick's mansion, his visitors are immediately struck by the enormous rooms, high ceilings, chandeliers, and paintings. Famous paintings are everywhere. Within his mansion, Frick has a covered courtyard resembling something out of ancient Greece or Rome, complete with a garden and pool. He has a large pool room, bowling alley, and swimming pool. His library contains thousands of volumes of which many are the first edition. It is here in his impressive library he plans to meet with the others.

After the butler pours the brandy, Frick orders him to get out. Now alone in his library, the bastard and his brethren share the kind of counsel they all know so well.

"A toast to the demise of King Teddy the Wretched; a traitor of his own social class! We weathered the storms he created and beat back his slings and arrows of contempt and control. As we proclaimed in the beginning, we would outlast the son-of-a-bitch, and we did. He can now take his big stick and bully pulpit, and go straight to hell," the host proclaims.

Frick's proclamation is met with a round of salutes. His guests are not necessarily fond of Frick. He is just a very nasty sort with a disgusting personality. However, Frick has a place and a purpose of benefit to them all. He is the devil's workhorse.

"Gentlemen, I must congratulate all of us on a most perfect ruse with the Panic of 1907. Through our manipulation of the business environment, we successfully convinced the public that the anti-corporate policies of Roosevelt were the cause of a near failure of the American economic system," J.P. Morgan exposes his pride in the manner in which financiers control and manipulate the economy.

"Mr. Frick, you are to be commended for this outrageous idea. Your evil scheme helped us create a setting in which we could act as saviors of the American economy. It was a stroke of brilliance," J.D. Rockefeller the wealthiest man in the world proclaims.

"It is most satisfying when the wool can be so easily pulled over the eyes of an unsuspecting public. Thanks to their economic ignorance, the people are like putty in our hands," Frick notes.

"J.D. is to be lauded for his contribution to this scheme. To use his money to prop up the American economy was nothing short of genius. He not only made himself but the rest of us look like knights riding unselfishly to the aid of our country," Morgan says taking a long draw on his cigar and exhaling a victorious plume of smoke.

"I didn't mind doing this, gentlemen. As a part of this conspiracy, I knew the risk was but a phantom ruse. Once I pumped my money into the economy, the rest of you unleashed the power of production to ensure Roosevelt a black eye. I got my money back with interest. Hardly a sacrifice," Rockefeller ensures.

"But what if it were not a ruse? What if another president, someone worse similar to William Jennings Bryan were ever elected? We must find a way to protect ourselves from the threat someone like this presents to our fortunes. The greatness of this country is found in its capitalistic and free enterprise system. We have earned and deserve every penny we have made, and no one of any socialistic leanings has a right to put our fortunes in jeopardy," Andrew Carnegie declares. "J.D. is your son not married to the daughter of Senator Nelson Aldrich?"

"Yes, he is, Abby is a dear child whom I am proud to call daughter-in-law. Why do you ask?" Rockefeller wonders leaning forward in his overstuffed chair.

"Well, we need someone to run interference in getting the government to adopt the Federal Reserve idea as a means of protecting against a real panic. Can we count on your son to see to it his father-in-law takes the lead in this work?" The shrewd-thinking Carnegie leaves no stone unturned.

"We shouldn't need young Rockefeller's help, hell, Senator Aldrich owes me many favors for the inside information I have channeled his way. He is a wealthy man because of me," Frick has worked tirelessly to put many men in his pocket.

"That might be true, but young Rockefeller could do this discretely and help insulate us from such unsavory business," Carnegie reminds the group of the need for deniability should anyone suspect collusion.

"Now is the time to use our influence on a full range of issues. In one week, Bill Taft will be inaugurated as president. I think we all know he is not up to the task," Morgan says knowing this cabal of financial tyrants has an abundance of favors to call upon.

"Taft is more interested in traveling and playing golf than he is in being president. He doesn't have the slightest idea about how to run the country. This is a time to solidify our influence," Rockefeller proclaims.

"What is more important gentlemen is we use our power with the press to ensure President Taft is seen by the people as President Daft. In the next four years, we must work to change the nature of politics in this country. Politics is the key to controlling the government. If we work it right, politicians can have all the glory and great riches too if they do our bidding. The government that works for us belongs to us," Carnegie sets the stage.

"I offer a toast to the next four years," Frick raises his glass high.

William Howard Taft was no sooner inaugurated than a schism between him and Roosevelt began to emerge. Taft is quite clear he doesn't agree with the bully pulpit approach taken by Roosevelt. While he may agree with the former President in principle, he doesn't agree with the approach. While Taft may be a big man, he is small on ideas and lacks the willingness to use his high office for the promotion of high ideals. In one of his first meetings in the White House, Taft set the tone for his administration with Secretary of State Philander Knox, Secretary of the Treasury Franklin MacVeagh, and Attorney General George Wickersham.

Philander Knox served Theodore Roosevelt as Attorney General. Knox is a wealthy elitist with deep ties as a corporate lawyer, especially with U.S. Steel. Franklin MacVeagh came from a wealthy family and achieved great success in the banking business. His brother Isaac MacVeagh served as U.S. Attorney General under Presidents Garfield and Chester Arthur. Franklin and President Taft were Skull and Bones members together at Yale. George Wickersham became a law partner with Cadwalader, Wickersham, and Taft; one of the most successful and influential Wall Street Law practices. Henry Taft, the President's brother is a partner with this firm.

"Good morning, Secretary Knox, Secretary MacVeagh, and Attorney

General Wickersham it is an honor to meet with you in these hallowed halls," greets the new president.

"Good morning, Mr. President, we trust you slept well."

"I slept well indeed. I am going to find this job much more to my liking than Secretary of War. I am in charge of my own agenda now, and I do not need to be in the office until 10:00 a.m. How can things be any better," the president admits he enjoys a late start to his day.

"Well, a game of golf would not hurt," Secretary Knox knows the president likes to play a round of golf.

Giving off a huge belly laugh for which William Howard Taft is well known, he responds, "So right you are Secretary Knox I see a game in the near future."

"Now my friends, we need to get down to business. We have a country to run, and challenges to address. Let me be clear, I do not see the executive branch as some independent authority outside the realm of Congress and the courts. While I agreed with most of the positions taken by my predecessor, I do not agree with his approach which often showed disdain for the law. Are we clear on that?" the president declares.

"We are Mr. President, and how do you see your cabinet functioning?" the Attorney General inquires.

"General, I do not believe in extending responsibility without the corresponding authority needed to fulfill your duties. I want you to run your departments with the confidence I will support your decisions and actions. I cannot nor do I plan to tend to every aspect of government."

"Mr. President, what are your plans with the tariff issue looming on the horizon?" inquires the Treasury Secretary.

"Secretary MacVeagh, as you of all people are well aware, we have been running a deficit budget the last few years. We must take steps to bring our revenue in line with our spending."

"The Republican Party has long been the champion of high tariffs to protect manufacturing at home. Yet there is a significant movement to see tariffs on certain goods reduced to bring the prices of these goods down. We are looking at a possible split in our party over this issue," injects Secretary Knox.

"Secretary Knox is correct Mr. President. Tariffs are the biggest issue facing your administration. This is what might be called a wedge issue within your party."

"Mr. Wickersham, I have inherited a progressive agenda from the most progressive president we have seen since Lincoln. And yet, progressivism must follow the same course of law as conservatism, and herein lies our dilemma. House Speaker Cannon is not likely to give an inch to the progressives on the issue of tariffs. Senate Leader Aldrich has long been in the back pocket of the industrialists who support high tariff policies. From a legislative perspective, this will be a real battle," President Taft acknowledges.

"But the battle will be fought. The progressives LaFollette of Wisconsin, John Dolliver of Cummins, Iowa, and Beveridge of Indiana will press forward in every way possible to see tariffs reduced on imports important to their constituents. Furthermore, they will expect you President Taft to stand with them in this fight," continues Knox.

"I do not stand with them and I do not stand against them. These men are egotistical fanatics who will stop at nothing, even the destruction of the Republican Party to achieve their goals. We must find a way to negotiate ourselves through these rocky shoals," the president acknowledges the dilemma.

"Gentlemen, I must take your leave, it is time for lunch and then a round of golf. Walter Travis and I have a 1:00 tee time at the Chevy Chase Club in the event any of you would like to join us."

"I shall be there Mr. President."

"Very good Philander, very good indeed!"

The tariff issue looms large over the Washington D.C. political landscape. Senator Aldrich and Speaker Cannon are well aware of the battle that lay ahead. They also know the President will put a great deal of pressure on them to come up with a plan agreeable to all Republicans. They are not certain this is something they can or are willing to do.

Both Aldrich and Cannon hold the president in low regard. They like him as a person, who wouldn't? The president possesses a congenial and affable personality. However, they both feel Taft is ill-suited for the Presidency. They are fearful of the damage his incompetent management of the executive office might do to the Republican Party and therefore the nation. Meeting in the Speaker's office, Aldrich and Cannon plot their course of action.

"Mr. Speaker, you are in the process of drafting a new tariff bill which I assume will reflect our party's historical commitment to protection," Senator Aldrich states the fact.

"Absolutely Senator, as we both know times require change, and the old tariff law needs updating, but it certainly doesn't need an overhaul. The Republican Party has stood staunchly behind our manufacturers and industries to protect our goods from unnecessary competition with inferior and cheap imports. The strength of our economy is based on the protection of American-made products," Speaker Cannon says what they both know.

"I know you enjoy a very large majority of progressives in the house. While I enjoy a majority in the Senate, I have some damnable progressives from the Mid-west who will work tirelessly to undermine anything they do not support."

"Our biggest problem Senator is in the White House. Taft is a bumbling idiot whose only use for his backbone is golf. He will try to play both sides of this issue and end up splitting the party."

"What I ask Mr. Speaker is a tariff bill I can maneuver through the Senate. We need a bill which provides American business the protection which will keep their confidence, and keep the progressives at bay."

"I guarantee we will send legislation from the House which will maintain high tariffs. Once it reaches the Senate, it is your job to maneuver something through to the passage. You have a sound majority in the Senate, and you must trust your membership will stand behind your leadership on this."

"I do not worry about the passage of strong tariff legislation. I worry about the state of the party when the dust on this issue settles."

"We will not get help from the White House. We must stand united and push a bill through which is favorable to big business. We must never forget that it is big business that undergirds this nation and gives it vitality. I truly believe that once passed, the President will have no choice but to sign it into law."

"Mr. Speaker, we must be prepared for a rider on the bill dealing with an income tax. The progressives claim the income tax is the only way to hold the wealthy accountable to pay their fair share of the nation's financial burdens."

"Yes, and such a tax would reduce the benefits we gain by aligning ourselves with the wealthy. Such legislation would be bad for us and bad for the party."

"I have an idea which I believe will waylay any move on an income tax, and it will give the appearance of placing more responsibility on the wealthy. It is called a Corporation Tax of 2%. Our wealthy friends can still claim the profits they so justly deserve, and pass off the corporation tax in reduced wages and benefits or reduced employment."

"But won't the progressives yell foul?"

"Of course, they will, but who will be listening? On the surface, it is holding companies accountable but underneath provides the legalese necessary to hold our friends harmless. This will also keep the burden of financing this country on working-class people. After all, they represent the majority of the people in this country, it only makes sense they bear most of the burden."

"So, you believe the corporations will find this tax acceptable."

"In relation to an income tax which takes money directly out of their pocket, they will find the corporation tax an easy pill to swallow. I have spoken with my son-in-law about such a strategy, and he finds it to be an acceptable alternative."

"Well, I suppose if the Rockefellers find it acceptable, we can rest assured the American Aristocracy will be fine."

Aldrich and Cannon do not realize that President Taft doesn't support an income tax on the grounds that it violates the Constitution. If such a tax is included in the Tariff Bill, Taft will veto the legislation.

As Taft considers the mid-term elections of 1910, he is hopeful that Senator Aldrich will not run again, and that House Speaker Cannon might retire. These two conservatives have kept his presidency caught in the middle of a battle between conservative and progressive Republicans. He does not want the mid-term election to be a repudiation of his leadership. And yet, a split in the party makes mid-term success very difficult.

In his first two years, Taft tried to run the middle of the gauntlet between conservative and progressive Republicans. In doing so, he successfully alienates both sides of his leadership. This approach also has the country wondering about his abilities as President.

As the mid-term elections drew near, Theodore Roosevelt returned from his hunting trip to Africa and tour of Europe. Roosevelt felt Taft had let him down by taking such a feeble approach to governance. Other than a tariff bill that makes no one happy, Taft failed to advance the social causes so important to the former President.

Taft never knows quite what to do, so he travels. He became the most traveled president in U.S. History. He views traveling combined with a speaking tour as a panacea for the troubles his administration faces. As a procrastinator, his speeches are often poorly drafted efforts to sway voter opinion. While he draws large crowds to listen, he often speaks like a lawyer to a jury in making his case.

The mid-term elections of 1910 were a disaster for Taft and the Republican Party. Before the election, the Republicans controlled the Presidency and both Houses of Congress by significant margins. Following the election, the Democrats control the House of Representatives by a wide margin, and neither party has the votes to control the Senate. Progressive Republicans are more likely to vote with the Democrats rather than support the President. Taft finds himself in a quandary as he looks to the last two years of his first term and the possibility of re-election in 1912.

With the Republican Party at war between conservatives and progressives, the future looks bleak for President Taft. As for the high and mighty on Wall Street, the future looks bright. Nothing serves their interests better than a government at odds with itself. The political and business environment offers the opportunity for the accumulation of greater wealth and increased power.

For President Taft, the time seems right for another speaking tour of the country. He needs to explain the political environment and make his case for the next two years. As the train pulls out of Union Station in Washington D.C., Presidential Secretary and advisor Charles D. Hilles, Secretary of Treasury Franklin MacVeagh, and Attorney General George Wickersham are on board. The first leg of this trip will provide these men with an opportunity to speak frankly about the challenges ahead.

"After all you have done to support the policies of your predecessor, the egotistical progressives did nothing to help your cause in the mid-term election," his advisor Hilles intones.

"Mr. Hilles, the progressives are only interested in bringing this country to ruin. If given the opportunity, they would tear down any and all of our sacred institutions in the name of the common man."

"I fail to understand Mr. President how they failed to see the benefits and wisdom of keeping the party united through your approach of compromise with the conservatives," injects Treasury Secretary Franklin MacVeagh.

"Hell Franklin, I am a conservative myself. I believe in a strong protective tariff, and I believe in the importance of big and successful businesses. I believe every man is due to the rewards of his work. And yet, I recognize the merits inherent in some of the ideas of the progressive wing of the party. I have tried to be flexible and accommodating."

"You have been more than accommodating Mr. President. The problem is the progressives have tunnel vision. They can only see things their way and if they cannot have it all their way, they would rather destroy it all."

"I agree Franklin, but the progressive press has demonized the president as someone owned and controlled by the power elite. They do not report anything positive President Taft has done to support progressive causes," Attorney General Wickersham notes.

"They have not just demonized the president, they have also demonized you, George. The progressive press is constantly pointing out that this administration has an attorney for the big businesses and financial interests of New York as the Attorney General."

"The real problem Mr. Hilles is Theodore Roosevelt. While away in Africa, he kept busy hunting trophies to bring back to Oyster Bay to enhance his image as the rugged individualist which means he had little time for politics. But he is back in the United States now, and he needs to be center stage. As the Secretary of the Treasury, I do not trust Theodore Roosevelt."

"He is still pissed that I canned his old buddy Pinchot. He took this as a direct affront to his legacy and as an indication I was anti-conservation. Does he not know I am president now, and I do not need to seek his approval to do the things I feel are in the best interest of the country?"

"Teddy thought you would simply be a Roosevelt shadow. He thought you would maintain his cabinet and bureaucratic appointees. He thought you would advance his policies. He believed you would reflect a third Roosevelt term."

"Mr. Hilles, Theodore Roosevelt is a menace. No one in our history has ever been so dangerous and so powerful because of his hold upon the less intelligent voters and the discontented. He uses his dynamic personality and loud thundering voice to shake the rafters of sensibility and enlist the dispossessed in his war against the American Aristocracy."

"But Mr. President, Theodore Roosevelt is a product of that very aristocracy. He still lives in luxury unknown to most people in this country. Such hypocrisy cannot go unnoticed."

"George, it is all about Teddy Roosevelt and power. As long as he draws breath, he will not be still until he has brought down the mighty and installed himself on the throne of public adulation."

"What are we to do Mr. President? How can we keep Theodore Roosevelt at bay, satisfy the progressives, unite the party, win you the nomination and a second term in 1912?"

"Franklin, I plan to do all I can to renew an amicable relationship with Teddy Roosevelt if for no other reason than to keep him from seeking the nomination. I plan to appeal to the people on tours such as this, and I plan to do my job. If nominated, as I expect to be, I plan to stay removed, as have most of my predecessors from the unsavory activities of campaigning. Should all this come to pass, I will appoint Mr. Hilles to chair my campaign and secure me a second term."

"Very wise Mr. President and I believe Charles is capable of seeing you through. I also know that George and I as well as all those who work for you will do all we can in this effort."

"Gentleman, politics makes strange bedfellows. I have no illusions about the task which lies before me, or about Teddy. The fact of the matter is if Roosevelt is not a socialist, he is intent on following policies that lead directly toward the appropriation of what belonged to one man, to another. We must put a stop to this now whatever the cost."

The next two years were brutal for President Taft. Every time something seems to be going right, the United States Congress steps in and brings it to a halt. The progressive press not only portrays him as a traitor but they along with the Democratic Party, portray him as something worse, ineffectual.

Taft's situation only grows worse through an on-again, off-again relationship with Roosevelt. Finally, as 1912 nears, it is apparent that Theodore Roosevelt will seek to claim the Republican nomination from a sitting president. Taft now must use the power and influence of his office to command the party leadership and muster the support needed to prevail at the convention. It is a damned if you do, damned if you don't situation. Defeating Roosevelt at the convention certainly assures a divided party. Taft remains optimistic, but he knows the reality of such a situation.

With the help of the conservative wing of the party, William Howard Taft secured the Republican Nomination for the presidency in 1912. Repudiated and angry at how Taft subverted his candidacy and took command of the convention through old-style bossism, Roosevelt splinters the party by running as a progressive third-party candidate.

As he looks to the election, Roosevelt meets with three close advisors who have likewise bolted the Republican Party for the Progressive or Bull Moose Party. Meeting in Oyster Bay, in the same library where he met four years before with William Howard Taft, Theodore Roosevelt now meets with California Governor Hiram Johnson, former Indiana Senator Albert Beveridge, and Jane Addams.

Hiram Johnson is the son of Grove Lawrence Johnson, a California politician whose career was marred by accusations of election fraud and graft. Albert Beveridge had been abandoned by his parents as an infant and rose to political prominence in Indiana of his own accord. Jane Addams is a leader of women's rights and founder of the Hull House in Chicago. She is the daughter of John Addams founding member of the Illinois Republican Party, and a personal friend of Abraham Lincoln.

"Thank you, dear friends, for taking the time to meet with me!" Roosevelt begins.

"It is our pleasure and honor, Mr. President."

"Four years ago, William Taft was a wolf in sheep's clothing. He did everything possible to cast himself as a progressive when underneath he harbored deep resentment for the progressive cause. He led me to believe his administration would reflect the policies and work initiated during my seven years as president. He has been sorely disappointing."

"Taft has done grave damage to this nation with his appointment of five justices to the Supreme Court along with the current Chief Justice. These six individuals comprise a conservative bastion on the court which could beat back our progressive agenda for years to come unless we have a strong and determined leader in the White House," Albert Beveridge is a champion of the progressive cause.

"Mr. Beveridge speaks the truth about a matter over which we have little control. What causes me great concern is the president's lack of interference with business. True, he and his Attorney General have prosecuted many trusts under the anti-trust laws, but the laws have become ineffectual, and the trusts find ways to circumvent legal barriers to control the market," comments Hiram Johnson the newly elected governor of California and a true progressive.

"While you both touch on important issues, the crux of the problem remains the immoral gap that exists between people of money and those who strive to make a life for themselves and their families. Taft did not acknowledge the right of workers to organize and he squashed unions at every opportunity. Millions of workers, women, and children suffer every day across this nation because to the rich go the spoils and to the rest the crumbs. Something must be done about this," Jane Addams has seen it all. Her work with immigrants and the poor convinced her something must be done to eliminate the disparity between the wealthy and the poor.

"Miss Addams, you are a champion for the poor and dispossessed. Your voice resonates with compassion and reason but no one is listening. Everyone with money and power believes the poor should take care of each other. The question is, with what? They toil day and night and walk away with literally nothing. They can verily afford shelter let alone housing. The clothes they wear are tattered and torn. They struggle to put food on the table. How in God's name can anyone expect them to take care of each other? They can hardly take care of themselves. We need a strong federal government led by people of conviction and courage willing to do what is right for the best interest of the people of this great nation. All people, not just the privileged few," Senator Beveridge is incensed by the thought.

"Mr. President, we must make it easier to amend the Constitution of the United States so the will of the people gets done. The Constitution, as glorious a document as ever existed, makes it easy for people of money to gain power and control. The Constitution must give unto the man working in the foundry as much authority as the man with a wad of cash. It is the government's responsibility to make this happen, and yet when the government is controlled by those who benefit from the current system very little or nothing of substance occurs," Governor Johnson not only sees the system as the problem, he sees the system as the solution.

"Well said Governor, no man is worth his salt in public life who makes on the stump a pledge which he does not keep after election; and, if he makes such a pledge and does not keep it, he should be run out of public life. Our government is filled with such men. When it is time to be elected, they say whatever might appeal to the voters and act differently once in office. These are spineless men, puffed up with self-importance pursuing their self-interest at the expense of the people they were elected to serve," Roosevelt is tired of incompetence and dishonesty in government. He speaks like a man ready for battle.

"The Declaration of Independence and the Constitution promise a nation where people are free to pursue their own lives, and yet, the economic and social injustice in this nation makes the realization of these promises impossible for all but a select few. We have millions of men working for subsistence wages. We have millions of women and children living in squalor. We have farmers wearing their fingers to the bone to produce food for a hungry nation. Amid all of this, there is no protection, there is no help, and there is little hope. We need you, Mr. President, we need your courage, your conviction, your determination to do the right thing," Jane Addams knows and believes in Teddy Roosevelt.

"And it is the right thing I will do Miss Addams. Not unlike my charge up San Juan Hill, I want to lead a charge on Washington. It is time to wage war on the infidels who occupy the citadel of power and demand they do the right thing or we will shut it down," T.R. is in charge mode.

"In two weeks, we will meet in Chicago for the first National Convention of the Progressive Party. I have been thinking long and hard about a platform, and I suggest we call our platform "A Contract with the People."

"Very good Governor and I would suggest our contract specifically address worker's compensation as a protection against loss of wages due to circumstances beyond the worker's control. We need to make a firm stand on behalf of American workers."

"I couldn't agree more Senator, and I believe we need to offer a social welfare program as a protection for our women and children."

"And farm relief which protects farmers from floods, droughts, pests, and other hazards to their crops."

"Women need the right to vote. How can a country based on democracy leave nearly half its population disenfranchised? Never has a political party taken up the banner of women's suffrage. We have the opportunity to begin this march together."

"Yes, everything you have mentioned needs to be part of our contract. The opposition will call us big spenders and ask where the money to support these programs will come from. Well, our contract needs to take on the wealthy in this country and say it is about time they pay their fair share. The Roosevelt family has long believed that "to those whom much is given, much is expected."

"Mr. President, they will call us socialists and say we want to redistribute the wealth that rightfully belongs to those who have earned it."

"With my big stick Mr. Johnson, I will clean the threshing floor. The wealthy have not earned their wealth; they have taken their wealth from the resources of this nation and off the backs of workers. They have greedily stolen the wealth of this nation and claimed the lion's share as their own. They have built themselves palaces complete with all of the luxury life can provide, and they have used their money to purchase influence and power as a means of securing the future of their dynasties. They do all this while leaving scraps for the vast majority of people in this country who scrape by trying to make a living just to put a roof over their families, clothes on their backs, and food on the table. So let them call us whatever they may like, the fact is, we are coming."

During the campaign of 1912, President Taft did as he said and remained above the fray. Theodore Roosevelt took to the stump with a vengeance hoping to marshal the progressive spirit of the American people. Woodrow Wilson on the other hand campaigns in a relaxed and confident manner knowing that a split Republican Party increases his chances of victory. The Democrats are a unified party, and Wilson knows he has the mathematical edge to victory.

Nobody is tougher than the old rough rider. While campaigning in Milwaukee, Wisconsin on October 14, 1912, Theodore Roosevelt survived an assassination attempt by a former saloonkeeper John Flammang Schrank. A bullet fired by Schrank lodged in Roosevelt's chest after penetrating his steel eyeglass case and passing through a thick (50 pages) single-folded copy of the speech Roosevelt was about to give. Despite the wound, Roosevelt went on to give the speech to the gathered crowd and began with, "Ladies and gentlemen, I don't know whether you fully understand that I have just been shot, but it takes more than that to kill a Bull Moose."

On election night, it doesn't take long to know who will be the next President of the United States. Wilson's mathematic edge gave him just over 42% of the popular vote to Roosevelt's 28%; Taft's 24%; and 6% for Socialist Candidate Eugene Debs. The Electoral College gave Wilson an even larger victory based on a winner-takes-all system in each state. Combined, Roosevelt, and Taft secured 51% of the popular vote. If the Republicans had remained united, it is likely they would have prevailed.

The progressives which include socialist voters are the hardest-hit group. Thirty-four percent of the voters in 1912 wanted to see the nation turn towards a fairer economic system. This percentage is probably higher because many progressive Republicans remained loyal to Taft.

With Wilson, the new President-elect, Roosevelt, and Taft fade into history. Progressivism has been stilled and the nation stands on the threshold of a new capitalistic era. An era in which the unbridled force of capitalism will extend beyond American shores to every corner of the globe. The capitalistic beast will be unleashed perhaps to never be caged again.

Chapter 14

MESSIAH COMPLEX

As an academician, Wilson possesses neither the political nor leadership senses needed to steer the ship of state toward a more promising future for the common people of America. As an orator, he possesses the power of persuasion much lacking in William Taft. As the son of a Presbyterian minister, he believes people's lot in life to be preordained by God. Therefore, the rich are entitled to their wealth as a result of being favored by God. The poor and downtrodden suffer a lot in life as a lack of worthiness in the eyes of God. As for Wilson, he feels strongly that God wants him to be President. He loves to hum the tune of "Onward Christian Soldiers." It is one of his favorite songs.

As a card-carrying bigot, Wilson's bigotry extends far beyond a matter of race. As a former member of the Ku Klux Klan, Wilson's bigotry includes the poor and dispossessed, as well as Catholics and Jews. As a member of the intellectual as well as economic elite, Wilson feels that unions are an aberration of society. He indeed has lofty ideas and goals, but these ideas are rooted in an internationalism aimed at bringing Christian principles and democratic ideals to an unworthy world.

The people Wilson brings into government are like letting the fox into the hen house. Internationalists all, these men want to extend the influence and power of the United States around the globe as a matter of superiority based upon Christian principles. These men are the embodiment of American exceptionalism, the idea that the people of the world would be better off under the guardianship of the United States. Of course, in exchange, the United States should benefit from the natural resources these countries can provide.

It is hard to imagine a more pompous ass has ever before or since occupied the White House. Wilson grew up in a Presbyterian household and his father helped found the Presbyterian Church of the Confederacy. His religious faith guides all of his beliefs and actions. Devoid of a real personality, Wilson relies on his keen power of intellect and oratory to command any situation. Without the great divide within the Republican Party in 2012, it is possible history would hardly note the existence of Woodrow Wilson.

This is not to say Wilson did nothing of value. He serves two terms, and this alone is a notable achievement for a President even if he just squeaks by to a second term. He also does some things good for the people of the nation. However, all in all, Wilson ushers in the beast that has consumed the heart and soul of this nation for nearly one hundred years.

"Mr. Bryan, so good of you to come." William Jennings Bryan has been a Democratic power all his life. He was the Democratic Party's nominee for president in 1896, 1900, and 1908. While he lost all three elections, he never lost his prominence as a Democratic leader.

"My service is at your pleasure, Mr. President-elect."

"Mr. Bryan I can honestly say my elevation to this most sacred office is in many ways due to your hard work on my behalf."

"I appreciate your kindness, but I believe you offer me far too much credit."

"What I would like to offer you William is a spot on my cabinet as the Secretary of State."

"This is certainly a great offer, and one which any person would be honored to accept, but are you sure this is the best spot for me."

"Why would you think differently?"

"My entire life I have focused on issues of domestic importance. I have been called the Great Commoner because of my interest in securing an economic system that allows all people to rise above their current station in life. I would think I am more suited for a position of domestic importance."

"And what do you have in mind, Mr. Bryan?"

"Without being presumptuous, I believe I am much better suited to serve you and the nation as Secretary of the Treasury or Attorney General."

"I see, it is not many men who would try to negotiate their position in the administration of a new president."

"I understand that sir, and I am most grateful for your offer, but I am just thinking of you and the country. I am a strict isolationist, and you are an internationalist."

"That is precisely why I need you at State. With the unsettling events going on in Europe, the drumbeats of war make our people nervous. I need a calming influence in my administration, and you Mr. Bryan are best suited to be that influence."

"I understand, yet the most important thing which can be done for the American people is to provide them with domestic and monetary policies which open up opportunities for economic growth."

"You seem to lack faith in my ability or determination to lead the way on domestic affairs."

"No, that is not true, I just feel I can best serve you in a domestic capacity. However, I offer my service at your pleasure, and if it is State for me, then I most gladly and humbly accept your offer."

"Good, then that is done. I shall make the announcement in the morning. You are doing your President and country a great service, William."

With Bryan's agreement to serve at State, Wilson lays the groundwork for the pursuit of his secret agenda. Wilson believed that war in Europe would require his intervention for a successful resolution. He sees himself as an agent of God in bringing peace to the world. It is a noble aspiration, but one steeped in visions of grandeur. Wilson did not want the United States involved in a European War, and he truly believed Bryan's pacifism would help the U.S. maintain neutrality so important to his goals.

Wilson had been the Governor of New Jersey, but his roots are in the South as a son of Virginia. He grew up a Southerner, and much of his thinking reflects a Southern mindset. He does not believe monopolies are good for the country because of how they control the economy;

however, he does believe people have a right to their wealth. He believes capital to be the driving engine of a strong and dynamic economy. His religion refutes every aspect of Darwinism, and yet Wilson believes the American Aristocracy represents the greatest ideals and aspirations of the country. He accepts Social Darwinism as a precept of God's intervention on earth.

The great industrialists and financiers of the country continue to wrestle with the new political environment of governmental intervention. For over a century, the United States Government maintained a laissez-faire approach to business. Now the government itself tilts between a hands-off and a hands-on approach. This environment constantly calls for these men of wealth to work together to secure influence and discover ways to circumvent governmental intrusion as a means of maintaining control over their economic future. Men such as Rockefeller, Carnegie, Mellon, Morgan, Payne, Clark, Ryan, and Baker hold sacred their millions of dollars of wealth and investments. These men of privilege are not about to allow the government to deny them their due.

Col. Oliver Hazard Payne served on the Union side in the Civil War and considers himself a patriot. As a child of wealth, he became one of the nation's wealthiest men following the war by investing in tobacco and oil. He built an estate along the Hudson River at Esopus, New York. Col. Payne owns a two-hundred-sixty-foot, one-hundred-fifty-ton steam Yacht, the Aphrodite. This sleek vessel trimmed out in the finest wood contains all the amenities of his mansion. Concerned about the direction of the federal government, Payne invites the nation's wealthiest men to join him for a cruise on the Hudson in the Spring following Woodrow Wilson's inauguration.

Among this den of thieves are such proven schemers as William Rockefeller, brother of John D., William A. Clark, Thomas F. Ryan, and George F. Baker. Rockefeller pioneered the Amalgamated Copper Mining Company by creating it as a paper organization and then selling millions of dollars in manipulated stocks. William Clark used his money to bribe party leaders in his effort to gain a seat in the United States Senate from Montana. Thomas Ryan amassed millions through tobacco and then schemed his way to a controlling interest in thirty different companies. George Baker is a creative and highly successful financier with investments in twenty-two different corporations. J.P. Morgan Jr. helped ensure the House of Morgan was the sole underwriter of War Bonds in Britain and France should war come to Europe. He could not make the trip. These men were highly adept at business on the shady side of the street, and they were not about to give in to what they considered misguided politicians.

"This is a marvelous ship Col. I don't believe I have seen anything quite like it."

"Thank you, Mr. Clark, I take great pride in this vessel and I must say it is the largest steamship built in the United States. I welcome you all aboard and invite you to the dining saloon in the deckhouse."

"Col., your deckhouse is most impressive. The intricate woodwork creates a very imposing setting. I am rather taken aback by the view which can be obtained from your deckhouse. I can see why this ship has been dubbed the Sea Palace," comments William Rockefeller.

"Gentleman, we will be underway within minutes. May I offer you something from the bar?"

The bar on board is pure mahogany and takes up an entire corner of the deckhouse. The bar like the rest of the ship is completely stocked with everything and anything a person could want. The Aphrodite is accustomed to voyages to Europe and the Mediterranean. It is always ready to go wherever the Col. would like to travel. The ship is fully manned, and two stewards in white coats stand ready to tend to anyone's needs.

With drinks and cigars in hand and the ship underway, these men of position and prestige settled in to talk business. As they cruise along, the beautiful rolling hills lining the Hudson River lush with Chestnut Oak, Black Birch, Hickory, and White Spruce are in full view. If the business before them was not so important, it would be easy to get lost in the tranquility of the region. It is little wonder why so many of the nation's wealthiest men have purchased land and built estates in this area of New York near the Catskill Mountains.

"Gentlemen, I hope you enjoy the next couple of days. I have done everything possible to make this a suitable place for us to do business with the highest degree of confidence. I also trust you will find all the accommodations appropriate to your social standing."

"Col., we all have things weighing heavily on our minds. You invited us here saying our deliberation is necessary for our future as well as that of the nation. A vague invitation, and yet one which necessitates our attendance. What exactly is it you would like to discuss?"

"I would like to discuss the future of this country and how our economic future is imperiled by a political process run amuck. Since the death of William McKinley, the rising tide of progressivism threatens to consume both political parties as well as candidates."

"I could not agree more Col., the federal government is growing tentacles which threaten our economic power and strengthens the government's ability to impede the free exercise of capitalism."

"George speaks the truth. Teddy Roosevelt instigated this entire mess, and now we have a socialist president and Congress. Wilson's attack on protective tariffs and trusts is a shot across the bow of the ship of capitalism."

"I completely agree, but the fact is our problem is two-pronged. First, we must find a way to nullify a Democratic President and Congress that threatens to undermine free enterprise and bring about our ruin. Second, we must find a way to control the process to ensure that whoever gets elected, from whatever party, remains loyal to capitalism above all else."

"What is it you suggest Mr. Rockefeller?"

"The winds of war are blowing across the European Continent. Woodrow Wilson pledged to the American people that the United States would stay out of war should it occur. We must see that this does not happen. War is our salvation gentlemen."

"But Wilson is a pacifist. War is contrary to his religious doctrine."

"Mr. Clark, Woodrow Wilson is the Commander-in-Chief of this nation. He is also an internationalist with a big ego. As he is forced to view the world from a vision of grandeur, he will hear the voice of God calling him to mount a crusade to save Europe. I assure you President Wilson will ride high in the saddle at such an opportunity."

"How do you think this is possible with William Jennings Bryan as Secretary of State? There is no bigger isolationist in the country than Bryan. Why he would not entertain such a thought as intervention."

"My dear Mr. Baker, Secretary of States come and go. All we have to do is create a wedge issue where it appears to Mr. Bryan that President Wilson is going against his wishes and advice. Bryan never wanted to be Secretary of State in the first place. If he thinks war is possible, he will resign of good conscience."

"So, what is it you suggest Mr. Rockefeller?"

"We all have friends involved in running the newspapers and magazines across this country. These are men with similar interests and concerns. We must urge them to be ready should the winds of war blow in our direction. Through the media, we can fan the flames of public outrage which will capture Wilson's attention."

"That sounds well and good, but how do we know the winds of war will blow in this direction?"

"Do you know the Kaiser, Mr. Ryan?"

"No, I do not, but I have read some things about him."

"Well Kaiser Wilhelm II has a bigger ego than Woodrow Wilson. His appetite for conquest and power is relentless. Word has it that his war industry has developed an underwater warship and the Kaiser will be itching to try it out."

"I spoke with young J.P. Morgan the other day, and he told me the House of Morgan is positioning itself to be a financial player should war break out in Europe. He indicated that their representatives are in discussion with the English and French about underwriting war bonds should the continent become engulfed in war."

"That is excellent news, Mr. Clark. Nothing will connect the United States to war and especially the winning of the war more than linking that war to the American economy. It would be wise for all of us to consider how we might make such a conflict beneficial."

"What is your second point Col., since it seems we are at the mercy of the Kaiser?"

"Gentlemen, we must take control of the political process. Up to this point, we have yielded to political parties and their bosses with mostly favorable results. And yet, in the last eleven years, the long arm of the government has reached further and further into the business sector. Fortunately, we have continually found legal means by which to either circumvent new laws or turn new laws into new opportunities. It is like a game of chess, and I don't like that the government has the upper hand on a checkmate."

"You are right Col., and in my experience, I have never found a man who wasn't for sale."

"Your proficiency at buying men is well documented Mr. Clark, but we have reached a point where buying men is no longer the efficient way to do business."

"I agree with the Col., it is time we take things to an entirely new level. We must own the process on both sides of the aisle to ensure that no matter who is elected, they understand who they really work for. This means we must intently but discretely become the power behind the political parties, the legislative process, and the government itself."

"And how would you do that Mr. Ryan?"

"It is all about money and message. It takes money to run political parties, and money is something we all have in spades. If we control the party, we control the message. If we control the message, we control the candidates. Candidates who don't stay with the message before or after being elected live short lives. We also control the great publishing houses across this country. This allows us to control the message which goes out to the people. Through this medium, we can impact public opinion, and therefore control the public."

"This sounds good in theory Mr. Ryan, but are you sure it will work? And if given time, won't those elected to office find ways to curtail our activity?"

"Let me ask you a question, Mr. Baker. As the government increases in size, who will possess the greatest amount of power: The president with a four-year term, a congressman with a two-year term, a senator with a six-year term, or a career bureaucrat who may hold a position of prominence for thirty or forty years?"

"I guess I am not certain Mr. Ryan."

"Well let me ask it this way; Why would a person want to be the Commissioner of the Port of New York?"

"Because the Commissioner has a great deal of authority as well as a very lucrative position from which to feather his own nest."

"That is exactly my point, as the government increases in size, we have a vested interest to see that people friendly to business assume key positions in the bureaucracy. Key people in these positions can make life a great deal easier for us all. And, in subtle ways, we can make life much easier for them."

"I like what you are suggesting Mr. Ryan. We must diversify our investments as well as our activity. We may be few, but we control the resources needed to shape the course of the future. I suggest we take our conversation to others of like mind. We must find a way to hang together, or as Franklin suggested, we will hang separately."

Over the next couple of days, the Aphrodite serves as a nest of conspiracy and a den of iniquity. Col. Payne who never married liked his women young. On the first evening out, the captain makes port long enough to take on five extremely attractive young women. The party ensues well into the morning hours with more than enough booze and debauchery for everyone. Just before the dawning of the morning sun, the captain makes port once more and the cargo, so important to a night of playful sin, slips off the ship unnoticed.

Rising late, this five-man conspiratorial group meets a second day to continue their conversation. During the morning hours in the throes of a semi-slumber, a few things occur to William Rockefeller. At a breakfast of fruits, juices, meats, cheese, potatoes, and eggs, he could hardly contain his desire to speak. After breakfast, everyone reconvenes in the deckhouse.

"I should like to begin our conversation this morning if I may do so."

"Absolutely, Mr. Rockefeller, the floor is yours."

"Gentlemen, we touched on some very important topics yesterday, and I would like to share with you a thought I have about the growing federal government and expanding bureaucracy. Historically governments and nations often grow so big they are unmanageable and ineffective. In these cases, the central government often appears to be more powerful, and yet, they are not. What happens is that they grow so big the central government loses control and has little idea regarding the things which are going on!"

"What is your point, William?"

"Consider reconstruction following the Civil War as an example. The entire effort was so huge that the right hand had no idea what the left hand was doing. Throughout that entire ordeal which in many ways is still going on, men made fortunes by taking advantage of the process. Thanks to an overburdened federal government, men charged excessive amounts and skimmed millions of dollars from public coffers. During this entire time, presidents and politicians came and went but those amid the process remained."

"Your illustration is correct, but in what way is it relevant to our conversation?"

"Mr. Ryan, just because the government is getting bigger does not need to be a problem for us. My father would say to turn every disaster into an opportunity. Well, we can turn a growing government into our opportunity."

"And how do we make that happen?"

"We work to ensure that key posts in the growing bureaucracy are filled with friends of capital. We work to see that these people and their subordinates are entrenched in a way that outlasts the politicians, my dear Mr. Clark. We find ways to make loyalty to us far more lucrative than serving the government."

"What about the politicians Mr. Rockefeller?"

"We must use our resources to the fullest to keep them at odds with each other. This will not only promote inefficiency but also foster compromise which waters down legislation and nullifies the real impact it has on the free enterprise system. Their legislation in name appears to do something, but in actuality does nothing."

"I recently had a conversation with Andrew Carnegie. He told me "The morality of compromise sounds contradictory. Compromise is usually a sign of weakness or an admission of defeat. Strong men don't compromise, it is said, and principles should never be compromised."

"Precisely Col., in most presidents or members of Congress, we do not find strong men let alone men of principle. The task is not that difficult, it will just take time and money."

"The other thoughts which occurred to me this morning, involve the Sixteenth Amendment to the Constitution, and the pending Federal Reserve Act."

"Do share Mr. Rockefeller."

"The Income Tax provision within the Sixteenth Amendment is a carefully crafted duck blind. To the people, it appears to be "Soak the

Rich" legislation when in fact it takes very little of what we own. Why, we could all light our cigars with a $10,000.00 bill and not notice a loss! A six percent income tax is peanuts. However, as Congress crafts legislation based on this amendment, we must make sure the onus falls more and more on the backs of labor."

"How do we make sure this happens?"

"Influence Mr. Baker, Influence. Regardless of what we may talk about, unless we gain control of the process, all is lost. We must be like those people who work backstage at the theatre ever-changing the scenery but never seen."

"What about the impending Federal Reserve Act, it does seem like a bit of mischief."

"I have some thoughts on that also Mr. Ryan."

"Please go on Mr. Rockefeller."

"The Federal Reserve Act is going to be passed because the panic of 1907 scared the hell out of the government. Every time there is an economic downturn, the president and Congress come running to the nation's financiers for help. You can speak to that Mr. Baker."

"The fact of the matter is when the economy begins to go sour, politicians run around like Chicken Little proclaiming the sky to be falling. Regardless of who is in control of the presidency or Congress, the opposition has a hay day placing blame. The fact is both parties have fallen victim to economic downturns, and neither party has any idea what to do. So, they always turn to the nation's bankers and financiers for help."

"So, Mr. Baker, are you saying the Federal Reserve Act is creating a governmental agency for regulating the economy."

"Better than that Mr. Clark, the government is creating an agency that exists outside the government comprised of financial experts for regulating the economy. It is our proverbial fox in the hen house."

"But I think it calls for close oversight by the government."

"How the hell can they hope to oversee something of which they have no knowledge or understanding? The agency will be made up of monetary experts. Capitalists are devoted to the perpetuation of capitalism. The government and the American people will have no idea what hit them. It is the perfect cover."

"I believe you are right Mr. Baker. My friend Henry Ford said, "It is well enough that people of the nation do not understand our banking and monetary system, for if they did, I believe there would be a revolution before tomorrow morning." We can be thankful for ignorance."

"Oh, so true Mr. Rockefeller, oh so true. But we must take it beyond ignorance to misinformation. We must educate the American people to believe that capitalism is sacred even when it goes against their best interest," Baker is convincing in his argument.

"Well, gentlemen it is time for lunch. I then insist everyone get some rest this afternoon. Of course, you are all welcome to enjoy the ship. I must warn you we will be making port again towards the evening to pick up a few guests. If you thought the young beauties last night were delightful, be prepared to enjoy the company of some vivacious young women. I believe you will find each young woman ready and willing to live up to the name of this ship. Until then, I am going to retire to my quarters."

That evening, Col. Payne moves the revelry to the saloon below the main deck. There, the men and guests enjoy the free use of alcohol amidst a large buffet of food. It doesn't take long, and the men and women are paired up in a rather agreeable and joyful manner. As the evening progresses, things move to the wild side with all the young nymphets naked dancing about freely sharing themselves from man to man. William Clark proclaims it the most wondrous night he has ever experienced. Of course, Clark always rose to the occasion meriting the description of him by Mark Twain, "He is as rotten a human being as can be found anywhere under the flag; he is a shame to the American nation, and no one has helped to send him to the Senate who did not know that his proper place was the penitentiary, with a ball and chain on his legs. To my mind, he is the most disgusting creature that the republic has produced since Tweed's time."

During the cruise of the Aphrodite, these five members of American Nobility laid the groundwork for things that would shape the next twenty years of American politics. Little do they know or probably care that their schemes will impact the course of American history in profound, complicated, and unsavory ways. The next morning the Aphrodite pulls into port to quietly disembark the young female passengers before returning to Col. Payne's estate. With all of their preliminary planning complete, these five members of the American Aristocracy know exactly what needs to be done next.

Chapter 15

CONFEDERATES

Back in Washington D.C., President Wilson prepares to meet with his full cabinet to map out a strategy for the next three years. If anyone questioned whether the South would rise again, they simply need to examine Wilson's cabinet. Having been born in Virginia, Woodrow Wilson's roots are in the South. Of his ten cabinet members, five hail from the South with direct connections to the confederacy. President Wilson himself grew up in a home in which his father owned slaves and served as a chaplain for the Confederate Army.

Since the newly built West Wing always seems in disarray, Wilson plans for this cabinet meeting to be held in the historic Red Room on the State Floor of the White House. This small but beautiful room will accommodate the meeting nicely. Wilson will sit at the head of the table facing the Italian Marble fireplace supported by twin caryatids reminiscent of those found on the Acropolis of ancient Athens. An imposing portrait of George Washington looks down from his lofty position above the fireplace. The walls of the room are covered in burgundy silk velvet dotted with gold-framed portraits of former presidents and first ladies. A large golden chandelier hangs in the center of the room from a pure white ceiling. On the floor rests a huge Persian Carpet upon which set a large Oak Table surrounded by immaculately carved oak chairs.

Entering the room before the President, Secretary of State Bryan takes it upon himself to welcome the others. As a man who ran for

President and lost three times, Bryan feels as if the White House should be his home. He is proud to serve in a Democratic Administration but bitter that he is not the president.

Secretary of the Treasury William McAdoo hails from Georgia with a law degree from the University of Tennessee. McAdoo's uncle had been a Civil War general from Texas. His father served on the Texas Supreme Court. Attorney General James C. McReynolds grew up in Kentucky in a very strict southern Christian home. Of all cabinet members, McReynolds rivals Wilson for the biggest ego. Secretary of War Lindley Garrison came from north of the Mason-Dixon Line. Unlike Wilson, Garrison welcomes the hostilities occurring in Europe and wants to flex U.S. muscle whenever possible. Postmaster General Albert S. Burleson comes from a wealthy southern planter family and his father served as a Confederate officer. Burleson possesses even greater bigotry than his boss. Secretary of the Navy Josephus Daniels' father accumulated great wealth as a Confederate shipbuilder in North Carolina. Secretary of Agriculture David F. Houston completes the southern contingency on the cabinet hailing from North Carolina. William Wilson a northerner with coal mining roots serves as the nation's first Secretary of Labor. Rounding out the cabinet are two northerners, Franklin Lane at Interior and William Redfield at Commerce.

Many of these men share significant things in common with the new President. First, they are conservative Christians possessing the belief that they are doing God's bidding. Second, they are internationalists believing that God wants to use the United States as an instrument in bringing freedom and democracy to the people of the world. Third, while they feel trusts and monopolies need to be brought under the control of the government, they are disciples of a free enterprise system that believes the obtaining of massive wealth fits into God's plan. Fourth, many of them including the President are outright bigots. Fifth, they all enjoy significant wealth.

The President sits at the head of the table facing the portrait of Washington. Secretary Bryan positions himself to assume the seat at the other end of the table with the other members filling in the sides. As Wilson enters the room, the men stand to acknowledge their leader.

"Be seated gentlemen, be seated. We shall not get much done

standing up. I expect you have all had time to look over the agenda. We have a real opportunity to get things done. It has not been since the end of the 53rd Congress in 1895 that the Democrats have controlled one house of Congress, let alone both houses."

"Mr. President!"

"Mr. McAdoo, how are you this morning? I hope you are finding everything satisfactory at Treasury?"

"I have sir, and I am honored to be serving as a member of your administration. What I would like to address is the significance of the 16th Amendment which took effect March 1st, and the prospects of the Federal Reserve Act which will find its way to your desk later this year."

"Could you be more specific Mr. McAdoo?"

"The 16th Amendment which empowers the federal government to levy an income tax has been promoted by progressives as a "Soak the Rich" piece of legislation. I think it is paramount that we tread with caution as we unveil this new revenue-generating activity to the public."

"Why should we tread with caution, Mr. McAdoo? The 16th Amendment is aimed at making those individuals with the wherewithal to pay income tax do so. It is far too long that men of wealth have done little to promote the common good of this nation," the secretary of state immediately jumps into the conversation.

"Mr. Bryan, everyone knows that you are far more progressive than the most progressive Republican. It is because of individuals like yourself that Democrats have difficulty shedding the label of socialist."

"And what Mr. McAdoo is so wrong with certain socialistic principles which would uplift the masses out of their meager existence and allow them to live with a certain degree of dignity," as the Democratic nominee for president three times, William Jennings Bryan is not interested in being challenged.

"And I suppose you would just turn the country over to the poor Mr. Bryan. Well while you are at it, why not include women and coloreds?"

"Mr. Burleson, you may be the Postmaster General, but God help us all should you be elevated to anything more. Your bigotry threatens to drive a wedge deep into the social fabric of this country. You are a small man by any measure," Secretary Bryan is not about to be challenged by lesser men.

"Gentlemen, I must demand such intercourse stop immediately. I will not have this administration brought down by internal bickering. I have selected each of you for your post because of your eminent qualifications. While I encourage disagreement, I insist on civility."

"As you wish Mr. President."

"Now, let us get back to the issue at hand, the 16th Amendment. What do you propose Mr. McAdoo?"

"As the leader of the party in power, I believe you and your administration should actively promote income tax legislation in line with the 16th Amendment which would in essence increase revenue, but do no harm," As Secretary of the Treasury, McAdoo is already initiating a policy of smoke and mirrors.

"I agree with Mr. McAdoo, we must take the lead and we must do so prudently. This is a new Amendment and legislation fashioned under this amendment will surely be tested by the courts. The more we can avoid a legal battle the better, so the income tax needs to be rolled out gently. We also do not want to cause a panic on Wall Street," the attorney general offers his legal advice.

"Mr. Reynolds offers wise advice; the income tax needs to be brought into existence slowly. The men on Wall Street would not take to it kindly if we promoted something drastic. These men of finance and industry control the levers of commerce. No matter what you say or do, they still control productivity in this country, and productivity is the engine that drives this nation," adds the interior secretary.

"Secretary Lane, McAdoo, and Attorney General McReynolds, I do not question your motive, but where do the common people of this nation fit into all of this? I thought this was a country of, by, and for the people. I thought public officials were to serve all the people, not just a select few. What is happening to the Democratic Party of progressive ideas?" William Jennings Bryan doesn't want to be secretary of state. He prefers a cabinet position where he can be true to his progressive ideals.

"That was your party, Secretary Bryan. We all oppose monopolies and trusts. We recognize the dangers inherent in huge conglomerates that can manipulate prices, and we believe the government has a role to play in keeping such financial and corporate power in check. We also believe wholeheartedly in the free enterprise system. Under such a system a man has a right to accumulate great wealth and material possessions without the interference of the government. For the government to unduly intercede in the free enterprise system will bring the wheels of capitalism to a halt," Secretary McAdoo holds the position Bryan covets.

"Mr. McAdoo is correct, and as for "of, by, and for the people", that was used by Lincoln, a Republican as a means of inspiring the North to fight on in the Civil War. Might I remind you Mr. Bryan that the South still clings tightly to the cause of state's rights!" Postmaster Burleson still hoists a confederate flag in front of his residence and considers Dixie his national song.

"I am sorry gentlemen, I know we all have deep-seated beliefs that drive our service, but can we try not to digress? I would like to hear some kind of proposal," Wilson is off to a slow start with his cabinet.

"Mr. President, as your Secretary of the Treasury, I would like to suggest we impose a 1% income tax on all single workers who make more than $3,000.00 a year, and all married couples that make over $4,000.00 a year. All workers below this range would be exempt from paying any income tax."

"I could support such legislation; however, I do feel 1% is a rather meager assessment of someone who has a greater ability to pay. I believe there needs to be a surtax on anyone who makes more than a certain amount."

"Mr. Bryan has a point worth considering. I am appointing Secretary McAdoo, Attorney General Reynolds, and Secretary Redfield to draft legislation that we can consider as a recommendation to Congress. I would like to see such a draft include a surtax. Mr. McAdoo, you also desired a discussion of the pending Federal Reserve Act."

"Yes Mr. President, I am certain Congress will have such legislation on your desk before the end of the year."

"What makes you so certain about this when bankers across this country are up in arms about such legislation? Will Congress move forward with this against such opposition?" the president asks.

"Mr. President, everyone but the common people know the Federal Reserve Act is but a ruse to place the nation's economy in the hands of bankers," the attorney general has studied this act.

"How is this so Mr. McReynolds, and why would bankers be making so much noise in opposition to this act?" the president is curious regarding his attorney general's assertion.

"The noise is not against the act; it is against the limited inclusion of bankers on what would be the Federal Reserve Board."

"Mr. McReynolds, if it looks like a duck, walks like a duck, and sounds like a duck, it is probably a duck. The Federal Reserve Act is nothing more than a smokescreen to put bankers and high finance in charge of the nation's economy. The bankers know that each of the Federal Reserve Districts will be run by bankers. They also know that the President is not going to appoint individuals to the Federal Reserve Board unless they have the knowledge and experience in banking and finance needed to run the economy. The banking community is making noise in order to convince the American people that this must be a worthy act if they oppose it," Secretary Bryan can see through the ruse.

"Why are you always so suspicious Mr. Bryan? Do you not see the good in anything?"

"I do, Mr. McReynolds, I see good in the hard work and labor of common people. I see good in the people who toil day in and day out to make a living for themselves and their families. The people who live on the bottom rung of society which is, by the way, the large majority of our people whose labor generates great wealth for the few who live in luxury."

"What do you make of John D. Rockefeller's newly formed Foundation Mr. Bryan? J.D. allocated $100 million of his fortune to this foundation. It seems to me that is not indicative of some old miser. What about the philanthropic activities of other men of wealth?"

"Secretary Lane, the philanthropic activities of wealthy men look just fine on the surface, and I am sure there is a great deal of good that comes from it. But let us not lose sight of the fact these philanthropic activities represent but a small portion of their wealth. Let us also not forget that such activities are designed to diminish inheritance tax. Furthermore, there is the power to be gained through such activities. To extend such activities around the world is a stroke of genius when it comes to gaining a foothold in foreign lands. I would suggest "If it looks too good to be altruistic, it probably isn't altruistic."

"I believe the issue of philanthropy is out of our hands. As for the

Federal Reserve Act, I will see what comes to my desk, and I will then decide to sign or whether not sign such legislation. I have a meeting with the British Foreign Secretary Sir Edward Grey in one hour, so let's move things along," Wilson can only tolerate so much bickering between his cabinet members.

"Mr. President, I would like to discuss something rather significant to foreign policy."

"Well Secretary Garrison, welcome to the conversation. I trust you have not been too bored with our previous deliberations," the president addresses his Secretary of War.

"Not at all, while I believe most of the discussion to be out of my bailiwick, I certainly am interested in any discussion which might increase revenues to help strengthen our defense posture."

"So, what seems to be your topic?"

"I am not sure everyone is up-to-date with what has been happening in the Balkans, but I find these events a bit disturbing. I am fearful that the conflicts in the Balkans could very much turn into a forest fire should the winds blow in the wrong direction. I do not believe we are militarily ready in the event such events get out of control."

"I agree with Secretary Garrison. The navy needs to be upgraded as soon as possible to be ready for action should it be needed," adds Secretary of the Navy Josephus Daniels.

"Now wait a minute Mr. Daniels. As the Secretary of State, I am maintaining constant vigilance on the activity going on in the Balkans. These issues are of no concern to us, and we must not do anything which sends the wrong message to the nations of Europe," As secretary of state, issues of foreign importance are within Bryan's area of interest.

"Don't be foolhardy Mr. Bryan, this world is rapidly shrinking so that what goes on in the Balkans may have repercussions in America. In the event you were not paying attention, an industrialist in Russia recently built and successfully flew a four-engine aircraft. It will not be long, and nations will have the capability to fight wars from the air," Daniels responds.

"We are still separated by big oceans of water which means we can and should stay out of the affairs of nations across the seas. The only thing we accomplish by increasing our military size or preparedness is to raise the concern of other nations about our intentions," Secretary Bryan has always been an isolationist.

"I understand the desire to keep the United States out of unnecessary conflict. I also understand what Mr. Daniels is saying, we need to be prepared for all possibilities. We are currently strong but not prepared. We also need to develop an air capability. This will only happen with your support, Mr. President," Secretary of War Garrison makes clear his position.

"I shall take this under advisement. I would like the Secretary of War along with the Secretary of Navy to prepare a plan for preparation that can be presented to myself and the Secretary of State. I would like to see this plan by the fall of this year," President Wilson directs.

"Mr. President, I wanted to thank you for throwing out the first pitch at the Senators and Yankees game on April 10. You not only threw a strike, but your pitch helped the Senators topple those darn Yankees," Secretary of Agriculture David Franklin Houston is not a Yankees fan.

"Thank you, Secretary Houston, but I must admit to remaining unbiased about the outcome of the game."

"Mr. President, I would urge you to send a delegation to the Panama-Pacific International Exposition in San Francisco to explore all of the wonderful innovations occurring around the world. We must stay abreast of new inventions and developments," injects Secretary of the Interior Franklin Lane.

"Thank you, Secretary Lane, I believe I have just put you in charge of that event. Now, gentlemen, we must adjourn. Thank you for a very lively and productive meeting."

Chapter 16

SMOKE AND MIRRORS

On April 8, 1913, the ratification of the 17th Amendment to the Constitution of the United States changed the playing field of national politics. Prior to the 17th Amendment, United States Senators are elected by the state legislatures as specified in Article 1, Section 3 of the United States Constitution.

Prior to the 17th Amendment, state political parties were in full control of the machinery that selected United States Senators. The old system secured state loyalty within the federal government to act as a check and balance to centralized control. The weakness of the system lies in the corruptibility of state political parties. While illegal, it was not unusual for a person of affluence to purchase the support needed to be selected for the United States Senate by a state legislature.

During the progressive era of the early 1900s, the direct election of senators emerged as a way of removing the shackles of state political parties and advancing the cause of direct democracy. On the surface, it certainly seems like a move in the right direction. What could be nobler than bringing officeholders into closer accountability to the general populace?

On a trip to New York, Andrew Mellon stops at Matinecock Point on East Island in Glen Cove to see his old friend J.P. (Jack) Morgan Jr. Morgan's father J.P. Morgan passed away while traveling abroad on March 31, 1913. Jack has just assumed the reigns at his father's financial firm. As his estate nears completion, he is taking time to enjoy the spoils of his wealth.

Upon seeing Mellon, Morgan Jr. asks, "What brings you to this part of the world?"

"I happened to be in the city, and I wanted to speak with you about a point of interest."

"What is on your mind?"

"First, I wanted to know how things went on your voyage down the Hudson with Col. Payne?" Mellon inquires having made such a voyage himself.

"Evidently you did not hear. I had a bit of a crud and missed the trip. I did hear it went very well. William Rockefeller contacted me about the things discussed. I believe they are on the right track."

"As do I Jack, but this must all be kept highly confidential," Mellon reveals that he already knows the finer points of the trip. "If word slips out as to our plans, we could suffer a huge setback from which we might not recover."

"I am sorry I missed the revelry. Col. Payne plans some of the most wicked events and he brings in the youngest and most lovey girls," J.P. Jr. likes his debauchery young and sweet.

"Hell J.P., you can bring in young and lovely girls anytime you choose."

"I know Andrew, but there is something of grand fun about the debauchery of several young pubescent girls all together at one time. Naked bodies are everywhere for the taking. It is the kind of sinful fun that allows me to forget everything else."

"Before we digress too far J.P. let me talk to you about the 17th Amendment to the Constitution," Mellon knows he must interrupt Morgan or run the risk of losing his opportunity to address this important issue.

"What about it other than the damn progressives are upsetting the apple cart? Trying to turn this country over to the common people. What the hell are they thinking?"

"They aren't thinking, that's the point," Mellon charges.

"Go on," Morgan says having turned his attention to the conversation.

"The 17th Amendment threatens to unravel the entire fabric of the existing federal system. Under Article 1, Section 3 of the Constitution, the method by which states select their United States Senators serves as a check and balance on the power of the central government."

"Enlighten me a bit," J.P. Morgan Jr. urges.

"State legislatures are controlled by state political parties. State political parties are closely aligned to special interests important to each specific state. Each political party selects a candidate for the U.S. Senate to be chosen by the state legislature. The candidate aligned with the party in power usually gets selected. If the candidate gets out of line, they lose favor with the party and are gone. Or if a new party gains control of the state legislature, a new candidate will be selected the next time around."

"I am not very politically astute, but that system certainly seems preferable to direct election," Morgan suggests quizzically.

"Not really, the current U.S. Senate is referred to as the Millionaire's Club because the senators are bought and paid for by special interests in each state. In many cases, these special interests are our competitors on a local or regional basis. These special interests are always looking to gain an advantage at our expense."

"So how does the 17th Amendment help us deal with this situation?" Morgan is a bit confused.

"Imagine trying to influence two different political parties in each state with so many different interests working against us. It is a managerial nightmare. The 17th Amendment neutralizes the state political party when it comes to United States Senators. They may still play a role, but they must now appeal to all people. The state political parties and smaller state interests must now spread their limited resources in an effort to impact all the people," Mellon has a keen understanding of the political system.

"I am starting to see what you are saying, but how is that beneficial to us?" Morgan remains a bit confused.

"Direct election of senators elevates this process to the national level. State boundaries begin to fade and the significance of national political parties extends beyond the presidency. Now rather than trying to influence and control numerous state parties, we can focus on two national parties. We J.P., you, me, and our capitalist friends have the resources to play on a national level. We can control the medium and the message that influences common voters across the country. The 17th Amendment plays right into our hands," Mellon is making it clear that the big players, the men of great wealth are in a much better position to influence voters, than are those interest groups of lesser means.

"I agree with your vision, Andrew. A stronger central government is to our advantage if we control the levers of government. Certainly, a senate with diminished loyalty at the state level could work to our advantage. I urge you to draft a confidential memo to this effect to be shared with only those of a common mind."

"Have no illusions about this J.P. It will take time, but I truly believe we have been presented with a real opportunity."

While there is maneuvering in the United States to leverage influence over the political system and the government, there is maneuvering occurring in the Balkans which raises concern across Europe. In July 1913, Romania declared war on Bulgaria, and Turkish troops got involved. While this war is quickly settled, tensions remain in the region. At the end of September, Serbian troops marched on Albania. To reduce tension in the United States, Woodrow Wilson proclaimed the United States would never attack another country.

1913 is a big year for automobiles. On October 7, Henry Ford started up his first assembly line which produced a car every 2.38 minutes. Ford says his objective is to make automobiles affordable for the average American. While Ford was already wealthy, the assembly line assured the establishment of his dynasty. On December 1, the first drive-up gasoline station opened in Pittsburg initiating a new oil boom.

In December 1913, Wilson was assured the Federal Reserve Act would reach his desk before the end of the year. In preparation for this event, he meets with Secretary of the Treasury McAdoo and Attorney General McReynolds in his office.

"Good afternoon gentlemen. As you know, the Federal Reserve Act is on its way to my desk within a couple of weeks. I would like to gain your input regarding my appointments to the Federal Reserve Board."

"You know I will be sitting as an ex officio member," Secretary McAdoo reminds the president.

"Yes, I do Mr. Secretary and I am confident you will help this new instrument of the federal government establish a solid and effective footing in economic oversight. What I am hoping the two of you can offer me is advice regarding the names I am considering for appointment to the Federal Reserve Board."

"Absolutely, we are honored to be part of the process."

"I am considering Charles S. Hamlin as the first Chairman of the Federal Reserve," the president announces.

"I think this is an excellent choice, Mr. President. As a former Assistant Secretary of the Treasury under Grover Cleveland, and now you, I think Charles is an excellent choice," says Secretary McAdoo.

"I would agree Mr. President. As a Harvard graduate and highly successful businessman, Charles would bring confidence to the business and financial community," adds Attorney General McReynolds.

"I am considering Frederic A. Delano a very successful and powerful railroad executive as a board member," suggests the president.

"I like Mr. Delano, and while he was born in Hong Kong, he is a United States Citizen and a very capable man."

"I don't believe citizenship is a requirement for membership on the board Mr. Attorney General, but he is indeed a citizen," the president reminds his attorney general.

"Mr. Delano would bring practical experience to the board table. Again, this should help shore up the confidence of the business community."

"Thank you, Mr. Secretary. So far so good," the president directs to McAdoo.

"Paul M. Warburg would be my next appointment," President Wilson continues his list.

"I do have some concerns about Paul Warburg. Paul was born in Hamburg, Germany and only recently (1911) became a citizen of this country. With everything going on in the Balkans, this seems like a risky appointment."

"I agree with Mr. McReynolds that Paul Warburg is a risky appointment, but I do believe he is an excellent choice. Paul M. Warburg's entire life has been banking, and he has been involved in international banking which I feel is a real plus as we monitor our economy," Secretary McAdoo affirms his belief in Warburg as a choice.

"You are both right about Paul, but I like his credentials and experience. He seems to be a man of high integrity and I believe he would be a good member," The president always holds the trump card.

"William P.G. Harding is a banker from Alabama," the president suggests.

"I don't know much about Mr. Harding, but perhaps the Treasury Secretary does."

"What I know is Mr. Harding is a banker's banker. Right now, we have a banking community that is highly suspicious of the Federal Reserve Act. I think it is a masterstroke to ensure two bankers of Paul Warburg and William Harding's caliber are members of the board," notes the treasury secretary.

"My final consideration is Adolph C. Miller," says the president.

"Perfect Mr. President. Adolph Miller graduated top of his class at Harvard. He is a highly respected economist. There needs to be a theorist on the board, and I cannot think of anyone better suited than Adolph Miller," affirms Secretary McAdoo.

"Gentlemen, this has been too easy. Mr. Attorney General, I would like your agency to do thorough background checks on all of these individuals. If you find even the slightest concern, I want to know. Otherwise, I will begin making preparations for their formal appointment."

Chapter 17

SUNLIGHT AMONG THIEVES

President Woodrow Wilson began his day working in his West Wing office. He did not sleep well during the night with thoughts of his Federal Reserve Board appointments running through his head. What if these are not the right men to initiate the work mandated by the Federal Reserve Act? What if bankers are serious about it being the ruination of the economy? What if conservative Republicans are right about it putting the banks in charge of the economy? All night he tossed and turned about either scenario with the outcome of each being equally bad. He wonders if he should even sign the legislation when it arrives at his desk.

"Mr. Burleson, you shouldn't just barge in on the President."

"It is all right Mr. Tumulty, I appreciate your concern, but let Albert in."

Albert Burlson is the Postmaster General. Born in Texas, Burlson came from a wealthy Southern Plantation family. His father was a Confederate officer during the Civil War. Burlson served in the U.S. Congress from 1899 to 1913. A devoted racist, Burlson as Postmaster General received permission from President Wilson to institute racial segregation in the US Post Office.

"Those damn Yankees are determined to ruin the very fabric of this nation." Burleson stomps in with his hands waving.

"What damn Yankees are you talking about Mr. Burleson?"

"Roosevelt and Taft are who. They have no respect for social order and position in our society," Burlson declares.

"So, what is the problem?"

"Niggers that is the problem. Roosevelt and Taft allowed niggers to work side by side with whites throughout the bureaucracy. How is a person expected to run an efficient and effective department when the workforce is compromised by mixing those who should never be mixed?"

"I do see your concern." Burleson has taped into Wilson's deep-seated bigotry. Wilson does not see blacks as equals to whites in any way especially mentally.

"Mr. President you believe as I do that white folk can perform much more complicated tasks than niggers. The inferior mental capacity of niggers makes it impossible for them to accomplish tasks which require a higher intelligence."

"I do believe that to be true Mr. Burleson but what can I do about the situation?" the president asks.

"You can issue an executive order which requires the heads of all departments to segregate their workforce. I implore you to do so sir before the ruination of this country," the postmaster general is an evil and mean-spirited man.

"I shall check with the Attorney General to make sure such an order is within my purview as president."

"Do not hesitate Mr. President. Time is of the essence!" The Postmaster General departs the room as abruptly as he enters, emphasizing his departure by swinging the door shut behind him.

President Wilson is convinced that Albert Burleson is correct in his assessment regarding the impact of race-mixing in the federal bureaucracy. During his campaign for President, Wilson promised coloreds that his administration would be fair in dealing with race issues. He saw the topic of mixing races in the federal bureaucracy as beyond the scope of fairness. He justified his stance on segregation by claiming it to be in the best interest of colored people.

Attorney General McReynolds abhors the idea of mixing coloreds and whites in the federal bureaucracy. He too believes it will lead to nothing but bad. He confirms Wilson's ability to segregate the bureaucracy through executive order, but he advises the president to take a different approach. Assured the heads of other departments will follow suit, McReynolds suggests that Wilson tell Burleson he has the ability to segregate his department if he wishes to do so.

As a result of Wilson, Burleson, and McReynold's involvement, most federal departments and agencies adopt policies of segregation in which white and colored workers are assigned separate working areas screened or walled off from each other. Furthermore, these workers are required to use separate restrooms, cafeterias, and drinking fountains. Throughout the federal government, the status quo of segregation that exists in the Deep South becomes the status quo for the federal government across the nation.

Outside the government and world of high finance, inventors like Wilbur and Orville Wright, Thomas Edison, Henry Ford, and Harvey Firestone are trying to make the world a better place through creativity and innovation. During this time, Thomas Edison and Henry Ford become very close friends. Prior to 1916, they spend a great deal of time together. After 1916, they own property in Ft. Meyers, Florida which shares a common property line. Although there exists a fence along the shared property line, there is a gate in the fence that always remains open. They call this "Friendship Gate".

On a trip to Ft. Meyers in 1913, Henry Ford stays at the Edison Estate.

"It is wonderful to have you visit Henry. How are things going in the automobile industry?"

"Exceedingly well Thomas. No matter what I do I seem to make money. Now I am implementing an entirely new concept for the assembly line based on a conveyor belt. It should increase productivity manyfold," Ford announces.

"Please tell me, it sounds so very interesting and profitable."

"Thanks to Eli Whitney and the interchangeable part we have always been able to standardize production. However, in the past, we have had individuals with specialized jobs moving from car to car contributing to the overall production of a car. This process was tedious and slow. It seemed like it took forever to produce one car."

"So how does this conveyor belt system work?" Edison wonders.

"Rather than have specialists move from car to car, we now place the car on a conveyor belt which brings the car to the specialist. A specific job is completed at each stage along the conveyor system. Now, we are able to produce a car in far less time."

"So, what will be the impact of producing so many more cars?" Edison continues to investigate.

"Because it takes so much less time to produce, and we can produce so many more cars each day, we will be able to reduce the cost per car and make them affordable to a greater number of people," Ford says with delight.

"Why that is sensational and exciting. How did you ever come up with such an idea?" Edison says with astonishment.

"You know better than most that thinking is the hardest work there is," Ford declares.

"Which is probably the reason why so few engage it," Edison completes the thought.

"Anyway, no one can do it all alone, every invention or innovation has some basis in the progress attained by others. We knew something needed to be done to increase productivity if we were ever to achieve our goal of making a car that would be affordable to everyone. So, we looked at productivity models. The assembly line appealed to us, and so we just needed to find a way to move our cars along that line," Ford says rather matter-of-fact.

"Congratulations Henry, I readily absorb ideas from every source, frequently starting where the last person left off. It is an integral part of the inventing process. So, Henry, what are your plans for your increased revenue?"

"Thomas, I wanted to speak with you about that."

"How can I help?"

"First, I would like to invest a certain amount in research aimed at producing an alternative form of rubber. I am wondering if you might take on this research," Ford inquires.

"Henry I would be honored to work with you on such a project. We will need to work out the details of such an agreement. You are my friend and I have great faith in your integrity but we will need to handle this as a business," Edison knows the slippery slope in the competition of ideas.

"I would expect nothing less. Second, I want to increase wages for my workers and perhaps reduce work hours. I would also like to implement a type of profit-sharing," Ford has always been interested in sharing his success.

"Look Henry, an opportunity is missed by most people because it is dressed in overalls and looks like work. For far too long the captains of industry have done little to recognize the importance of labor to their success. It is a noble and wise idea to increase the quality of life for those who do all the work. I applaud your idea," Edison is genuine in his thoughts.

"Thank you, Thomas, but you know such a move will send shock waves through industry and labor across this country. I can tell you for a fact it will gain the ire of men such as Rockefeller, Carnegie, Mellon, Frick, Payne, Clark, Duke, and others. They will consider it treason to make such a move without their approval. They will call me a socialist hell-bent on ruining capitalism," Ford understands the risk involved.

"Henry, those criminals will never approve of anything which might reduce their profits. They have no interest in advancing the good fortune of the common man. You and I have long been considered outcasts by this greedy group of highwaymen," Edison lets his success speak for itself.

"What do you suggest?" Ford asks.

"I suggest you do what is best for your company and your workers. I can tell you without reservation that Secretary of Labor William Wilson will view your actions as those of a brave and honest man. I can also say with assurance that common laborers across this country will applaud your unselfishness and concern for your workers," Edison's words of admiration for his friend.

"If you were in my shoes, Thomas what might you consider? I currently pay workers $2.32 for nine hours a day six days a week with no profit sharing," Ford is looking for some advice.

"How much do you anticipate productivity to increase?" Edison asks in a pragmatic manner.

"In 1912, we produced a total of 78,440 cars, but we did not successfully sell them all because the cost still remained too high for commoners. I believe the assembly line will allow me to produce over a quarter-million cars, reduce cost, and sell them all," Ford says with excitement.

"If you have increased productivity by over three times, then it would not be unreasonable to increase wages by two times. I would suggest you raise wages to $4.64 per day and create an 8-hour workday," Edison suggests a bold move on Ford's part.

"That is in line with my thinking, I am just not sure the timing is right."

"Do it. Henry, it is time to shake things up a little bit. You will be hailed as a working-class hero. Someone must break away from the predatory practices that are all too common in industry and finance. You are at the top of your industry and in the perfect position to lead," Edison is excited for his friend. Leadership is a powerful thing.

"I am not afraid of leading, but I am not so certain anyone will follow," Ford knows that without followers, there is no leader.

"One thing we can be certain of Henry is no one else in the industry will take this lead. If you do not do this, the opportunity may very well pass."

"What about the government?" Henry Ford asks. "Will not the government step in and demand that workers be treated more fairly? Will not the government see to it that all people are afforded access to the good life this country has to offer?"

"There is a war occurring in this country. It is a subtle war for the control of the government. Men of great wealth are fearful the government will act in opposition to their personal interests. These pompous men whose wealth has been achieved at the expense of our natural resources, and the hard work of labor watch over their fortunes like Midas with his gold," Edison can illuminate more than a light bulb.

"But Thomas, wealth has always been the gateway to power. Even in the founding of this great nation, it was the wealthy that rose to prominence in government and society," Ford knows the history and dynamics of wealth and power.

"That is true Henry, however before the Civil War, the power struggle existed between the merchant class in the North and the agrarian class in the South. It created a sort of balance of power. The Civil War changed all of that. Industrialization unleashed a mighty force across this country. Men with machines have found ways to exploit this nation to establish kingdoms over which they can and do rule. In a free and democratic society, independent kingdoms cannot be allowed to exist. Teddy Roosevelt understood this," Thomas Edison is a student of history.

"So, what is the reason for the war you claim is currently occurring in this country?"

"Men of great wealth have discovered their power and kingdoms are threatened when men of great principle and courage rise to prominence in government. They have also discovered they can be most effective when acting together to control the levers of government. They believe that government like anything else can be purchased at the right price," Edison shares.

"History suggests they are right. All of history is about the wealthy leveraging their power to get their way. Progress for the masses only occurs with the rise of courageous and just leaders. Unfortunately, courageous and just leaders usually meet an untimely fate," Ford speaks the truth.

"So true Henry, but that is where the war occurs in this nation. Are we a nation of, for, and by the wealthy, or are we as Lincoln suggested a nation of, for, and by the people?"

"Thomas, are we not among the wealthy?"

"We are Henry, and that is what makes us unique. We see our role in this world differently than others of great wealth. We believe our work is of great value only if we use it to uplift all people, not just ourselves or a few. That is why your idea to increase wages, reduce hours, and profit share with your workers is so very powerful," Edison is telling his friend that wealth in the right hands can be used for great good.

On January 5, 1914, Henry Ford announced a new minimum wage of five dollars per eight-hour day, in addition to a profit-sharing plan. It is the talk of towns across the country; Ford is hailed as the friend of the worker, as an outright socialist, or as a madman bent on bankrupting his company. Many businessmen -- including most of the remaining stockholders in the Ford Motor Company -- regard his solution as reckless.

Ford shrugs off all the criticism: "Well, you know when you pay men well you can talk to them."

Recognizing the human element in mass production, Ford knows that retaining more employees will lower costs and that a happier workforce will inevitably lead to greater productivity. The numbers bear him out. Between 1914 and 1916, the company's profits doubled from $30 million to $60 million.

"The payment of five dollars a day for an eight-hour day was one of the finest cost-cutting moves we ever made," Ford later tells his friend.

There are other ramifications, as well. A budding effort to unionize the Ford factory dissolved in the face of the Five-Dollar Day. The most cunning of all, Ford's new wage scale turns autoworkers into auto customers. The purchases they make return at least some of those five dollars to Henry Ford and help raise production, which invariably helps to lower per-car costs.

As Spring arrives in Washington D.C., President Wilson, Secretary of State Bryan, and Secretary of War Garrison are keeping a close eye on the Mexican Revolution. Near the prosperous oil town of Tampico, Tamaulipas, revolutionaries are closing in on the defenses of the de facto head of state Victor Huerta. Tampico represents a major American interest due to the concentration of U.S. citizens and the immense investment of American firms in the local oil industry.

"Mr. President, the developments occurring near Tampico represent a direct danger to U.S. Citizens and our national interest."

"Tell me what you know Mr. Garrison."

"Should the Mexican Revolutionaries overrun the government forces protecting this prosperous oil reserve, many Americans could lose their lives, and millions of dollars of investment by U.S. citizens lost. We need to act now to protect this vital interest."

"Mr. President, what Secretary Garrison says may very well be true, but is it the role of the United States Government to intervene in a domestic issue such as the Mexican Revolution? While I sympathize with the U.S. citizens in that region, they are there of their own accord. As for the oil investors, they are exploiting the natural resources of Mexico. Are we going to use the protection of their exploitation as grounds for military intervention? I highly recommend we do not!" It is again important to recognize Secretary Bryan for the isolationist he is.

"Mr. Bryan, I share in your desire to keep out of business that belongs to the Mexican Government. But when that business is a revolution that threatens the lives and interests of U.S. citizens, I do not see how I can turn a blind eye?" the president retorts.

"You cannot turn a blind eye, Mr. President. It is your responsibility to defend and protect the lives and interests of U.S. citizens wherever they may exist," injects the secretary of war.

"Mr. Garrison you have been itching to use U.S. military might since assuming your current position. How dare you be willing to put an entire nation on the line for U.S. fortune seekers who knew the risk when they took it," Secretary Bryan is at odds with his counterpart at the war department.

"Mr. Bryan is a pacifist who would surrender the image and position of the United States as a great nation by abdicating action to a group of thugs fighting for control of the Mexican Government. Abdication is not the path of a great nation!" Secretary Garrison fires back.

"Gentlemen, I do not want to overreact, but I do feel compelled to act. Secretary Garrison, who is in the best position to offer protection to U.S. citizens and lives in Tampico?"

"Rear Admiral Henry T. Mayo commands several warships which are in a position to respond."

Secretary Garrison, "I want you to order Rear Admiral Mayo to post his fleet in the area for the stated purpose of protecting American citizens and property."

"Yes sir!"

"This is a dark day Mr. President. Military action to protect U.S. acts of imperialism and exploitation is a dangerous precedent. I shall support your actions, but I do it with protest."

"Your protest is noted, Mr. Bryan."

As a result of this military action, the United States begins the occupation of Veracruz that results in a severing of diplomatic relations with Mexico. The occupation lasted six months until U.S. troops were withdrawn on November 23.

Throughout world history, nations have used their military power to protect or advance economic interests under the guise of national interest. For the United States, the policy begins with the first and second Barbary Wars of the early 19th century. However, since the turn of the 20th century, the grounds for such intervention become far more imperialistic and capitalistic with the Roosevelt Corollary to the Monroe Doctrine and Taft's Dollar Diplomacy.

Things are supposed to be different under Wilson. While an internationalist, Wilson also possesses pacifist leanings. During his campaign for the presidency, Wilson said he would keep the United States out of armed conflict. Here in Tampico and Veracruz, Wilson shows he may be a hawk in dove's clothing. His Secretary of State doesn't like what he sees in Wilson's decision. William Jennings Bryan recognizes Wilson's actions for what they are, the use of the U.S. military to promote the power of capitalism.

While Wilson is lending military assistance to protect U.S. interests in Mexico, his Secretary of Commerce William Redfield and Secretary of Labor William Wilson are meeting with Alabama Congressman Henry Clayton Jr., Oklahoma Congressman Dick Morgan, and House Speaker Champ Clark about the Federal Trade Commission and the Clayton Antitrust Act. As Speaker Clark doesn't maintain a specific Speaker's Office, this group of men meets in a side office of the House complex.

"My friends, we are on the cusp of a new era in the management and oversight of corporate power in the United States. I offer each of you my sincere thanks and congratulations."

"Thank you, Secretary Redfield, we have labored hard and built upon initiatives of the past to bring about the Federal Trade Commission Act," acknowledges Congressman Morgan.

"You of all men Congressman Morgan have sustained a vision for bringing corporate power under the control of the United States Government."

"Thank you, Speaker Clark, with the passage of this act, and the president's signature, we will once and for all have an instrument from which to promote consumer protection and prevent coercive monopolies."

"This is true Congressman Morgan, but without the leverage

provided by the Clayton Antitrust Act, the FTC will have little basis for action. We all know the futility of the Sherman Antitrust Act and the manner in which corporations and financiers have circumvented that law," the speaker reminds everyone.

"It is still too soon to celebrate my friends. There is little doubt the Federal Trade Commission Act and the Clayton Antitrust Act will be passed by the House and Senate, but it will not be without the influence and opposition of Henry Cabot Lodge, Henry A. du Pont, and company. These men will be working behind the scenes to undermine the power of this legislation. It is not a matter of what gets proposed, but what gets passed. We must work diligently to ensure the most powerful legislation reaches the president's desk," warns Secretary Redfield.

"We must pay close heed to Secretary Redfield's point. We cannot rest until the strongest legislation possible demands the stroke of the president's pen. As for me, I want to see the safe harbors created for union activity in the Clayton Bill enacted. It is far past time the government officially recognizes that the labor of a human being is not a commodity or article of commerce. Labor organizations must be allowed to carry out their legitimate objectives through boycotts, peaceful strikes, picketing, and collective bargaining."

"Secretary Redfield is indeed a friend of the working man. It is not enough to regulate commerce unless it results in a marketplace friendly to the common man. Labor must be allowed to implement the tools which will give it a level playing field in seeking a fair shake for workers."

"We are all friends of the working man Congressman Clayton and it is, for this reason, we must diligently move these two important pieces of legislation through the House and Senate. President Wilson's signature must be a strong stroke of action for fairness in this great nation. Thank you, gentlemen, for taking the time to join me in this humble setting for this meeting," closes Speaker Clark.

The Federal Trade Commission Act receives the signature of President Wilson in September of 1914, and three weeks later he signs the Clayton Antitrust Act. These two pieces of legislation set the stage for the regulation of corporate activity and commerce for years to come. And yet, the corporate world has no interest in rolling over and exposing its soft underbelly. Faced with a new challenge, corporations and financiers are even more determined to find ways to circumvent the law and continue to reap the lion's share in a capitalist society.

Chapter 18

A STORMY HORIZON

As President Wilson attempts to stay focused on domestic issues, the conflict in Europe is about to alter the course of history. On August 4, 1914, German troops invade neutral Belgium which prompts Britain to declare war on Germany. This means that the entire British Commonwealth and Empire are now at war. Wilson declares neutrality but knows events could rapidly spin out of his control.

Calling a full cabinet meeting in the Blue Room on the State Floor of the White House, Wilson plans to discuss the events unfolding in Europe with his cabinet. He finds the size and design of the Blue Room to his liking. The oval shape of the table gives the feeling of King Arthur's Round Table. Wilson wants his cabinet members to feel an equal part of any deliberation. Using an oval table in the Blue Room creates the effect of giving equal value to all participants in a meeting. The topic before them requires the utmost candor and participation.

The deep blue walls of the Blue Room are set off with light blue curtains and patriotic sashes conveying a feeling of intimacy. The large windows facing the south lawn let in a natural light that fills the room. In fact, what looks like a window is actually a door that leads to the South Portico porch. In the center of the room hangs an early 19th-century French chandelier made of gilded wood and cut glass, encircled with acanthus leaves. The walls of the Blue Room are adorned with portraits of presidents and patriots along with scenes of early American life. Most prominent are the portraits of President John Tyler (who became a Confederate traitor in 1861), and Grover Cleveland. As President, Cleveland married his young bride Frances Folsom (the youngest first lady at 21 years of age) in the Blue Room accompanied by John Philip Sousa and the Marine Band.

On this last day of August 1914, President Wilson stands on the South Portico porch considering the view across the south lawn as his cabinet members arrived. The President is in a pensive mood as he takes his place at the table. His cabinet can tell something very significant is about to unfold. Speaking in a soft and somber voice, "Gentleman, the entire European Continent is on fire and we are faced with the dilemma of isolation and neutrality in a world at war."

"I applaud your statement of neutrality Mr. President. It is imperative to the American people that we remain above the fray and out of this war at all costs," Secretary of State Bryan is a pacifist and an isolationist.

"I could not disagree more with Secretary Bryan. If we are to ascend to a position of world power, we must be prepared to demonstrate our power and protect our interests," Secretary of War Garrison is an internationalist.

"I understand Secretary Garrison's desire to flex the military might of our nation. We are indeed the most industrialized nation of the world, and our involvement could determine the course of the war, but where do our greatest interests lie?" the attorney general is a pragmatist.

"Mr. Attorney General, I believe you are aware of Wall Street's involvement in this war. While we as a nation sit idly by, the House of Morgan and other financiers are moving swiftly to underwrite the war effort of Great Britain and France. If these nations were to fall to the Kaiser, our economy would be greatly weakened," Secretary of the Treasury McAdoo is in the back pockets of the industrialists and financiers.

"So true Mr. McAdoo, but can we allow this nation to be manipulated by the independent actions of Wall Street? It seems to me this should be their risk and not something that requires the sacrifice of the American people. Why should our young men be sent to sacrifice in a world conflict to protect the interests of the House of Morgan?" Secretary Bryan is also progressive and has an ax to grind with those of incredible wealth.

"Secretary Bryan, you and the president have identified this emerging conflict as a world war when in fact it is more of a family feud."

"How is this so General McReynolds?"

"They are all related Mr. President. The Kaiser is the grandson of former British Queen Victoria, nephew of former British King Edward VII, and the first cousin of King George V. He is also the first cousin of Empress Alexandra of Russia, Queen Victoria of Spain, Queen Marie of Romania, and Queen Maud of Norway. The Kaiser has long been snubbed by most of them because of his arrogant manner. He in turn is out to secure his position within his family as the true master of Europe."

"This may all be true General, but we cannot deny the dangers this family and national entanglements hold for the United States. As the President, it is my duty to protect the United States, and the best way I believe this can be done, for the time being, is to remain neutral."

"I am not sure I appreciate the assertion of remaining neutral for the time being. I believe it is imperative to set our feet firmly in the ground of neutrality and to leave them firmly planted there," as Secretary of State, Bryan is determined to be the instrument of international policy.

"Secretary Bryan speaks with such foolhardy notions when we all know we must remain pragmatic. There are factors within and outside our control. Who among us can say what may happen tomorrow which might alter our view of things? Our national economy is greatly dependent upon a healthy and successful Wall Street. We have no choice but to see their interests as our interests. Furthermore, we rely a great deal on international trade of which the bulk of it occurs with European nations."

"Well said Secretary Redfield, as the Secretary of the Treasury, I believe it will be difficult for us to remain isolated when we depend so much on trade around the world. I understand that many of the European royalty are related to each other, but can we disregard the fact that Japan entered this war on the side of the Allies? Fighting has emerged in Africa, the Ottoman Empire, and Italy, which seems poised to join the Axis powers. This looks to be a long and bloody conflict."

"My friends, as Secretary of the Navy, I have become privy to information regarding the Kaiser's intention to make widespread use of "U" Boats. The design of these boats has been a work in progress since 1870, and while other nations possess such boats including ourselves, the Kaiser seems to be the first willing to make them an integral part of his war effort."

"The use of such machines is tantamount to criminal activity. To use a weapon that cannot be seen or heard is nothing more than a surprise attack on an unsuspecting victim. If the Kaiser deploys the use of these "U' Boats despite world condemnation, we will have little choice but to get involved," implores Secretary Garrison.

"As the Secretary of War, you would like nothing more than to have the Kaiser's use of these "U" Boats as a justification for U.S. intervention in this war. Why is it so hard for this distinguished group of men to see that the conflict in Europe is nothing more than wealthy people, many of them relatives all proclaiming nobility, fighting for more wealth and power? Now some of you proclaim this nation should get involved to protect the wealthy elite in this country who are trying to capitalize on war by underwriting certain nations. This war is about imperialism at its worst, and we must stay out at all costs!" Secretary Bryan will not stand down.

"Gentlemen, as President, I appreciate the insight and perspectives you bring to the table. I am heartened that no one seems to believe we need to be militarily involved at this time. I am not so concerned about Wall Street and the House of Morgan, but we all know when they fall on bad times, this nation falls on bad times. I do recognize the importance of not allowing this war to disrupt our trade, and as a neutral nation, we will maintain open trade with all nations involved in this conflict. I want Secretary Bryan, McAdoo, and Redfield, to be actively involved in securing and maintaining all current trade agreements with nations on both sides of this conflict. I want Secretary of War Garrison and Secretary of the Navy Daniels to ensure we are militarily prepared should God forbid our involvement is required. Good day, the president says ending the meeting."

As the war heats up in Europe, Robert Lansing an expert on international law serves as a special counsel to the Secretary of State. Lansing grew up in Watertown, New York a member of a prominent upstate New York political family and following his graduation from

Amherst Law School, he joined the family practice of Lansing and Lansing. He married the daughter of John W. Foster, President Benjamin Harrison's Secretary of State. Prior to becoming Secretary of State, John W. Foster served as Ambassador to Mexico, Russia, and Spain. The epitome of the American opportunist, Foster uses his experience in government to create a legal practice that lobbies for large corporations seeking favor in Washington and a chance to expand abroad." Despite the conflict of interest, Foster uses his government and political contacts to secure legal fees as counsel to several foreign nations. He also continues to serve presidents (when requested) on diplomatic missions which further establishes his personal knowledge of world leaders and his ability to do international business. Acting on behalf of American companies, he brokers agreements that place American corporations on foreign soil for the purpose of exploiting national resources and using cheap labor. It is with this background and association that Robert Lansing seeks to exert influence on U.S. foreign policy.

On a visit to Lansing's Georgetown Brownstone, Col. House, President Wilson's closest and most trusted advisor, seeks to have a conversation regarding the international scene with Robert Lansing. Col. House never served in the military, but he bestowed the title of Colonel upon himself because he likes the status. Col. House comes from a prominent Texas political family, and he is a close advisor to Woodrow Wilson as a result of his unwavering support of Wilson for the presidency in 1912. An astute observer of the international scene, Col. House wants to hear what Robert Lansing has to say.

"Come in Col. House, it is a pleasure to see you, and may I ask how is the President these days?" Lansing welcomes Col. House to his home.

"President Wilson is doing quite well. However, he has found it difficult to concentrate on domestic issues with all the noise in Europe," Lansing's visitor reveals.

"As well he should. The war in Europe and beyond is about to reshape the world," Lansing says with a definitive tone.

"That is why I am here Robert. I know that you have a long history of international experience going back to your father-in-law, Secretary Foster. How is he doing?"

"The Secretary is quite well for a man of 78 years. His mind is sharp and he continues to correspond with many world figures, as well as important corporate figures whom he befriended over the years." Like so many people of service, John W. Foster uses his unique experience and knowledge gained as a trusted public servant to advance and feather his own nest in retirement.

"So, what do you make of this war in Europe?" Col. House gets to the point.

"I believe we are on the cusp of great opportunity if we only know what to do with it. I just met with William Rockefeller and Andrew Mellon the other day. These men have jumped into the fray by joining the House of Morgan in underwriting the war effort of the British and French."

"Does that not seem foolhardy when the outcome of the war is uncertain?" the Col. Inquires.

"They do not see the outcome of the war as so uncertain. They are counting on the United States to enter this war and bring victory to the allies."

"That seems a bit presumptuous, doesn't it?" Col. House wonders how they can be so certain.

"Not when the United States economy is riding on the outcome. If the Kaiser and the Axis powers win this war, not only will Wall Street take a hit from which it may never recover, but all of Europe will fall into the hands of an egomaniac who believes the world must bow to his demands."

"Do you see the Kaiser in that light?" the Col. is seeking clarity.

"Kaiser Wilhelm is an arrogant snob who is dangerous as the head of a nation let alone a European Empire. In such a position, he will attempt to dictate trade and business around the world to the detriment of the American economy."

"So, what are the benefits of the United States entering the war?" Col. House can see how the deck is being stacked for war.

"I realize the President is hesitant to go to war, but he must eventually see this as his only option. By entering the war on the side of the Allies, he will assure victory. He has an opportunity to establish himself as a hero on the world stage," Lansing has this right.

"But he abhors war, and he cannot stand the thought of young Americans dying on the battlefield."

"Col. House, you must help him get beyond this. Those who die are serving their country. It is their chance to make something meaningful of their otherwise meaningless lives. Through their sacrifice, a great nation of great men can endure and take its rightful place among the great nations in world history."

"Your dismissal of human life is reprehensible! It is this kind of twisted elitist thinking that endangers the very essence of our nation. Whatever happened to "All men are created equal?" Col. House is taken aback by Lansing's most egregious comment.

"Face it, House, there is a reason wealthy men and women stay above the fray when it comes to fighting a war. Every society sacrifices the less significant for the greater good. That will never change," Lansing is a scoundrel.

"While you have provoked my ire, this is not about me. Convincing the president is easier said than done," Col. House is pessimistic.

"I know President Wilson admires Lincoln above all other presidents. He admires Lincoln for the tough decisions he made on behalf of this nation. Now it is Wilson's turn to make those tough decisions, and he must come to the conclusion that it is so."

"Robert, you may be right, but Secretary of State Bryan has Wilson's ear and he is a staunch isolationist and pacifist," the Col. tells Lansing what he already knows.

"Then replace him with someone who can lead in the right direction. With an Allied victory, our economy will be stronger than ever. We will see the German, Austrian-Hungary, and Ottoman Empires fall which will open up opportunities for American corporations all around the world," Lansing is offering Col. House a glimpse into his personal agenda.

"But if the President goes to war now, he will face possible defeat in the next election."

"So, wait Colonel, there is no hurry. This war could stretch on for years. By waiting, the President can remain true to his promise to keep the U.S. out of the war. By waiting, all participants in the war will be weakened. Then, after re-election, when the time is right, we send our boys to sacrifice for the salvation of the Allies and the glory of the United States of America!" Robert Lansing sees everyone as a pawn in this international game of chess.

"You seem to have the vision needed to see us through this international mess," Col. House detests Lansing personally, but he is impressed with Lansing's power of deduction.

"There are three things I want to see happen Col. House. First, I want to see all nations involved in this conflict weakened to a point that when the war is over, it is the United States which stands alone as a world power. Second, I want to see the United States exalted as the savior of democracy and capitalism. Third, I want to see American corporations and investors reap the spoils available in the wake of such a conflict."

"Robert, you make a case that is difficult to refute."

"There can be no refuting Colonel, we either make the most of this opportunity, or we shall fall victim to the outcome."

"Thank you for your time, Robert. I must be going. You have given me much to consider." As Col. House departs Lansing, he shakes his head in disbelief as to how such a sinister person could interweave his own personal interests with that of the nation. Based on Lansing's argument, war is a matter of time.

In late 1914, few American businessmen can command the attention of such financial and corporate giants as William Rockefeller, J.P. Morgan Jr., George Jay Gould I, and Andrew Mellon like Charles M. Schwab. Schwab feels the need to speak with his colleagues about capital and corruption. Taking an unusual step, Schwab invites W. Averell Harriman the son of Edward Henry Harriman to a meeting with this powerful group of men. Averell as he is called has just recently graduated from Yale and inherited one of the great American fortunes in railroading, shipping, and banking. He is by far the youngest man to ever attend such a gathering. Schwab feels a sense of urgency regarding the conflict in Europe, and he has significant business to discuss. He asked for the attendance of Henry Ford and Thomas Edison, but both men declined. They suspect the gathering might be up to no good. Henry C. Frick got word of the meeting, and not being one to be left out of any conversation about profiteering, shows up uninvited.

The men gather at Immergrun, Schwab's plush estate in Loretto,

Pennsylvania which resembles a combination of Versailles and Napoleon's Fontainebleau. As the men arrive for the meeting, they are ushered through the mansion to the back terrace overlooking a broad and beautiful lawn dotted with tall evergreens and Sycamore trees. The stairway cascades down the hill from the center of the terrace and then divides into a left and right-curved stairway to the garden below. Rectangular cement pools stretching into the distance greet the bottom of each staircase. Hundreds of yellow Lilys line each side of the pools. Looking back at the mansion from the garden, the observer is overwhelmed by the large stone wall at the base of the hill, the length, and dynamics of the staircase, and the incredible mansion whose red roof and tall chimneys remind one of Henry VIII's Hampton Court. It is in this setting that these men of wealth and power meet to discuss the events in Europe and the manner in which they can benefit.

"What a beautiful fall day! I appreciate all of you attending this afternoon. I know we all have a great deal to share when it comes to the conflict unfolding in Europe. Before we get started, I want to introduce Averell Harriman. If you don't already know Averell, he is the son of our dear departed friend Edward. I hope you will make him feel welcome as a part of our group."

"Thank you for inviting us, Charles, we are all quite interested in the events unfolding in Europe, and I for one am a bit nervous as to how this will all play out with a president who seems determined to be an observer," J.P. Morgan Jr. jumps in quickly.

"We are all a bit nervous J.P. but perhaps not to the degree you are," Jay Gould I remarks.

"As you all know, the House of Morgan has gone all-in with our financial backing of Britain and France. We see no alternative but to support these two nations as well as other members of the Allies. We thought the Kaiser might see the folly of his aggression and seek a quick resolution of these hostilities. However, it appears Germany has gained members of the Axis powers, and the war could stretch on for months if not years. We do not like this game of isolation and neutrality being played by our President."

"I too have considerable investments in Britain and France. I do not foresee any acceptable outcome other than complete victory by the

Allies. Britain and France are our close friends. We conduct a great deal of trade with these nations, and their success is critical to not only my personal financial wellbeing but that of the nation," declares Andrew Mellon.

"Gentlemen, there is a great deal of money to be made from this war. The demand for oil, steel, and munitions creates an incredible opportunity for profit. And yet, the war itself represents small potatoes in comparison to the outcome. Hanging in the balance of this war are the oil reserves of the middle east, the raw materials of Africa, and command of trade around the globe," William Rockefeller has a keen eye on the family fortune.

"William is right, and furthermore, regardless of the outcome, the nations of Europe will be left weak. They may still call themselves empires, but these empires will be but a shadow of their former selves. This is the opportunity we have all been waiting for. We are looking at the rise of American dominance around the world if only our president will join the fray and tip the balance our way."

"I agree Charles but what can we do?"

"I suggest we all do the very thing which Morgan Jr. and I are doing. Act independently to tie yourselves to the Allies. The tighter we make the connection between American business and the Allies, the more we ensure the president will have no other choice but to join the fighting and bring victory to the Allied cause," Schwab reveals the very reason he called for this meeting. He is seeking an alliance of financial power.

"That sounds good, but the president has made it clear American businesses are to remain neutral."

"Truly Mr. Gould, you are going to sit back and allow Wilson to play dictator. Where is your backbone man? If we all act in our own self-interest to do what we can to support the Allied cause, the president will have no choice but to acquiesce and allow it to occur," Schwab continues to make the case. "Mr. Frick certainly knows a thing or two about self-interest and to hell with anything else."

"Yes, I do, and if you don't believe it just ask around. I can tell you now, that Henry Frick is all in!"

"Let me share something which gives us all a more solid basis for action. I have been in conversation with Robert Lansing at the State

Department. Robert is not one to pass up a good opportunity to line his pockets. I guess he follows in the footsteps of his father-in-law John Foster. Based on his legal background in international law and business, Robert says there are ways to do business with the Allies which are not illegal."

"I believe we are all ears, Charles."

"Well William, my company is currently involved in selling munitions to the Allies. We are able to achieve this by funneling the munitions through Canada and then on to Britain and France. I must tell you this is a very lucrative trade. Because we are going through Canada, which is a viable trading partner, we are well within the law."

"This almost seems too good to be true. I am sure every one of us would like to have a piece of that pie."

"Yes, we would William and the more engaged we become in trading with the Allies, the greater the entanglement that will pull our nation into the war on the side of the Allies. This is a win-win for all of us."

"I know I don't have the experience of the rest of you, but I still don't see how this plan of trading with the Allies will force President Wilson into the war. He has adamantly stated the United States will stay out of the war. He has a Secretary of State who will argue to stay out of the war at all costs. It seems like a stretch to me," Harriman finally speaks up.

"Averell, there are people who wait for things to happen to them, and there are people who make things happen. We have Winston Churchill in Britain and the Rothchilds in France with the ability to manipulate events. We have the Kaiser who will act without thinking about the consequences. I assure you based on conversations which occurred aboard the Aphrodite last spring, there will come an event which will define America's involvement in this war."

"And just what would that be Mr. Rockefeller?"

"I cannot say, Averell. I am not even sure I know what that will be, I just trust it will be. The important thing about these meetings is our sworn oath to each other and secrecy. When we agree on something such as our need to support the Allies, we do so not only out of self-interest, but because we know that our interest is also in the nation's interest."

"William speaks the truth, Averell. You are part of a very elite club.

Through our hard work and ingenuity, we have accumulated great fortunes. We cannot say why we were chosen for this responsibility but we were, and it is our responsibility to do everything in our power to keep and increase our wealth. We are the financial backbone of this country, and if we go under, so will this nation."

"So true J.P. and the winning of this war is paramount! Averell, you are in the merchant shipping business. If the Allies win this war, you will be in a position to be the master of the shipping lanes around the globe. We all will be in a position to experience a financial boom such as never before. Our goods and materials will be in demand all around the world."

"Thank you, Jay. Gentlemen, I believe we are all on the same page. I would encourage your attorneys to begin mapping out a strategy for trading with the Allies immediately. We must leverage our power and influence for the Allied cause. For those of you who do not need to rush off to other business, my butler will be having a mid-afternoon lunch as well as drinks brought onto the terrace for your enjoyment."

The wheels of history are turning, and the men at the helm of finance, business, industry, and government are busy attempting to make them spin in their direction.

Chapter 19

A MUST TO AVOID

War is a beast best known for its consuming rage in the destruction of everything it encounters. It matters not to war who may be right or who may be wrong, for a war unlike other things in society does not discriminate. War lays low edifices which have stood for centuries; and buries beneath its ruble treasures passed down through the ages. War consumes the breath of the innocent as well as the guilty. War dehumanizes unlike any other activity contrived by the villainous nature of man. War is an act of failure on the part of nations whose mission should be a world of peace. War is mass murder. In all these definitions, World War I bring forth a new meaning and dimension to war. It brings forth new horror, a nightmare of epic proportions.

In mid-January 1915, Germany employs the Zeppelin in a bombing raid against Great Britain. By the end of the month, the Germans use chemical weapons. In February, Germany extends their submarine warfare to include merchant vessels. And, by the end of April, the Germans are employing the use of poison gas.

All of these things horrify the world, but none of them move the United States from its position of neutrality. Then, on May 7, 1915, the British liner Lusitania traveling from New York to Liverpool enters the waters off Great Britain proclaimed a war zone by the Germans. Acting on orders from the Prime Minister, the Admiralty issued directives for the British navy to provide the Lusitania with a convoy of protection. However, the communication and codes are so beyond comprehension they make the mission impossible. The Germans serve warning regarding the dangers of traveling on the Lusitania in American newspapers believing the Lusitania to be carrying war supplies for the Allies. With the Lusitania in its sights, the German U-Boat strikes with one torpedo. The strategic blow causes an explosion tearing a big hole in the Lusitania. Of the 1,959 passengers on board, 1,195 lose their lives of which 128 are citizens of the United States.

The sinking of the Lusitania causes an international outcry. However, the Germans claim justification on several points including the fact that the Lusitania carried fifty-one tons of fully loaded three-inch shells produced by Bethlehem Steel. It is no secret Great Britain wants and needs the United States to join the Allies in the war. It is also no secret that American financiers and captains of business and industry want and need the Allies to win the war. There is just too much coincidence to believe the Lusitania simply fell victim to submarine warfare.

The British know German submarines patrol these dangerous waters and yet they do nothing to divert the Lusitania to a safer route. The British cover their ass by ordering a protective convoy for the Lusitania, yet leave channels of communication impossible to establish. This ship with the ability to outrun any U-Boat is ordered to reduce speed in the war zone. How can one of the biggest ships in the world fall victim to a single torpedo strike? There are too many questions and no one providing answers.

In Washington and across the United States a firestorm of public opinion seems to favor U.S. involvement in the war. In actuality, the vast amount of U.S. public opinion continues to favor neutrality. President Wilson himself demands a German apology while ignoring British contraventions of international law. Still wanting to remain neutral it appears the sinking of the Lusitania moves Wilson closer to hostility.

Following the sinking of the Lusitania, President Wilson calls his Secretary of State, Secretary of War, and Attorney General to the White House for a meeting in the Treaty Room. Sitting behind the Resolute Desk, President Wilson invites these three advisors to have a seat. On the wall, pictures of General Washington, Pres. McKinley addressing his cabinet, Independence Hall, a Civil War Battle, and a Rocky Mountain Landscape serves to remind these distinguished men of this nation's greatness. There are books filling the waist-high shelves all around the room with historic mementos including a bust of Abraham Lincoln by Gutzon Borglum, a bust of Henry Clay, a pair of 1917 vases, and a mantel clock by Thomire and Co. adorning the top. The mantel clock reminds the men that they are involved in precarious times. In one corner of the room can be found a Duncan Phyle Work Table, and along the walls, a gold-plated Pier Table, and a 1902 Double Eagle Console Table by A.H. Davenport. In the middle of the room hanging from the ceiling, Christoph Palme and Co. Crystal Chandelier conveyed to these men they are in an important historical room doing important historical business.

"My friends," begins the President. "We are presented with a dilemma from which there may be no return."

"Mr. President, the sinking of the Lusitania amounts to a fiendish crime by the Germans, but to suggest it is an event from which there may be no return does not need to be true. As with every situation, there are options, and it is our responsibility to explore all options."

"At least Secretary Bryan recognizes this tragedy as a war crime, but he continues to downplay the serious threat the Germans pose to the United States. We may have options, but they are few."

"The attorney general is correct, we not only have few options, we have no option but to declare war on Germany. We lost 128 citizens of the United States in this criminal act by the Germans. We lost several significant members of our society including Lindon Bates, Arthur Henry Adams, Phyllis Hutchinson, Mary Picton Stevens, and Alfred Gwynne Vanderbilt to name a few. We cannot allow this act to go unpunished!"

"Always looking for a reason to flex U.S. military muscle aren't we Secretary Garrison? Ever since you assumed the position of Secretary of War you have been looking for a good fight. Now there is a fight and you want to jump in," the Secretary of State is upset that his pacifism and isolationism are taking a beating.

"Mr. President it is not a matter of looking for a fight. The war going on in Europe calls for our intervention. This war could rage on for years with a massive death toll unless we interject ourselves on the side of the

Allies. Now, Germany has acted in a way which has killed 128 of our citizens of which many are of a highly notable character."

"Mr. Garrison, there is reason to believe that the warmongers in this country, which includes a large number of the wealthy class, would like to see U.S. intervention as a means of opportunism. The sinking of the Lusitania plays conveniently into their hands."

"Mr. Bryan, you see evil behind the eyes of anyone with money. Do you honestly think the rich would have anything to do with such an atrocity when it resulted in the death of their own? Is everything a conspiracy to you?"

"Mr. Attorney General, conspiracy is at the heart of human history. Since the beginning, man has been killing man regardless of who that man may be to protect self-interest or gain an advantage. We know from our limited information that the Rothschilds have been in communication with Churchill as well as several U.S. financiers and industrialists. It gives good reason for one to pause to wonder?"

"Mr. Bryan, Winston Churchill is not the Prime Minister of Great Britain."

"No, he is not Mr. McReynolds, he is the First Lord of the Admiralty which puts him in a position of leadership when it comes to the activities of the Royal Navy. There are significant questions surrounding the Lusitania which we must demand to be answered."

"And just what might these questions be Mr. Bryan?" asks the Attorney General.

"We have reason to believe the unauthorized loading of British ships in U.S. harbors with war weapons and supplies has been occurring. We have reason to believe that J.P. Morgan & Co. invested $1,100,453,950.00 dollars in the Allies and shipped their materials and supplies to the United Kingdom via British ships. We have reason to believe that one of these ships was the Lusitania. These questions need to be answered for the American people," Secretary of State Bryan asserts.

"Mr. Secretary, let me make it perfectly clear we will not be questioning the motives or the actions of the British Government. The Lusitania may give us pause, but it does not give us reason to suspect Great Britain. Am I understood on that matter?"

"Yes, you are Mr. President, but when it looks like a skunk, walks like a skunk, and smells like a skunk, there is a good chance it is a skunk," Secretary Bryan responds in his homespun Nebraska manner.

"Gentlemen, we lost 128 citizens in the Lusitania tragedy. Among those lost were notable citizens of this country including a member of the Vanderbilt family, the niece of Andrew Carnegie, and Mary Stevens the wife of our ambassador to Spain. Yet, we must not allow ourselves to act foolishly in the face of such tragedy. I am opposed to war, and I remain so," Wilson remains adamant in his position.

"Mr. President, the citizens of this country are going to demand justice for the Lusitania. There shall be such an outcry of support for U.S. entrance into the war that you will not be able to withstand such pressure."

"I believe you are wrong Mr. Attorney General. I believe the President like myself stands on the right side of this issue. Americans will certainly denounce the Lusitania, but they will remain staunchly opposed to entering the war."

"I agree with Secretary Bryan, but I wonder how long we will be able to sustain such a position. The Lusitania is but one factor attempting to force our hand. As this war rages on, the demands for our involvement will grow," the president recognizes the challenges ahead.

"As much as I hate to hear you make such a proclamation, you may be correct. What I do believe is if you enter the war now, you will not see a second term. The American people remember all too well your promise to keep them out of war. Should you break that promise, the Republicans will once again take control of the White House in 1916."

"Yours is wise counsel Secretary Bryan. I did not make that promise lightly, and I do plan to keep it. I also plan to be prepared should I be given no other choice. Therefore, I want you Secretary Garrison to prepare our military in the event we run out of options."

Leaving the White House, Secretary of State William Jennings Bryan is overcome with disappointment by the President's unequivocal support of Great Britain in the face of possible conspiratorial conduct. He feels certain he must leave his post. He cannot act as a good and faithful advisor to a president willing to ignore wrongful acts regardless of who commits them. Furthermore, he senses Wilson is moving towards U.S.

military involvement. He must resign. On June 9, only three weeks after this meeting, William Jennings Bryan steps down.

Sitting alone in the Treaty Room following the meeting, President Wilson doubts he is getting the best counsel from his Attorney General and Secretary of War. The President values a heated debate, but he wants that debate on the facts, not a personal bias. In this meeting, Attorney General McReynolds often came across as too confrontational for objective consideration of a topic. He appointed McReynolds because of his reputation as an ardent trust buster. Yet McReynold's support of laissez-faire economic policies often put him at odds with the president's agenda. Now, on the issue of the Lusitania and war, McReynolds seems to have his mind made up. As for the Secretary of War Garrison, the president needs to keep him in check. From the very beginning of his administration, he knew Garrison wanted to extend U.S. military force whenever and wherever possible. Up until now, this disposition has served the president well.

After receiving Secretary of State Bryan's resignation, Woodrow Wilson goes looking for a new Secretary of State. He doesn't need to look too far to find Robert Lansing who serves as a Counselor to the Secretary of State. Lansing comes from a prominent family which includes his father-in-law former Secretary of State John Foster. Lansing's qualifications include training and experience in international law. He possesses a vision for the United States as the predominant power around the world which appeals to Woodrow Wilson's visions of grandeur for himself as an internationalist.

"Good afternoon Mr. Lansing."

"Good afternoon Mr. President."

"Robert, Secretary of State Bryan has tended his resignation and I need you to fill in as Secretary of State ad interim while I seek to fill the position."

"I serve at your pleasure, Mr. President. May I toss my hat into the ring for consideration for the top spot in the state department?" Lansing does not appear too disappointed at Bryan's exit.

"Absolutely Robert! In fact, one of the reasons you are here is to have a conversation about the position of Secretary of State. Tell me, Robert, what is your vision, and what would be your priorities should you ascend to the top spot at the State Department?"

"We have never been in such a precarious position and yet been presented with such opportunities as we face now at this time in history. The outcome of the war in Europe will dramatically alter the balance of power around the globe. If we allow the Allies to fall victim to Germany, we will have unwittingly collaborated in our own demise."

"What do you mean by such a statement, Mr. Lansing?"

"Mr. President, isolationism has never been an option for this nation. Since the inception of the union, we have sought to expand our trade and influence around the globe. That is the business of great nations, and the United States is destined to be a great nation. With the rise of industrialization, our exports can be found everywhere. Our businesses gained vital footholds in regions where resources are plentiful and cheap. We have important financial investments around the world. A German victory could reduce all of that to shambles and deny the United States its rightful place on the world stage."

"And as Secretary of State, you would advocate?" the president inquires.

"You must be re-elected, and that will not happen if the American people feel you have broken a promise. You must keep us out of the war until after the 1916 election and your second term Mr. President."

"But what about the Allies and all of the innocent people? The war becomes more brutal every day, the loss of life is beyond comprehension," President Wilson is testing Robert Lansing.

"Mr. President, history is calling your name, but it will never be heard if you act too soon. The Allies will hold for another year and a half despite the brutality and cost of life and treasure. We can do some subtle things to provide aid and ensure this happens. For you to take us into this war too soon will be a huge political mistake which will cost you re-election, and the nation the benefit of your visionary leadership."

"And what do you see happening after the election of 1916 Mr. Lansing?"

"I see the United States mounted on a white charger coming to the rescue of a desperate Europe in need of salvation. I see the United States emerging as the preeminent world power with you hailed as a great leader around the world. I see all the pre-war spheres of influence broken down and the United States arriving to capitalize on the great financial opportunities which will exist. Our time will soon come Mr. President. God has ordained our nation to be the missionary of democracy and capitalism around the globe," Robert Lansing knows how to appeal to the president's sense of grandeur.

"Very bold Mr. Lansing. As an internationalist, I do believe it is the Manifest Destiny of this great nation. Thank you for providing me with such an enlightening vision for the days and years ahead. I shall give your thoughts my every consideration."

"Good day Mr. President."

"Good day Mr. Lansing."

In and of himself, Robert Lansing is a rather benign character in the history of the United States. However, Lansing represents a family connection that provides fertile ground for the emergence of two of the most-dastardly characters in American History. Father-in-Law John Foster lives long enough to provide Lansing and his grandchildren with a philosophy of using governmental positions as a means of self-perpetuation through the advancement of American capitalism around the globe. To John W. Foster, Robert Lansing, and his grandchildren, the work of American foreign policy has as much to do with advancing the cause of Christianity as it does Democracy. In fact, the prevailing philosophy for this family of American diplomats is to view their religious, economic, and political beliefs as one and inseparable. As the future reveals, this philosophy paves the way for the unthinkable. John W. Foster's connections to world leaders and men of high finance opened doors for Lansing and his grandchildren which will change the course of U.S. history forever.

As a result of his marriage, Robert Lansing rises to prominence otherwise inaccessible to him. As a partner of Lansing and Lansing Law Firm, and with his connections through his father-in-law, Robert Lansing finds himself involved in the arbitration of a number of international disputes which allow him to establish international contacts of his own. As a counselor to the Secretary of State, he displayed unwavering loyalty to President Wilson. As Wilson had appointed William Jennings Bryan as his Secretary of State in appreciation for Bryan's support in securing

Wilson the Democratic Nomination for President in 1912, Wilson now feels compelled to appoint Bryan's second in command to the top post.

Ascending to the post of Secretary of State appeals to Lansing as a stepping stone to his ultimate goal of receiving the Democratic Presidential Nomination in 1920. What Lansing quickly learns is disheartening. Woodrow Wilson's personality will not allow anyone to assume a position of prominence which might cast a shadow on the president. Woodrow Wilson views his subordinates not as advisors to be considered, but as instruments for carrying out his plan. President Wilson can't see how his own ego is subversive to the goals he hopes to accomplish in a second term.

Chapter 20

STEPPED RIGHT IN IT

Woodrow Wilson belongs to the Bohemian Club, an organization founded in 1872 originally intended to provide a place of rest and respite for entertainers, writers, musicians, and other artists which quickly grew to include powerful men from all parts of society. The club's motto "Weaving spiders come not here," taken from Shakespeare's "A Midsummer Night's Dream," suggests the club doesn't serve as a place of business. Despite such a motto, the Bohemian Club evolves into a forum for high-powered lobbying and planning.

Through the Bohemian Club, Wilson feels the direct impact of pressure levied by capitalistic giants such as Rockefeller, Carnegie, Mellon, Curtis, Frick, Clark, Davis, Ryan, Duke, and H.L. Hunt. Many of these men provide Wilson's re-election campaign with funds vital to his success. With money comes strings important to allowing the puppeteer to manipulate the puppet. In this case, the understanding is clear. Once re-elected, Wilson will move quickly to engage the United States in the war on the side of the Allies.

On the first of September, under the cloak of secrecy ensured by the camp at Bohemian Grove just north of San Francisco, the President meets with these titans of business and industry. Bohemian Grove has many camps, and the president prefers the Owls Nest whenever in the Grove. However, the president agrees to meet at Mandalay Camp as requested by these men of wealth. Sitting around a campfire among the 1000-year-old 300-foot-tall Redwood trees at Mandalay Camp, the president sits in awe of his surroundings as he enjoys the blazing fire and the smell of burning wood. Confident in the privacy and security of the setting, these men of great wealth, power, and determination speak freely and frankly with the president.

"President Wilson, I along with my friends want to know why we should back you for re-election. You have done nothing to move this country closer to war knowing full well that many of us have invested heavily in the allies."

"Mr. Mellon, my administration has been closely monitoring the situation in Europe. Each day we grow more concerned about the fate of the allied powers."

"Growing concerned is well and fine Mr. President, but should we support your re-election? What guarantees do we have that you will do everything within your power to protect our interests?"

"Mr. Frick, I do not and will not take lightly the commitment of our boys to the brutality in Europe. On the other hand, my Secretary of the Treasury Mr. McAdoo who you know is also my son-in-law has made it quite clear that an allied loss would have serious financial repercussions for this nation."

"The men you are sitting with Mr. President are the backbone of the American economy. You allow the allies to go under, and you are sinking your own ship. We have done everything possible to give you a reason to enter this war. The Lusitania did not sink on its own sir, and yet you allowed a perfectly good reason to enter the war to slip from your grasp."

"I have not forgotten the Lusitania Mr. Clark, but I will not be goaded into this war. I am the President of the United States, not some patsy to be toyed with."

"Don't get on your high horse, Mr. President. Unless you have our help, you very well may find yourself unemployed in a matter of months. Nothing says we have to help you. You and Mr. Hughes are not all that much different. Don't give us a reason to do our shopping on the other side of the aisle," Clark makes his case almost a threat.

"Okay, Mr. Clark I believe you have stated your case. We need to remember Mr. Wilson is the president and as such deserves at the least our courtesy and respect" injects J.D. Rockefeller.

Continuing, Mr. Rockefeller addresses the president, "Mr. Wilson, we are all men of great success. We have hitched our wagon to this country, and we too want what is best. While we have not always seen eye to eye on economic matters, I think we can all agree that our success has been good for this nation."

"I would agree Mr. Rockefeller, while the rise of great wealth has created new challenges, it has certainly done good things for the nation."

"Thank you, Mr. President, that acknowledgment is important. I would hope you will also agree that the defeat of the allied powers could do great harm to this nation's economy. An allied defeat could bring on a depression which would create great hardship for the people of the United States."

"I recognize the truth of this assertion, Mr. Rockefeller."

"Gentlemen, I do not believe the Allied Powers can win this conflict without the help of the United States. I also do not believe the Republican Candidate understands this. My counsel has advised me to stay neutral until after the election. They suggest that my re-election is impossible should I commit the United States to the war too soon. Thus, my campaign slogan, "He kept us out of War!" the president feels obligated to show his hand.

"So, despite your slogan, you are personally committed to a declaration of war?"

"Mr. Duke, give me a reason to declare, and I will do so in my second term!"

"How can we be sure of this Mr. President? How do we know that once you have been re-elected, you will stay true to your word?"

"As I said, Mr. Duke, give me a basis for declaring war, and I will take the matter to the United States Congress."

"Once the election is over, you will be presented with a very good reason to enter this war. I sincerely advise you to act on this quickly. Time is of the essence, and we all know the clock is running out for the Allies."

"Thank you for that advice, Mr. Clark. I appreciate the candor with which this fine group of gentlemen has engaged me this evening. I trust your support will be forthcoming. I assure you I intend to act accordingly. I shall now bid you goodnight."

Returning to the Owl's Nest, President Wilson finds Col. House pacing back and forth with his hands behind his back.

"Col. House you seem anxious about something?" the president asks upon entering the cabin.

"For the past hour your re-election has hung in the balance, and you suggest I might be anxious," the Colonel responds. "Please tell me the news."

"I have secured the financial support of some very powerful men this evening Col. House. I do believe their help will make all the difference in this election. However, their support has come at a cost."

"They want war," Col. House suggests.

"Indeed, they do my dear friend. I had to do just about everything but sign a declaration this evening," the President notes.

"They certainly do not expect a declaration before the election," House says emphatically.

"No, they understand the importance of waiting until after the election," the President assures his closest confidant.

"Good," House says wiping his brow with his handkerchief.

"Col. a member of this group suggested tonight that the sinking of the Lusitania may have been planned. Do you think this is possible?" President Wilson asks.

"Mr. President, these men have incredible influence and power here at home and across the Atlantic. While they may seem good-hearted on the outside, they are ruthless on the inside. These men have amassed fortunes that rival the wealth of many nations. When they are threatened, they will do anything to protect their personal kingdoms," The Col. knows these men well.

"You realize Edward," the president becomes more personal with his friend, "If I did not intend to enter the war after the election in the first place, I just made a deal with the devil."

"There are devils all around us Mr. President. It is your job, along with the people around you, to navigate the ship of state safely down the river Styx. As Britain's First Lord of the Admiralty Churchill said, "When going through hell, keep going". This is good advice, Mr. President."

"Edward, William Clark suggested this group of men would give me a good reason to enter the war after the election. What do you suppose they have in mind?"

"You do not want to know Mr. President. You must always maintain the ability to deny any such allegations," his friend assures.

You are right Edward, and I am tired. I will speak with you again in the morning upon our return to Washington."

"Good night Mr. President."

On Wednesday, November 8, 1916, Woodrow Wilson found himself the victor in a hard-fought duel with Republican Charles Evans Hughes for the Presidency of the United States. Wilson pulls out a razor-thin victory on the slogan, "He kept us out of the war" thus making him the first two-term Democratic President since Andrew Jackson.

The realization comes quickly to Wilson that following the advice of close advisors to stay out of the war until after the election has indeed been the deciding factor in his re-election. The victory seals his messianic complex and puts in motion grandiose thoughts for leading the world out of war and creating a League of Nations to end all wars. He still hates the idea of war, but this war presents him with an opportunity for greatness unheard of in human history. Now, if only something will compel the American public to demand his action.

On January 16, 1917, British Intelligence intercepts a telegram sent from the Foreign Secretary of the German Empire, Arthur Zimmerman to the German ambassador of Mexico. The telegram clearly incriminates the German Empire in an attempt to recruit Mexico's help should the United States enter the war. The telegram represents a clear violation of the Monroe Doctrine, as well as announces Germany's renewal of unrestricted submarine warfare.

Attempting to protect their ability to break the German secret code, the British don't reveal the contents of the telegram to President Wilson until February 24, well after the renewal of unrestricted submarine warfare.

The Germans immediately deny the validity of the telegram. They claim they did not send this message, nor would they ever make such an overture. The Germans claim the British fabricated the telegram in an attempt to drag the United States into the war. They say they cannot apologize because they were not responsible for this message.

As news of the telegram became public, the revelation of the contents outraged American public opinion. Sitting in the private residence at the White House, President Wilson wonders who if not the Germans had sent this telegram to Mexico. He recognizes the seriousness of this alleged telegram and acknowledges the war fever it is creating across the nation. Thinking back to his encounter amongst the towering Redwoods last September, he wonders if this is the excuse William Clark suggested.

President Wilson does not like to be manipulated, but the telegram, combined with a renewal of unrestricted submarine warfare, has the American public demanding action. Looking for guidance, the President calls his cabinet members to the second-floor White House Cabinet Room on March 20, 1917.

The dimly lit Cabinet Room with its tall walls and fireplace at one end of the room is consumed by shadows moving back and forth in some historical dance. The Cabinet Room has been the setting for some important meetings over the years. The only furnishing in the room is a magnificent Victorian table used by every President since the Civil War. The size of the table and room require cabinet members to sit close together in a near huddle.

As cabinet members arrive, they file into the room solemn and somber. They know the business at hand could place the United States at war. Secretary of State Lansing enters the room anxious to take a leadership role in war planning. Lansing better than almost anyone else including the president understands the economic importance of an Allied victory. Secretary of the Treasury William McAdoo also enters the room convinced a declaration of war is critical to the defeat of the Axis powers and the survival of this nation. Secretary of War Baker and Attorney General Gregory (new to their positions) hold onto hope that war might be avoided. Postmaster General Burleson has long awaited this day. However, like the remaining cabinet members, he knows the limited extent of his influence.

On this particular day, it is noticed that one member of this administration is not present for this very important meeting. Vice President Marshall no longer has the confidence of the president. Kept on the ticket in order to avoid a rift within the Democratic Party, Marshall is kept at arm's length from the president and the nation's business. In fact, Marshall who once had an office in the White House compound has been moved to a different location.

"My most esteemed cabinet, over the past six weeks we have witnessed the German Empire's violation of their pledge to not engage in unrestricted submarine warfare. Since renewing their terrorist activity on the high seas, several hundred of our citizens have lost their lives traveling aboard merchant vessels. Less than a month ago, we became privy to an intercepted telegram in which Germany tried to enlist the Mexican Government to their cause should the United States enter the war. These provocative actions on the part of the German Empire are why I have asked you here today."

"Mr. President."

"Secretary Baker, how do you weigh in on the situation confronting our nation?"

"Mr. President, the German Empire has made it difficult for the United States to maintain a position of neutrality. The resumption of unrestricted submarine warfare is a blatant disregard for an earlier agreement. Furthermore, the Zimmerman Telegram is a shot fired across the bow of this continent. As this telegram indicates, the Germans are seeking to extend this war into our own hemisphere."

"You have stated the obvious Secretary Baker, so what is your opinion regarding the posture of the United States?" The president is seeking specifics.

"I believe we should protect the freedom of the seas through the use of naval convoys and patrols. We should make it clear to Germany that any hostility on the open seas will be met with force. We should also let Mexico know that any complicity on their part with the German Government will be viewed as an act of aggression toward the United States. I recommend you move troops to the Mexican border to show our resolve."

"Mr. President."

"Mr. Lansing, how might you weigh in on our current situation?"

"Mr. President, we have sat in the wings for far too long. We watched the Lusitania sink to the bottom of the ocean with little resolve. We have sat on our hands for months awaiting your re-election to a second term. Now, the Germans flaunt their submarine power anticipating

Britain's collapse before the U.S. can join the fray. They are confident in the inevitability of victory. They went so far as to send forth overtures to Mexico which threaten the United States of America. I say, Mr. President, it is time we go to war!"

"With his banner held high, I see Mr. Lansing is ready to lead the charge of U.S. forces into and across the perils of No Man's Land. I must wonder Mr. Lansing, are you willing to take responsibility for the thousands of young American soldiers who will be killed or wounded in this war?" Attorney General Gregory condemns Lansing's bravado.

"Mr. Attorney General, I take my high station in this government with all seriousness. Our nation has been assaulted on the high seas and through the back channels. We have been careful to not act in haste, but now the time has come to act."

"What will you say Mr. Lansing after thousands of young American men have died and it is discovered our merchant's vessels have been transporting war materials to the Allies? What will you say, sir, when it is discovered that the Zimmerman Telegram was contrived by the British in an effort to pull the United States into the war?"

"I take offense to such accusations from the Attorney General. I am not the enemy here, and I will not answer such questioning. The Germans have violated their promise to suspend unrestricted submarine warfare indefinitely. They have done so in the belief that they can bring the Allies to their knees before the United States can come to the rescue. Furthermore, they sought, as evidenced by the Zimmerman Telegram, to enlist the Mexican Government in an exercise that would retard the ability of the United States to focus on the war in Europe. There can be no greater reason for war," Secretary of State Lansing feels the wind of destiny in his sails.

As the Postmaster-General, I have limited say in this deliberation, but I have long advocated the involvement of the United States in this war. If we had entered the war prior to the Lusitania, we would be sitting around a peace conference table today. Now, I am fearful we have waited too long. If we enter now, it may very well look like we are trying to save face, rather than win the peace."

"I will not sit by and allow some of you to impugn the integrity of this Presidency. Much of the activity occurring aboard merchant vessels, including the Lusitania was undertaken by men of high finance and merchants of war. Such activities were not sanctioned acts by the United States Government. The situation before us is not about the past, it is about the current situation and the relationship it has to this country," the president is looking for sound advice.

"The President is absolutely right. Up to this point, we have faced public indifference to the cause of war. Now, due to unrestricted submarine warfare and the Zimmerman Telegram, the tide of public opinion has shifted at this most important time. As the Secretary of the Treasury, I can tell you that should the Central Powers win this war, the United States will pay a heavy price whether we are involved or not. An Allied defeat would have a catastrophic impact on our economy," says Secretary McAdoo.

"Of course, it would", invokes Attorney General Gregory, "Men of high finance and industry have invested heavily in the Allied cause. If the Allies go down in flames, so will many of these fortunes. Such a thing might be justice in disguise."

"You are so short-sighted Mr. Gregory. Are you not aware of the upheaval in Czarist Russia? Do you not realize that the greatest threat to this country is not Germany, but an economic depression that leads to a revolution? If the allies are defeated, and these important men fall into financial ruin, the economic foundation of this nation will crumble. We must recognize that the well-being of these men and the well-being of the nation are inseparable. We cannot allow the Allies to fail! Public opinion runs in favor of war, we must not allow this opportunity to pass," Lansing is not pulling any punches. He wants a commitment to war, and he wants it now.

"Mr. President."

"Mr. Burleson, do you have something to add?"

"I do. Secretary Lansing makes an excellent point even if it is laced with a bit of fear-mongering. I have known Mr. Lansing's father-in-law, former Secretary of State John Foster for a number of years. I am aware of Mr. Foster's strict adherence to Manifest Destiny and American Exceptionalism. Mr. Foster is a determined fellow, and I am sure he has taken great pains to instill his worldview in his son-in-law. While I would stop short of claiming Secretary of State Lansing has a conflicting interest in this debate, his family ties come from old money, the type rooted in the foundation of this nation's economy. I would be very disappointed if Secretary Lansing advocated anything but war."

"I resent such accusations from the Postmaster General. He might be wise to stay out of this debate," Postmaster General Burleson has struck a nerve with Secretary Lansing.

"Gentlemen, we are discussing the war in Europe, not attempting to start one here in the White House. I believe I know the arguments for and against war. I also know the final decision on whether to recommend war to the Congress of the United States rests with me, the president. Let me recap what I have heard, what I believe, and offer one last opportunity for comment."

Pausing a moment to gather his thoughts, the President begins, "When the war broke out in Europe, we had every reason to adopt and maintain a posture of neutrality. As the war waged on, we witnessed Germany initiate the brutality of gas in the trenches. We heard the appalling details of the dead. The use of gas evolved into the use of chemicals on both sides. While we were anguished at such conditions, we maintained our resolve to stay out of the fight. Germany then initiated unrestrictive submarine warfare which we protested and denounced. Then they sank the Lusitania causing the death of 1,198 passengers including 128 U.S. citizens. We pondered our response fully knowing the Lusitania carried thousands of tons of American munitions destined for the Allied forces. With a public outcry for vengeance fueled by the press, we considered a declaration of war only to step back as the public outcry subsided. Yes, re-election caused further delay. We had every reason to believe a declaration of war before the election would seal victory for the Republicans. So, we waited until after the election. Now, we have arrived at this point in our deliberation. History is awaiting our verdict, and it will not need to wait much longer. I am considering a message to Congress. I will announce a date within the week."

"Mr. President, I believe I can speak for the entire cabinet that we stand firmly behind you."

"Thank you, Mr. McAdoo." (This is followed by applause from everyone in the room.)

The endeavor facing President Woodrow Wilson immediately adds years to his appearance. Such a decision weighs heavily on his shoulders and impacts his countenance. For the next couple of days, his wife Edith noticed her husband in the evening sitting in the White House residence for the longest time looking off into the distance.

"My dear, you seem so far away, can I be of any assistance?"

"Sweet love, the hour is drawing near when I shall cast the die which will seal the fate of this nation and perhaps the world."

"Woody, there have been few truly great men who have led this nation, and destiny is determined you be one of them. I do believe in you!"

"I too believe destiny has saved me for this time, but I mourn for the many young men who will perish should we enter this war."

"What could you have done Woodrow? How could you have prevented this great calamity from arriving at our doorstep."

"I suppose nothing, but I do not like my hands being tied by the warmongering money machine within this country. Try as we might to avoid entanglements, the powerful financiers and industrialists do whatever they may to fill their coffers with money, even blood money. Now we have no options. If we stay out of the fray and the Allies fail, our economy will go to hell. Big money has made sure that if the Allies cannot get the job done of their own accord, we will come to the rescue."

"But dear, the Germans have given you two good reasons to enter the war."

"Things are not always as they seem, Edith! I need to get some rest. I am going to bed. Good night."

The President does not sleep well on the evening of March 23rd. War has been on his mind day and night. He tosses and turns, rolling from one side of the bed to the other often muttering to himself about the dead and dying. While no American soldier has set foot in Europe as of yet, the president has read the reports and seen the pictures. They are ghoulish and haunting pictures of men lying in the trenches one on top of another. These will soon be American boys and for what reason? His worst dream involves the increasing death toll as a mound of bodies grows steadily out of the ground while wounded soldiers without limbs all bandaged up and bloody march around the mound over and over and over saying "Why Mr. Wilson, Why?"

On the night of March 23rd, President Wilson woke at 3:15 a.m. His bedroom is dark and he feels compelled to get out of bed. He is awake and yet he feels as if he is dreaming. Something is urging him out into the hall of the residence. Stepping forth from his bedroom into the hall, he notices a silhouette at the end of the hall. It appears someone standing in dim light is beaconing him. As he approaches, it looks to be the image of General George Washington. With each step, the image gets clearer until he can actually make out the images of two people, Washington and Lincoln.

The President knows he should be frightened, but instead, he is calm, almost relieved to see these two iconic figures. As he nears, they both leave the hall and enter the treaty room where Lincoln signed the Emancipation Proclamation. Entering the room, President Wilson finds the apparition of George Washington sitting in a chair to his left, and Abraham Lincoln sitting to his right. Instinctively, Wilson takes a seat directly in front.

"Woodrow, you have been handed a mantle of great distress," says the apparition of Abraham Lincoln. "War at best is terrible. I have witnessed unspeakable horror and felt my soul being torn to shreds. Before all is done, the blood of hundreds of thousands of people will be on your hands which can only be cleansed through righteousness."

"I did not ask for this, and yet there is little I can do," Wilson is clearly distressed.

"What you must do Woodrow is cast aside passion for rational thought. Only cold, calculating, unimpassioned reason can furnish you with the strength to face the future," says Lincoln from a face lined with great sorrow.

"I am troubled as to whether I am up to the task," Wilson is wearing his soul on his sleeve.

"I know not how to aid you, Woodrow. I can only offer the assurance from one of mature age, and much severe experience, that you cannot fail, if you resolutely determine, that you will not," the ghostly Lincoln assures.

"But what am I to do, deep in my heart, I am afraid," The self-righteous Wilson seems far less than righteous.

"The occasion is piled high with difficulty and you must rise with the occasion. As your case is new, you must think anew, and act anew," says Lincoln. Continuing on, Lincoln's countenance shows all the signs of a man tormented by his past. "Politics is a dirty business, Woodrow. You will be asked to make deals with the devil, and only you will be able to determine if the ends justify the means. There is no way forward that will spare you from the anguish of the coming ordeal."

During this exchange, General Washington sat attentive to the things the sixteenth President of the United States is sharing with the 28th President.

"Mr. President," the apparition of Washington says. "You stand on the threshold of a new age, and yet, I believe you must adhere to an old axiom. Avoid foreign entanglements that create attachments and animosity which only cloud judgment in foreign policy."

"How can I do this when we are about to go to war in a foreign land taking one side over the other?"

"Europe has long been the most dangerous of continents Mr. President. Your challenge is not avoiding the war, because as you fear, you have already made a deal that makes war inevitable. Your challenge will now come after the war is over," says the General.

"What do you mean?"

"Woodrow Wilson, alliances between countries are a dangerous prospect, but alliances made between people are insidious at best. When you trade one thing for another, the Quid Pro Quo enslaves you to the deal. There is no room in public service for self-interest, and yet, you have allowed your self-interest to align with the self-interest of those with questionable allegiance to the country," Washington reveals he knows all.

"Are you talking about the Bohemian Club?" Wilson exclaims with surprise.

"You are not the first to sell your soul for election or re-election, and you certainly will not be the last. Your sin Woodrow is not in selling your soul, but in selling the future of the nation for your personal gain," Washington is making Woodrow Wilson face the facts.

"What if I had not been re-elected? What if my opponent assumed the mantle of leadership, and refused to go to the aid of the Allies thus sealing their defeat and condemning this nation to economic hardship?"

"Do you not have faith in our democracy? How can you be certain the people would have denied you a second term? How can you be so certain an Allied victory including any arrangement between the Allies and the United States would be in the best interest of this nation? Why have you cast your lot with men of high finance and industrial might over the wisdom of the American electorate? You betray the very essence of the democratic process," George Washington is scolding the president.

"Dear General, I believe God has chosen me to do his work here on Earth. Do you not believe in destiny?"

"If you believe as you say, Mr. President, you would not have needed to seal a deal among the giant Redwoods of Northern California. If you are a man of destiny, no intervention would have been necessary," Washington will not let up.

"Even God can use a little help, General Washington."

"The path ahead of you will be very difficult. You are destined to an eternity of blood-stained hands. You must take control of the situation. You will win the war, but you must not lose the peace. Save the world from alliances that only draw nations into more and more war. Distance yourself from the money changers, their interests cannot be your work. Find a basis to establish a world climate in which all nations feel treated fairly. Only if you can do this will the world be saved from a dark and dismal future" Washington advises.

"Tell me how I can do this, I need your help!" Wilson pleads as the images begin to fade into nothingness.

As the images fade into nothingness, President Wilson hears the haunting voices in unison, "Strive for the integrity of high-minded action!"

Sitting there alone in the Treaty Room, Woodrow Wilson begins to wonder if he was dreaming. A kind of peace has come over him and he realizes the thing he faces can only be faced by him and him alone. Whether a dream or truly a visit from Washington and Lincoln, Woodrow Wilson returns to his bed and falls asleep.

Chapter 21

WAR IT IS

Woodrow Wilson awakes the next morning immediately surveying his hands. He can vividly recall his encounter with General Washington and Abraham Lincoln, but brushes it off as a mere dream, or perhaps a message from God. He cannot escape the taunting phrase "Integrity of high-minded action". He feels the guilty sting that accompanies an act of betrayal and knows he should have never struck a deal with the wealthy and powerful men of high finance and industry. And yet, there is a calm about him that almost always precedes a storm.

Wilson is convinced war is inevitable. It all seems so clear to him now that war is the only way to catapult himself onto the world stage. The United States can win the war for the Allies and put him in a position to be the architect of peace and a new world order. He would follow the lead intended by Lincoln following the Civil War, "With malice toward none, with charity for all, with firmness in the right as God gives us to see the right . . ." This will be his victory mantra. This will be his integrity of high-minded action.

The idea of a League of Nations has been around for over a decade. Wilson has long been intrigued by such an organization for world peace. He can hardly wait to get to work as the architect of the new world order. But, a war message to Congress must come first. He would base the entrance of the United States into the war on the high-minded notion of it being the war to end all wars. He had first come across this idea while reading H.G. Wells's book entitled "The War that will end War". However, Congress will require something more than an idealistic notion about putting an end to war. Wilson decided that "the world be made safe for democracy" strikes a high-minded ideal that Congress could hardly refute.

Walking through the White House, President Wilson wants to be alone where he can think and draft his address. Instinctively he turns into the Treaty Room where he stands startled and transfixed on the lone chair sitting in the middle of the room facing the wall. It is the same chair of his dream. The Treaty Room is reserved for his personal use and meetings he calls with his advisors. Shaking his head as if to deny any possibility, he moves the chair to the table and begins to work.

On April 2, 1917, President Woodrow Wilson stands before the United States Congress and asks for a declaration of war against the Central Powers. Four days later, the United States House of Representatives and the United States Senate passes a resolution and the United States enters the war. On this day, Woodrow Wilson sits alone in the Oval Office of the West Wing and gazes for the longest time at his hands knowing the time will soon come when they will be stained by the blood of young American men.

President Wilson moves quickly to consolidate his power and influence over the conduct of the war. He already has a cabinet, but he needs something more specific to meet the needs of the coming struggle. Therefore, he creates the War Cabinet. Only one member of his Presidential Cabinet becomes a member of the War Cabinet, his son-in-law William McAdoo is put in charge of financing the war through the sale of War Bonds. Col. Edward House, Wilson's closest friend and advisor, also serves on the War Cabinet, as does Bernard Baruch, as head of the War Industries Board, Herbert Hoover, as head of the Food Administration, Henry Garfield, as head of the Federal Fuel Administration, and Vance McCormick, head of the War Trade Board.

Secretary of State Robert Lansing feels rebuffed by the President's failure to include him in the War Cabinet. Wilson tries to explain the rationale to Lansing, but big egos are difficult to penetrate. Lansing feels himself to be the most knowledgeable and capable person in matters of foreign relations. He can't understand his exclusion from the War

Cabinet unless Wilson feels threatened by his superior knowledge and grasp of international issues.

In June 1917, Secretary of State Lansing finds himself sitting on the veranda of the Watertown, New York home of his father-in-law John Foster with his two nephews John Foster Dulles and Allen Dulles. They are enjoying a beautiful sunset while sipping on some Swiss Wine brought home by Allen from his post in Bern, Switzerland. The family has gathered to spend some time with the ailing former Secretary of State and family patriarch John Foster.

John Foster has instilled in his family a sense of divine service. He believes that certain people are born to achieve great things and that like people, certain nations are destined to rule and lead. John Foster believes not only in American Exceptionalism but in personal exceptionalism. He believes great people and great wealth exist to do great things. He views the interest of the nation and the interest of wealth in the same light. Without wealth, the nation cannot be great.

As a public servant, John Foster found it only natural to nurture personal relations with world figures for personal benefit. By developing close ties with foreign leaders, he could pursue the nation's interests as well as his own. To the aging John Foster, it was all a natural part of the natural order. After leaving public office, John Foster invented a new type of legal practice by lobbying for large corporations in Washington as well as abroad. Using governmental and political contacts nurtured over the years, John Foster secured legal fees as counsel to foreign nations. As a result, the former Secretary of State filled his own coffers while brokering treaties advantageous to the United States, as well as other nations. This philosophy of duplicity was passed along to his son-in-law and grandchildren.

"So, Uncle Bert (as Robert Lansing's nephews call him), President Wilson finally decided to show some balls and jump into the war before it was too late," John Foster Dulles observes.

John Foster Dulles is the oldest son of Rev. Allen Macy Dulles a pastor of the Presbyterian Church. John's father and mother instilled ideals of Christian virtue in him which included the idea that at the heart of all work is missionary work. This piety, so firmly ingrained in John Foster Dulles, remained an important part of his life. He came to view internationalism as a means by which unbelievers were converted to true faith. As he negotiates the waters of international diplomacy, John Foster Dulles frequently grapples with issues requiring personal compromise. In every instance, he concludes that the ends justify the means.

"We are at war John but that does not mean the president knows how to make war, let alone peace. He is an academician well out of his element," Uncle Bert responds.

"Woodrow Wilson was my favorite professor at Princeton, he is a brilliant thinker. He was smart enough to make you his Secretary of State," John Foster Dulles asserts.

"That might be true John, but the president views the war as some form of a crusade to save the world, ignoring the opportunity to establish the United States as the preeminent world power. There are great opportunities inherent in this conflict, and we should do whatever possible to capitalize on this situation."

"What do you have in mind, Uncle Bert?" Allen inquires.

Allen Dulles is the opposite of his brother. While they grew up in the same home, Allen did not take to piety in the way his older brother and younger sister did. As Allen rises in the community of international espionage, he has no issues of conscience.

"Earlier this year, John displayed a great understanding of international dynamics during his mission to Cuba. While the regime there is totalitarian it is friendly to the United States. John saw the importance of protecting the existing government from liberal rebels in order to protect vital American financial interests in that country. By convincing me to dispatch two destroyers and the marines to Cuba, we brought stability to that Island nation," his uncle applauded.

"My Cuban experience taught me a valuable lesson about international power broking. I learned that a rich and powerful country guided by the wishes of wealthy corporations can impose their will on poor and weak countries," John Foster Dulles shares.

"How has that worked out for you so far?" Uncle Bert asks. He is leading John Foster to give his example.

"Recently, there arose a concern about the allegiance of the dictators in Costa Rica, Panama, and Nicaragua to the United States. United Fruit which is an important and lucrative client of Sullivan and Cromwell, the firm I have worked for since 1911, became very much concerned about the security of their investment in these three countries. Uncle Bert dispatched me to speak with these dictators and gain assurance that they would remain aligned with the United States should we enter the war. Their pledge of loyalty alleviated any concerns on the part of United Fruit."

"Allen, I recently moved you from the Embassy in Vienna, Austria-Hungary to our Embassy in Bern, Switzerland. How are you adjusting to your reassignment?" Uncle Bert knows how to keep it in the family.

"As you both know, after reading Rudyard Kipling's "Kim", I am enthralled with the world of espionage. I realize Kipling romanticized the world of a spy, but it is the world of intrigue that I seek," proclaims Allen. "My transfer to Bern provides me with a fertile international setting for collecting vital information while enjoying the spoils of the position.

"How can you enjoy snooping around in the shadows, it seems rather unsavory and certainly Unchristian," interjects John Foster Dulles.

"Let me assure you brother, the work I do provides intelligence valuable to this nation and our war effort. The ends justify the means, and in this case, the winning of the war rises above all other considerations."

"Well said nephew, the information you have sent us has been quite valuable. I trust you are also enjoying a rather freewheeling lifestyle," Uncle Bert inquires.

"I want to thank you for subsidizing a lifestyle that allows me to hobnob with the richest, most famous, and most important people in Europe. It is this hobnobbing that gains me the trust so important to my work. The more people trust me, the more willing they are to talk, especially after consuming a copious amount of alcohol or other drugs," Allen confesses.

Unable to help himself, Allen continues with a confession in a rather prideful manner, "About two weeks ago, I was having drinks in the bar at the Bellevue Palace Hotel when a worker from the British Embassy pointed out two incredibly beautiful women from the German Embassy. He told me they were twins, and bet me ten pounds I couldn't bed even one of them."

"Please go on, Allen," Uncle Bert encourages.

"It turns out these girls are twins and just barely twenty years old. These girls have long blonde hair and piercing blue eyes. They stand about five-ten with perfect bodies. My first move is to find out their favorite drink which I obtain with ease from the bartender. Walking to their table, I introduce myself, offer them a drink, and ask if I can join them. To my surprise, they speak English with ease."

"So, do you win the bet?" Uncle Bert asks while John Foster Dulles seems more appalled than interested.

"We have a couple of drinks when one of the girls pulls out three pills and explains they are MDA which makes you feel very relaxed. She giggles a very breathy and sexy giggle as the girls immediately take one and slip it down with a drink. I pretend to do the same but keep the pill in the palm of my hand and slip it into my pocket. I am not opposed to taking the pill, but in this situation, I do not want to take any chances," Allen stresses.

"Now what?" Uncle Bert says obviously wanting the hear more.

"One of the girls suggests we go up to their room. Soon I find myself with two gorgeous girls getting naked and laying on the bed. The two of them begin kissing me on the mouth and neck. Their lips are full and soft, their breath is sweet, and their fragrance is enticing. I do not have enough hands to touch all of the places I desire to touch at one time. My cock is rock hard, and I soon find one of the girls sucking up and down on it with a feverish passion. The other sister has positioned herself so I can suck on her full plump nipples. My mind vacillates from the pleasure of the blow job to the intense pleasure of making the other sister go crazy by sucking back and forth on her breasts. My hands are reaching and groping. My right hand firmly engages the soft moist pussy of the girl sucking my dick while my left-hand does the same to the other sister. I feel like I am being crucified in pleasure. As I feel the uncontrollable need to cum, I try to draw back from the girl with her lips firmly encompassing my cock, but she grabs my ass and holds on tight as I blow. She doesn't even flinch, but simply takes it all and laps up that which she cannot swallow. Both girls are screaming with ecstasy when they switch positions. This time, one sister sucks on my cock to make it hard enough to mount while the other sister lays her sweet soft cunt in my face. As the one sister bounces up and down moaning and groaning in delight, I use my tongue to massage the other sister's pussy. At one point, my tongue touches her ass hole, and she tells me she wants more. As my tongue moves back and forth between her puss and ass, she gyrates her hips until she finally collapses in exhaustion and delight. At about the same time, the other sister and I cum in unison, and she collapses on my chest. We all lay there on the bed panting as if we are about to die," Allen shares in graphic detail.

"And what does this have to do with espionage?" John Foster Dulles asks a bit sarcastically.

"Dear brother, this is the essence of espionage. Nothing brings people closer together than booze, drugs, and sex. When you have successfully engaged someone in this manner, their trust and confidence are not far behind. Before our evening was over, these girls felt compelled to share things going on at the German Embassy which I might not have gained any other way. These girls are now a personal contact I can use whenever the opportunity arises. Which gives rise to other things also," Allen declares with a fiendish smile.

"The bottom line here nephews is that you are both extraordinarily talented in the jobs you perform. You are making contacts and personal alliances with foreign officials which could be of benefit to you, your friends, and your nation for years to come. You must both come to realize that diplomacy and espionage are partners in achieving goals," Uncle Bert emphasizes.

"So where do we go from here Uncle Bert?" John Foster Dulles asks.

"John, I am going to appoint you a legal advisor to the War Trade Board headed by Vance McCormick. I want you to be my eyes and ears on this board. Furthermore, this position should allow you to recruit new clients for Sullivan and Cromwell which is also good for the United States. Furthermore, you will be able to create alliances with important businesses by helping them secure lucrative government contracts. This is all part of public service. If you can make deals beneficial to the U.S., Sullivan and Cromwell, and yourself, everyone is a winner."

"I would appreciate such an appointment, Uncle Bert!" John Foster Dulles will do anything to advance his career.

"Allen, you have the potential to be a spy in every sense of Rudyard

Kipling's romanticized version. As Secretary of State, I am committed to expanding the fledgling Military Intelligence Division of this country. I envision the things we do now as precursors to a full-fledged American Intelligence Network. I plan to keep you right in the thick of things for as long as you desire."

"Nothing would please me more Uncle Bert," Allan responds.

"John and Allen, I truly believe we are on the cusp of establishing an apparatus that will serve and direct this nation far into the future. I ask you to keep this quiet. There will be those who see what we are doing as a threat to democracy. I think we all three know what we are engaging will be the salvation of democracy," Uncle Bert concludes.

As the three men are concluding their conversation, a servant comes from the house to announce dinner.

Back in New York City at a Madison Avenue Penthouse, Andrew Mellon is hosting a visit from John D. Rockefeller. As the men sit to enjoy a glass of Cherie, Andrew initiates the conversation.

"It is good of you to come to New York at my invitation J.D."

"Andrew when it comes to business, I will travel just about anywhere to turn a profit."

"Well, a profit is what we shall turn. Our plan worked out wonderfully, the press and public easily bought into the authenticity of the telegram. With public sentiment running in favor of war, President Wilson had the perfect forum to ask Congress for a declaration."

"It occurred none too soon Andrew. There was more than a little concern that the Allies would fall before help could be secured. Such a fate would have been the ruin of a good many men," Rockefeller is a tycoon of the first degree.

"They were sweating it out on Wall Street. The market hung in the balance, but the war declaration saved the day," Andrew proclaims.

"Well, the war is not won yet, my dear fellow. The President cannot waste a moment in getting manpower, equipment, and supplies to the Allies."

"You must be patient J.D. Soon there will be a cry all across the country for an increased supply of oil. You are about to turn a very nice profit, my friend," Andrew Mellon is a master of high finance.

"I do hope so. After all, our plan is based on increasing our wealth and power base."

"The war is going to be a boon for the country. More and more people will be employed, and those who are not employed will be off to war. The demand for American goods and services will reach far around the globe. With more workers, there will be more money to spend which will fill our coffers," Andrew assures Rockefeller with a toast.

"What about foreign markets, how can we be assured the United States will use this war as an opportunity to expand our influence and access to valuable resources? Our entrance into the war is important for an Allied victory, but when the dust has cleared, it must be the United States which stands tallest and strongest among all nations," Rockefeller proclaims. It is the bottom line, always the bottom line.

"J.D., we have a friend on the inside. Secretary of State Lansing is a diplomat with a very keen eye for business and personal gain. As you may know, he is the son-in-law of former Secretary of State John Foster. When Foster retired, he formed an international consulting business. He has greatly increased his fortune as a private businessman by using the valuable contacts and friendships he made as an American diplomat. Robert Lansing is every bit as savvy as his father-in-law."

"That seems all well and fine for Mr. Lansing, but what about the rest of us?"

"You miss my point J.D. Robert Lansing is an internationalist. He believes in Pax Americana and clearly knows this can only occur if we plant the flag of American business in every country around the globe. It is his vision to make all nations subservient to the United States as a matter of economic necessity."

"And how does he plan to do this, he is only one man, and the mantle of high office can be rather fleeting," J.D. Rockefeller is a man who does not like to leave things to chance.

"As a good friend of Mr. Lansing, he has shared some of his ideas with me. He has a nephew who works for Sullivan and Cromwell a firm involved in many international dealings," Andrew Mellon is well networked.

"I am familiar with Sullivan and Cromwell, go on."

"Lansing is assigning his nephew John Foster Dulles as an advisor to the War Trade Board. This is a significant assignment, and we have every reason to believe his nephew will help assure profits from this war run in the right direction," Mellon assures.

"I like what I am hearing."

"Just wait, there is more. Secretary Lansing also has a nephew Allen Dulles, John Foster Dulles' brother who is perhaps the most devious young fellow I have ever met. This young man is every bit a believer of American Exceptionalism as his brother, and he is willing to go to whatever lengths might be necessary to make it happen. Where John Foster Dulles has a puritanical nature to him, his brother Allen is devilish."

"And how is that so?" J.D. is not interested in having his ass packed with sand.

"Secretary Lansing has sent this nephew Allen to Bern, Switzerland with the mission to gain intelligence about the Central Powers no matter how it must be done. The United States has always dabbled in espionage, but Robert Lansing believes espionage is critical if the United States is going to hold dominion around the world."

"Where does the President of the United States fit in all of this?" J.D. wonders.

"Wilson is too high-minded for these sorts of things. As long as he delegates responsibility to those who know how to conduct business, we will be well served."

"You have shared a great deal with me today Mr. Mellon. I am most appreciative of your candor. I am confident we are on the right path. I insist you keep me in the loop. For now, I must bid you a good day."

"Good day Mr. Rockefeller."

Chapter 22

IT IS ALL AN ILLUSION

The United States enters the First World War like a violent thunderstorm rolling across the American plains. The infusion of men, guns, artillery, and a thirst for conquest bring new life to the Allied forces mired down in the trenches all across the Western Front. The nearly defeated Allies find hope and a renewed belief in victory with the arrival of the American Doughboys.

With the United States committed to victory, on the war cry of President Wilson to make the world safe for democracy, the chief American warmongers, the American financiers, and industrialists settle in to reap the profits gained by what will be the death of 116,500 Americans along with 204,200 wounded. A small price to pay for American imperialism and the cause of international capitalism.

Of all to benefit financially from the war, those at J.P. Morgan Inc. delight most in the American sacrifice and what looks to be an inevitable victory for the Allies. Morgan invested heavily in the Allies early in the war, and an Allied victory will be an incredible windfall for the company.

Charles M. Schwab, the President of Bethlehem Steel and Ship Building revels in the news of the U.S. entrance into the war. In the years leading up to the U.S. entrance, the steel and shipbuilding business boomed. Now, with the United States an active participant in the war, the demand for steel and ships multiplies as do the profits.

Before the U.S. entrance into the war, DuPont Corporation under the leadership of Pierre S. DuPont found clandestine ways to ship munitions to the Allies. DuPont Corporation founded in the early 19th century as a producer of gunpowder emerged as a leading producer of explosives during the First World War. Prior to 1914, DuPont Company revenues reached $25 million dollars. Between 1914 and 1918, DuPont's revenues reach $1.25 billion dollars supplying 40% of the explosives used by the Allies for a profit of $250 million dollars.

According to General Smedley M. Butler, of the estimated $52 billion cost of World War 1, war industry profiteers pocket nearly one-third. More than 21,000 new American millionaires and billionaires emerge from the human ashes of the war, while the federal government is mired in post-war debt paid for by working people's taxes.

All the conspirators of the Bohemian Club, as well as many more, celebrate the financial benefits of the United States at war. The manipulation of democracy and the shrewd maneuvering of the financially powerful prevail to win the day.

Shortly after the declaration of war, President Woodrow Wilson calls a meeting of his Secretary of State, Secretary of the Treasury, Attorney General, and Postmaster General. Meeting in the West Wing of the White House, the President addresses the matter at hand.

"Gentlemen, I have called you here to discuss a matter of grave importance. Espionage has long been a part of a sovereign nation's defensive fabric. The gathering of information critical to thwarting any threat to a nation's security is essential to survival, especially during times of national crisis. Over the past three decades, the espionage capabilities of the United States have diminished as the American star has risen. Over the past couple of years, we have failed to prevail upon Congress on the urgent need for legislation supporting espionage and national security. We cannot afford to fail any longer."

"We have drafted legislation to the extent to which you have requested Mr. President," informed Attorney General Gregory.

"Mr. President, I believe the drafted legislation provides the basis from which we can monitor and control any domestic activity that might jeopardize the conduct and success of the war. You should prepare to submit this legislation to Congress for immediate action," adds Postmaster General Burleson.

"Does the legislation include our ability to censor the press when necessary?" asks President Wilson.

"No sir it does not. As you are aware, congress and the courts have been unwilling to allow for what they consider a breach of the First Amendment," interjects the Attorney General.

"Then of what good is this legislation if our efforts can be impugned and subverted by an unbridled press?" asks Wilson.

"The legislation will allow the United States Post Office to screen all material sent through the mail. Should we find the content of any publication a threat to national security, we can deny delivery," responds the Postmaster General.

"Furthermore Mr. President should any journalist conduct themselves in what we determine is an act of disloyalty, we can have them apprehended and tried under this law," proclaims the Attorney General.

"Mr. President, we are building a Bureau of Investigation under the Justice Department which will create a network of domestic spies ready to monitor the conduct of U.S. citizens across the country. All we need is for Congress to pass this legislation," adds the Attorney General.

"What do you think of all this Secretary Lansing?" asks the President.

"My concern sir goes beyond domestic espionage. While we must certainly guard against the enemies within our country, we must do a better job of our foreign espionage if we are going to assume our new role as a world leader," Lansing suggests knowing far more about the current state of foreign espionage than the president.

"What is it you suggest Mr. Secretary?"

"Our foreign intelligence system is very weak and disjointed. We currently have the Military Intelligence Division of the U.S. Army and the U.S. Office of Naval Intelligence, but there is no coordinated way of sharing information between organizations for the benefit of everyone involved in international activity. Starting last year, I took the initiative to activate an espionage group through the State Department for the purpose of the small-scale collection of intelligence valuable to our war effort."

"Seriously," the president appears a bit startled by this revelation. "You talked about the war effort well before the formal declaration of war? This seems rather unusual. So, how does this resolve your concern about a disjointed system?" asks the President.

"It doesn't Mr. President, but it fills a void at the State Department for vital intelligence. What I suggest is the creation of a central intelligence agency responsible for all foreign espionage and clandestine operations aimed at advancing the cause of the United States around the world. This one agency would act to gather all information and coordinate all activity relative to national security," announced the Secretary of State.

"Very bold Mr. Lansing, but you seem to forget that those things which appear to be needed now will lose their relevance once peace has been restored to the world. Furthermore, I am not so sure your idea will resonate well with the Secretary of War. Perhaps we should stay focused on obtaining congressional approval of the Espionage Act," points out the President.

"But Mr. President, after the war the United States through our international business connections will have a global presence requiring eternal vigilance. The vital interests of this nation will no longer stop at the water's edge. As a world power, we must keep our finger on the pulse of what is going on in nations around the globe," asserts the Secretary of State.

"Mr. Secretary, international businesses can take care of themselves. Democracy is the only thing that requires eternal vigilance, and once this war is over, we must seal the peace for the future of democracy. For now, I want each of you to do your job in seeing that the Espionage Act is passed as soon as possible," demands President Wilson.

Robert Lansing leaves this meeting irritated and disenchanted with the President. He is the Secretary of State, and he should be the architect of foreign policy. President Wilson could create a central intelligence agency with one swipe of his pen, and empower his Secretary of State now, and after the war, to oversee all espionage. Instead, he wants to micromanage foreign policy. He won't even share his vision for this world of peace he speaks about following the war. Lansing is frustrated. Now is the time for him to be consolidating the interests of the United States and business. Of course, his personal interest is a part of the family mantra. Lansing also has his eye on a much grander prize. If the president would share the glory, he could be living in the White

House following 1920. However, the president seems intent on stealing the show.

Even before becoming Secretary of State, Robert Lansing envisioned himself as President. Once he became Secretary of State, he could feel the mantel of power so close at hand. He remembers the early history of the Republic and how the Secretary of State had once been the stepping stone to the White House. He needs Wilson to grant him the authority so important to his rise to prominence. The fact that Wilson will not take his hands off the levers of power and decision-making causes Lansing a great deal of consternation.

Making a trip to New York, Secretary of State Lansing pays a visit to his old friend Andrew Mellon.

"Mr. Secretary, to what do I owe the pleasure of your visit?"

"Andrew, I have tried in vain to convince President Wilson that we must have a worldwide espionage network to protect the vital interests of this country. The president is an egomaniac who sees himself as the salvation of the world."

"Robert, you have long known the president as a person with a grandiose nature. Why do you act so surprised?"

"I am not so surprised as I am frustrated. As the Secretary of State, the world should be my stage. I have the vision best suited for our country and our businesses, you should know that," Lansing reveals his own ego is no small thing.

"I know you are frustrated, Robert, but there is still much you can do and accomplish. Look for the opportunities that exist and make the most of them. You have valuable resources at your disposal, you are after all still the Secretary of State."

"You are right, Andrew, I must find a way to seize the day."

"Don't forget you have provided a valuable service by helping to usher in this war. American businesses are poised to make a killing, pardon me that may be a poor choice of words. Through our direct involvement in the war, American business and industry will establish a firm foothold in many poor and underdeveloped nations. We will have access to cheap resources and labor far into the future. You shall reap a just reward from all this."

"My just reward will come with residency in the White House. As the president, I will be in a position to be of the most service to this nation, our businesses, and our position as a world power. We are on the threshold of a new empire Andrew, an empire in which our footprint will be found all around the globe. American industry, business, and financial institutions will realize huge profits by planting deep roots in underdeveloped nations. Our national interest will have no bounds, and we will need to establish a military and a clandestine presence to protect those interests," Lansing reveals his own grandiose nature.

"Return to Washington Robert and continue to shepherd the president toward an international posture that will establish the United States as the preeminent military and economic power around the world. Be patient, your time will come."

"I will return to Washington, but I am not a patient man. Should the President fail, I may be forced to find ways to do things on my own. Good day, Andrew."

As Lansing departs, Mellon leans his head back with his eyes closed and gives forth a huge sigh. Mellon is a man of no small ego himself. He knows that an all-consuming desire for power can drive men to do crazy and irrational things. He sighs again and hopes his friend keeps his wits. The last thing the country and business need is a crazed man as Secretary of State.

American military might and an industrial capacity rivaled by none soon turn the tide of the war. Nine months after the United States enters the war, an Allied defeat that once seemed inevitable turned into an inevitable victory. While there remains a great deal of fighting to occur, by the first of January, 1918, President Wilson decides to articulate his plan for winning the peace to the United States Congress.

To Wilson, the United States did not enter the war with the hope of gaining wealth or territory; instead, the United States entered the war to shape a new international climate and to ensure the well-being and continued growth of democracy around the world.

Wilson's Fourteen Points are the product of a group of academicians known as the Inquiry. The Inquiry was headed by Col. House and included journalist Walter Lippman, Supreme Court Justice Louis Brandeis, Lawyer David Hunter Miller, and Harvard President Abbott

Lawrence Lowell. Absent from membership in this esteemed group was Secretary of State Lansing.

Standing before the United States Congress and filled with visions of grandeur, President Woodrow Wilson proclaimed the following Fourteen Points:

1. Open covenants of peace, openly arrived at, after which there shall be no private international understandings of any kind but diplomacy shall proceed always frankly and in the public view.
2. Absolute freedom of navigation upon the seas, outside territorial waters, alike in peace and in war, except as the seas may be closed in whole or in part by international action for the enforcement of international covenants.
3. The removal, of all economic barriers and the establishment of equality of trade conditions among all the nations consenting to the peace and associating themselves for its maintenance.
4. Adequate guarantees given and taken that national armaments will be reduced to the lowest point consistent with domestic safety.
5. Free, open-minded, and absolutely impartial adjustment of all colonial claims, based upon a strict observance of the principle that in determining all such questions of sovereignty the interests of the populations concerned must have equal weight with the equitable claims of the government whose title is to be determined.
6. The evacuation of all Russian territory and such a settlement of all questions affecting Russia will secure the best and freest cooperation of the other nations of the world in obtaining for her an unhampered and unembarrassed opportunity for the independent determination of her own political development and national policy and assure her of a sincere welcome into the society of free nations under institutions of her own choosing; and, more than a welcome, assistance also of every kind that she may need and may herself desire. The treatment accorded Russia by her sister nations in the months to come will be the acid test of their goodwill, of their comprehension of her needs as

distinguished from their own interests, and of their intelligent and unselfish sympathy.

7. Belgium, the whole world will agree, must be evacuated and restored, without any attempt to limit the sovereignty which she enjoys in common with all other free nations. No other single act will serve as this will serve to restore confidence among the nations in the laws which they have themselves set and determined for the government of their relations with one another. Without this healing act, the whole structure and validity of international law are forever impaired.
8. All French territory should be freed and the invaded portions restored, and the wrong done to France by Prussia in 1871 in the matter of Alsace-Lorraine, which has unsettled the peace of the world for nearly fifty years, should be righted, in order that peace may once more be made secure in the interest of all.
9. A readjustment of the frontiers of Italy should be effected along clearly recognizable lines of nationality.
10. The people of Austria-Hungary, whose place among the nations we wish to see safeguarded and assured, should be accorded the freest opportunity to autonomous development.
11. Romania, Serbia, and Montenegro should be evacuated; occupied territories restored; Serbia accorded free and secure access to the sea, and the relations of the several Balkan states to one another determined by friendly counsel along historically established lines of allegiance and nationality; and international guarantees of the political and economic independence and territorial integrity of the several Balkan states should be entered into.
12. The Turkish portion of the present Ottoman Empire should be assured a secure sovereignty, but the other nationalities which are now under Turkish rule should be assured an undoubted security of life and an absolutely unmolested opportunity for autonomous development, and the Dardanelles should be permanently opened as a free passage to the ships and commerce of all nations under international guarantees.

13. An independent Polish state should be erected which should include the territories inhabited by indisputably Polish populations, which should be assured free and secure access to the sea, and whose political and economic independence and territorial integrity should be guaranteed by international covenant.
14. A general association of nations must be formed under specific covenants for the purpose of affording mutual guarantees of political independence and territorial integrity to great and small states alike.

In response to Wilson's 14 Points, Henry Frick sends an urgent message to his good friend and business associate Andrew Mellon. The telegram reads:

> MY DEAREST FRIEND ANDREW. WHAT THE FUCK IS WILSON UP TO? WE NEED TO CONVENE A MEETING OF THE MINDS IMMEDIATELY. HENRY

Andrew Mellon feels threatened by the president's proclamation. He agrees with his friend Frick that a meeting of America's most powerful men must be convened to avert the looming disaster. Andrew doesn't want to attract any attention to this meeting and therefore understands the necessity for a quiet pursuit of the urgent. He decides to respond to Frick's telegraph in the following manner:

> I AM STUNNED. NEED TIME TO PONDER THE RAMIFICATIONS. RETREATING TO RICHARDS ESTATE IN THREE DAYS. ANDREW

Frick knows immediately that Andrew is calling for a meeting at Richard Mellon's estate in Pittsburg. He understands the importance of distancing the financial hub of New York from the political hub of Washington. The topic before them will require a subterfuge of the highest order. Frick also knows his friend wants him to contact those he feels are necessary at such a meeting. Henry Frick sets to work cabling a simple message to the power elite knowing each will feel the same sense of urgency as he and Andrew.

The following message goes out to J.P. Morgan Jr., J.D. Rockefeller, Thomas Clark, Philander Knox, and W. Averell Harriman:

> GENTLEMEN. JOIN ANDREW AND ME FOR LUNCH AT RICHARD'S IN PITTSBURG. NOON ON JANUARY 11. HENRY

Richard B. Mellon built his incredible sixty-five-room mansion on Pittsburg's 5th Avenue in 1910. The imposing structure includes all of the trappings of the American aristocracy. It is a huge estate with gardens rivaling the great palaces of Europe. Every room contains an immense fireplace with sculptures and paintings everywhere. Guests strain their necks admiring the tall ceilings and huge chandeliers. The entrance to the mansion reveals an incredible open staircase descending from what seems the clouds. Built out of a beautiful red imported stone, the mansion sits high on a hill to remind all of Pittsburg of Mellon's massive power. In the basement of the mansion can be found a private bowling alley. The magnificent walled garden at the front of the mansion reflects the image of Nebuchadnezzar's "Hanging Garden of Babylon." Anyone approaching or entering this structure feels the presence of wealth and power.

As the men arrive on the 11th, the butler escorts each one of the guests to the 1600-square-foot library which also serves as a gallery for Mellon's extensive art collection. On the walls hang masterpieces from Raphael, Van Dyck, Rembrandt, Titian, and Botticelli. As this illustrious group of men takes a seat at the large table in the center of the room, they are surrounded by sculptures by Donatello, Gucci, Rossellino, and de Giovanni. These are all rare products of the Renaissance only available to the wealthiest and most powerful men on Earth. These rare artifacts serve to remind these men of the prominence that they and they alone hold in American society. They are the captains of commerce and industry, and as such must find a way to manipulate the ship of state often found in the hands of far lesser men.

With drinks served and cigars lit, Andrew Mellon looks about the table nodding as his eyes meet the eyes of each participant. Then, he begins "My friends, as Robert Burns' poem *To a Mouse*, 1786 suggests about the best-laid schemes of mice and men, we find ourselves in a predicament. We helped navigate this nation into this war to save the Allies and therefore ourselves only to have our nincompoop of a president proclaim it all for not in his recent address to Congress. If Wilson has his way, we stand to win the war and lose everything."

"Who does Wilson think he is Abraham Lincoln? What is this nonsense about charity for all and malice toward none?" chimes in Mr. Clark.

"Hell, he doesn't think he's Lincoln, he thinks he's Jesus Christ, come to save the world. Wilson thinks he can walk on water, and he has made it our business to see that he drowns in a sea of dissent," proclaims J.P. Morgan Jr.

"Has the bastard not heard "to the victors belong the spoils". Those Goddamn Germans need to pay and pay dearly for unleashing the demons of hell all across Europe," adds Rockefeller as he brings his fist down on the table.

Mellon stands looking directly at each participant, "If Wilson has his way my friends, we will suffer defeat in the midst of victory. All our investments will mean nothing. Our investments in an Allied victory will yield nothing if the Central Powers and in particular the Germans are not forced to pay reparations. England and France specifically will default on our loans and leave us scrambling to recover."

As Mellon sits, J.P. Morgan Jr. stands "I know that each of you has a huge stake in the outcome of the peace conference, but we at J.P. Morgan stand to lose substantially should the peace conference fail. We loaned $12 million dollars to Russia, and $50 million to France, and organized a $500 million dollar loan to the Allies through our syndicated banks. We must not only see the return of this money but a profitable return on this money.

"That may be true Mr. Morgan, but your company benefited a great deal by acting as the purchasing agent for Britain. At a 1% commission, your firm made a tidy profit," suggests Mr. Clark.

"Are you suggesting my firm has little to lose Mr. Clark?" Morgan says standing with an air of defiance.

"Gentlemen," Senator Knox calls out, "Every one of you has made a sizeable profit off of the war, but that is not why we are here. We are here to discuss the President's proclamation and how it undermines winning the peace. The most horrid part of Wilson's 14 points is his attempt to create a level playing field for all nations around the globe. By God, it is the strong and powerful who should rule the Earth and reap the reward to be had. This past war has left old empires in shatters. It is now time for the United States to ascend to its rightful place as the most powerful nation on Earth. Such an ascension will make you not only the captains of finance and industry in the United States but around the world."

Andrew Mellon stands once again, "The things Senator Knox proclaim is the very reason I included him in this gathering. He shares our vision and our concerns. We need his assistance in ensuring Woodrow Wilson's proposals are rejected here at home."

The ever-reactionary Frick snidely adds "Perhaps if Mr. Wilson wants to be like Lincoln or Christ, we should invite him to the theatre or nail him to a cross!"

Having sat quietly, young Averell Harriman chooses to speak. "It is absolutely imperative we do not make a martyr of Woodrow Wilson. He is already considered a Saint across much of Europe even though the Allied Powers are not happy with some aspects of his 14 points. At the moment, the president benefits from popularity here at home. Time is our greatest resource, given even the shortest amount of time, people will turn their attention to other things and Wilson's popularity will become vulnerable. We must beat him in the court of public opinion. There are mid-term elections in less than eleven months. We must go on an offensive and convince the American people that Wilson's plan is bad for the United States."

"Young Mr. Harriman is onto something. Wilson can make all the proclamations he wants, but if he does not have the votes to put his ideas into action, it will all go up in flames. We must work to at least place control of the Senate in the hands of the Republicans. The Senate must approve all treaties, and a Republican Senate would be a roadblock to Wilson's plans," notes J.D. Rockefeller.

"If we are going to go after the Senate, why not seek to increase the Republican majority in the House also? If we can help the Republicans gain control of both houses of Congress, Woodrow Wilson is done," adds Mellon.

Rising to speak, Senator Knox after straightening his vest and coat, grabs the right lapel of his coat with his right hand in a Napoleonic manner, "I assure you gentlemen, your best course of action is to beat Woodrow Wilson at the ballot box. This is the first election since the 17th Amendment has been in force, and the popular election of Senators puts several states up for grabs. Fly under the radar, and saturate the public with negative information regarding Wilson and his defeatist approach to ending the war in Europe. This is a solid plan to protect your interests at home and abroad."

"Knox is correct, we need to involve all those who stand to lose from Wilson's policies and marshal the funds needed to sway public opinion behind Republican candidates. We need to call upon our old friends in the press who were so instrumental in beating the drums of war to now beat the drums of victory," says Frick.

"We have just under-eleven months to get the job done. We must put Wilson on the defensive. We must force the President to waste valuable time, money, and energy defending that which we shall portray as indefensible," proclaims Rockefeller.

"What about Robert Lansing, Senator Knox? Do you see the Secretary of State being of any service to our cause?" asks Andrew Mellon.

"Robert Lansing is a pure internationalist with grandiose plans of his own. He is truly a friend of your cause. Nothing moves the Secretary like personal interest. Money and power are at the heart of his desires. However, Robert Lansing has no standing with Woodrow Wilson. Wilson made Lansing Secretary of State because he felt that, unlike William Jennings Bryan, he could control Lansing. As far as influence is concerned, Lansing has little, yet, he could be a great source of information," the Senator reveals.

"What about Lansing's nephews? Could they be of any benefit to our cause?" J.P. Morgan Jr. inquires.

"Let me put it this way," Andrew Mellon injects, "John Foster Dulles and his brother Allen are two of the most aggressive and predatory young men I have seen in decades. They have inherited in spades their grandfather's penchant for fame and fortune. Young John Foster holds a position with the prestigious law firm of Sullivan and Cromwell, and his brother Allen just took a low-ranking position with the State Department in Vienna. However, both these boys are very loyal to their uncle Bert. Any benefit we can derive from the Dulles brothers at this time will need to come from Lansing."

"I would recommend watching the Dulles brothers from a distance. They are still somewhat unproven regarding their ability to make things happen. True, young John Foster has displayed an uncanny knack for international law in advancing U.S. interests in Latin America. He could have a bright future in advancing the cause of the United States Empire. His brother Allen is a bit of an unknown commodity. He seems to like the spy business, and he lusts for sexy women. These two things don't always make good bedfellows. It seems his lust for a young Czech woman led to some carelessness and a breach of secrecy. The bad news is she passed along information as a counteragent, the good news is Allen had no qualms about her being liquidated. Very interesting brothers," adds the Senator.

"Okay, enough about the Dulles brothers, we have much bigger fish to fry at this time," Rockefeller insists.

"Just a second," cautions J.P. Morgan Jr., "I recently learned something about John Foster Dulles which I believe merits mentioning. I know this is not first or foremost on our minds, but we all need to stay abreast of developments that could have immediate or future consequences for our mutual interests. Just the other day, young John Foster took a leave of absence from Sullivan and Cromwell to accept an appointment by his uncle as an adviser to the War Trade Board. We all know the Foster, Lansing modus operandi when it comes to government service and personal interest. Old John Foster himself set the tone for tending simultaneously to government and personal interests. We must assume this approach has been inherited by his grandsons."

"I don't understand the problem?" injects Frick, "We all believe in self-interest or we would not be here. It seems to me that John Foster Dulles adheres to a philosophy which could be very much to our advantage."

"I agree," says Rockefeller, "Now let's get back to the matter at hand.

Are we in agreement to mount a unified effort to discredit Woodrow Wilson's peace plan in the months leading up to the election in November?"

With this question, all present give a sign of affirmation.

"I believe we need someone who can work under the radar in charge of coordinating our effort. I suggest Thomas Clark head this effort and recommend young Harriman to work closely with him in this endeavor," Rockefeller puts before the group.

With this, the group adjourns with each man going his own way. Before departing, Clark and Harriman agree upon a time and place for their first strategy session.

Chapter 23

ULTERIOR MOTIVES

President Wilson unveils his 14 Points before the United States Congress nine months after the United States entered the war, and eleven months before an armistice will be achieved. By January 1918, Wilson feels confident in an Allied victory, and he wants to take the lead in providing a vision for the war's end. Wilson's close advisors led by Col. House believe Woodrow Wilson is in command of an unprecedented place in world history. Never has one leader been in such a position to influence such broad sweeping global change.

The industrialists, businessmen, and financiers on this side of the ocean are not the only ones disenchanted with Wilson's 14 Points. While nations rejoice at the war turning in the allies' favor due to the United States, these nations are not so eager to see the United States impose a solution on Europe at the war's end. Peace without retribution against Germany is not acceptable. All across Europe, the cry for vengeance demands that a defeated Germany pay for this war of their making. Wilson's challenges at home are compounded by equal challenges in Europe.

As the war wages on in Europe, and U.S. Doughboys sacrifice life and limb to keep the world safe for democracy, Woodrow Wilson makes plans to win the peace. As Wilson plans to win the peace and receive the accolades of a grateful world, the Pittsburg Seven are hard at work consolidating their base of industrialists, businessmen, and financiers in preparation for an all-out assault on the President at the ballot box in November.

To the surprise of the Pittsburg Seven, inflammatory rhetoric comes easy for newspapers and publications across the nation. The New York Times, Washington Post, War Weekly, North American Review, New Republic, and publications for cities coast to coast are calling for the complete destruction of the Axis Powers in contradiction to the President's 14 Points. Once in the war, the majority of citizens of the United States want to fight for nothing less than unconditional surrender.

On the other hand, the President, every bit the academician, writes editorial after editorial making the case for an armistice and peace as if he is Abraham Lincoln seeking to reunite the country following the Civil War. The eleven months of 1918 prior to the election in November are long and brutal. As the election results come in on Tuesday, November 5, 1918, it becomes clear to the president that he will face serious odds as the United States House of Representatives falls overwhelmingly to the Republican Party, and the Republicans become the majority party in the United States Senate.

No President wants to face a situation where everything he tries to do can be blocked in Congress by the opposition party. But Wilson believes wholeheartedly in his vision and he believes that God has ordained him to lead the world from the darkness into the light of a new day. Republicans or not, he has a crusade to undertake, and he himself will lead the charge. Awaking on the morning of Wednesday, November 6, Wilson has two things on his mind: An armistice to end the war and the Paris Conference to win the peace.

Wilson feels his leadership will be buoyed as the nation celebrates an end to the war, and he feels that the Paris Peace Conference will vindicate his vision for the future. What President Wilson may see coming, but fails to acknowledge its formidable nature is the full-frontal assault of the Republican Party led by Senator Henry Cabot Lodge regarding the Treaty of Versailles and the League of Nations.

Henry Cabot Lodge has served in the United States Senate since 1893 and has risen to Majority Leader and Chairman of the powerful Senate Foreign Relations Committee. Few men possess the pompous, condescending, selfish, opportunistic, and nasty nature of Henry Cabot Lodge. Raised on Beacon Hill in Boston, and educated at Harvard, Lodge views himself as highly favored among favored men. His sharp intellect combined with the absence of any moral compass makes him an unyielding adversary of the President.

With the Armistice of Compiegne to end the war signed at 11:00 a.m. on November 11, the President turns all his attention to peace. In late November, President Wilson at the advice of his closest friend and adviser Col. House decides to lead the United States delegation to the Paris Peace Conference.

"Mr. President, you need to personally represent the United States at the Peace Conference in Paris!" Col. House proclaims stomping his foot to emphasize his opinion.

"I too feel strongly that I am best suited for this mission. However, I hesitate to know the precedent it could set for future chief executives. This seems like a role that should be played by the Secretary of State as my emissary," Wilson responds as he gazes at the globe near his desk.

"Mr. President this is your time on the world stage. All of Europe and the world, in general, exalt your name as synonymous with freedom and democracy. The Peace Conference offers you an opportunity to take your well-deserved bow as well as grab the reigns of world leadership," the Col. insists.

"But what about Lansing, he will not like this one bit?"

"To hell with Lansing, he is not worthy to even walk in your shadow. Lansing should feel fortunate to be able to bask in your glory. If he is smart, and I doubt he is, he will see this as an opportunity to use your acclaim as his own," the Col. asserts.

"Well, we need to let him know my decision before he learns it in some other manner," Wilson says knowing the difficulty in healing a bruised ego.

"I agree Mr. President, should I send for him?" House asks.

"No time like the present Col. House, no time like the present."

As a man of great ego and self-confidence, the president does not look forward to telling his Secretary of State that he the president, not him, will lead the U.S. delegation to Paris.

Sitting in his State Department Office, Secretary of State Lansing has been making plans for his emergence onto the world stage in Paris for the past couple of weeks. Robert Lansing saw this as his opportunity to establish himself as a world leader and catapult himself into the lead for consideration as the Democratic Nominee for President in 1920. When word arrives that the President would like to see him, Lansing is certain the President is looking for an update on his preparations for the peace conference. Quickly grabbing some notes, Lansing heads from the State Department to the White House.

As he enters the President's personal study, he finds President Wilson and Col. House sitting together in a private conversation. As he enters, the President and Col. House rise to welcome the Secretary.

"Mr. President, you asked to see me?" Lansing says with a twinkle of excitement on his face.

"Have a seat, Mr. Secretary," Col. House instructs.

Robert Lansing finds this kind of odd. He has been summoned to the White House by the president, and yet when he arrives, it is the president's unofficial adviser who instructs him to sit. Lansing tenuously takes a seat across from the president and Col. House.

"Mr. Secretary, you know how much the president values your work and the contributions you have made to this administration," House begins.

Now Lansing's mind is racing like some person lost in a maze and trying to find a way out. Why is the president not speaking to me himself, he is sitting right across from me.

Without receiving a response from a confused Robert Lansing, Col. House continues, "Mr. Secretary, you are a diplomat of the first order. Your knowledge, experience, and abilities will be greatly needed in the coming months," Col. House continues.

Sitting there listening, it feels to Lansing as if he is sitting on a trap door.

"Why is it the president who is sitting just a few feet from me is not addressing me personally?" Lansing inquires.

"The president feels a bit uncomfortable with the delicacy of this matter Mr. Secretary. He has great admiration for you."

"Well then, I would suggest he extend to me the courtesy of speaking to me directly. This meeting has all the overtones of a dismissal. Am I being dismissed?" Lansing is being direct.

"Oh no Robert," Wilson chimes in, "I just did not know how to tell you about a decision I have made regarding the Paris Peace Conference. Col. House is just trying to insulate me from that discomfort," the President says leaning forward to personalize the communication.

"Well, I have been working extremely hard in preparation for the Paris Peace Conference Mr. President, and I can assure you the United States Delegation will be ready," Secretary of State Lansing says quickly to ensure it gets said.

"Your preparation is invaluable, and I am counting on you to help me during this most exciting and challenging time. I have decided Robert, I will lead the United States Delegation myself," Wilson declares.

"Why you can't do that Mr. President, it is without precedent," Lansing asserts determined to deter the president's decision.

"Oh, I do believe President Roosevelt established the precedent of traveling outside the United States when he chose to visit Panama. I also believe Roosevelt set a precedent for a president to actively engage in diplomacy when he negotiated the Sino-Russian Treaty. So, I think the precedent has already been breached," President Wilson assures.

"This is not the way the foreign policy was intended to work Mr. President!" Lansing cannot contain his anxiety at losing what he sees should be his leadership role.

"You are so right Robert, but we are in a new century, and we are certainly in new times. What might have existed in the past can no longer remain the same in the future. Therefore, I will head the U.S. delegation and I will need you to be by my side," the president says as he rises indicating an end to the meeting.

Reaching out to Lansing with his right hand, the President clasps Lansing's hand with his left holding on firmly. "Robert, we have great things to do, and I hope you will stand with me as my partner in this great endeavor. Will you do that Robert?"

Offering the president, a look of disappointment, Secretary Lansing clasps his left hand on top of Wilson's, "I serve at the pleasure of the president." With this Lansing bows gently "Good day gentlemen," and departs.

This is a nasty blow to Robert Lansing's ego. All his hopes and dreams for the future seem to now be in question. The President wants him to be his partner, but what does that mean? He just usurped his position as Secretary of State, so what will keep him from further diminishing his role in such an important event in world history? Lansing heads back to his office only to pick up some things and retreat to his home where he can attempt to sort through this most unfortunate situation.

Robert Lansing's wife Eleanor, the daughter of former Secretary of State John Foster provides Lansing with an open ear and wise counsel. She has the benefit of growing up with old John Foster, and she inherited the family's propensity toward self-interest.

"I cannot believe the son-of-a-bitch would deny me the role of leading the United States Delegation to the Paris Peace Conference. I have been loyal to him in every way," Robert protests to his wife.

"Now Robert, watch your language. We are a Christian household, and we will keep a civil tongue," his wife chides him. "You have known all along that President Wilson is a man with a gigantic ego, and a penchant to keep the spotlight on himself."

"You are right, Eleanor, I should have seen this coming. Perhaps it is best if I resign," Lansing says as he lowers his face into his hands.

"You will do nothing of the sort Robert Lansing. There is much you can do to serve your country as Secretary of State even in the shadow of Woodrow Wilson. Furthermore, as Secretary of State, you are in a position to make important international connections in Paris which will serve this family well," Eleanor insists.

"What you say is true my dear wife. My international connections will be invaluable when I re-enter my private life. I also must not forget my young nephews John Foster and Allen Dulles. These two boys are benefiting from my position as Secretary of State, and they too will benefit from my international connections, as well as those of their own. If Wilson will not give me my due, I will go out and get it," Lansing says as he stands and moves in the direction of his home office muttering, "Self-interest is a powerful motive, why should I not benefit from all of this."

Woodrow Wilson and a small entourage arrive in Brest, France aboard the SS George Washington on December 13, 1918. From Brest,

Wilson travels to Versailles with Secretary of State Lansing, Col. Edward House, Henry White, and General Tasker Bliss. While the delegation is small, they are supplemented by a group of nearly one hundred advisors possessing expertise in European economics, geography, history, culture, and ethnicity.

The United States delegation took up residence in the Hotel de Crillon a converted palace with 103 guest rooms, 44 suites, 3 restaurants, a bar, and a number of salons. Inside, the Hotel has all of the trappings of a palace complete with high ceilings, gorgeous chandeliers, beautiful drapes, marvelous stonework, with magnificent sculptures and paintings at every turn. In 1778, then a palace, the Hotel de Crillon hosted another American Delegation headed by Benjamin Franklin in France to sign the French-American Treaty which recognized the Declaration of Independence as well as a trade agreement.

Outside the front door of the Hotel is the Place de la Concorde, the largest public square in Paris. To the right of the Hotel is an identical building that serves as a Government Office Building. Standing tall in the center of the Place de la Concorde is the Obelisque de Luxor which is 75 feet tall and weighs 230 tons. The obelisk once marked the entrance to the Amon Temple at Luxor in Egypt. The Obelisk, a gift to France by the Viceroy of Egypt in 1836, stands at the sight of the guillotine used to behead more than 1300 people including King Louis XVI, Marie Antoinette, and Robespierre in public executions between 1793 and 1795.

Paris is a beautiful city with historical landmarks and monuments. From the Hotel, the delegation can see the Eiffel Tower, at the time the world's tallest structure. Nearby the Hotel can be found the Conciergerie built during the 14th century. This fortress-like structure served as a place of imprisonment, torture, and death for many notable figures in French history. Near the Conciergerie is Notre Dame de Paris dating back to 1163, this Early Gothic Cathedral is a stark reminder of the role Christianity played in French History. La Sainte Chapelle is a small 12th-century Gothic chapel built by King Louis IX near Notre Dame to house relics from the Holy Land. Not far from these incredible landmarks is the Pantheon with its imposing dome and a portico of Corinthian columns. This vast temple houses the bodies of Voltaire, Diderot, and Rousseau three of the great philosophers of the Enlightenment.

Despite all of the alluring places Paris offers, Woodrow Wilson did not come to see Paris, he came to conquer it. As he traveled from Paris to Versailles, Woodrow Wilson met thousands of people wanting to get a glimpse of the savior from across the ocean. Men, women, and children lined Wilson's route waving, cheering, and crying in great joy. Woodrow Wilson took it all in, and with each passing mile, he grew more confident and more convinced that he and he alone would broker the peace to create a new Europe and a more stable world. Little did all of the people traveling with Wilson know that they would just be pawns in the President's quest for greatness.

Secretary of State Lansing becomes the first person to feel the sting of the president's aloofness. Wilson felt no need for his Secretary of State, so he delegated him to monitor the progress of each committee as it worked its way through some very difficult and complicated problems. It does not take Lansing long to realize the president is only seeking to keep him busy. Very seldom does the president ask his secretary of state to report on his observations or offer suggestions for conflict resolution.

It doesn't take long for Henry White, General Bliss, Bernard Baruch, and even Col. House to realize that they are of little use to the president. Despite their dedication to various committees ranging from economics, boundary disputes, and restitution, it is Wilson who brokers the final agreements without their advice and consent. And yet, Wilson will not deal with the press. He sends his commissioners to the Hotel salon uninformed and unprepared to meet with the press.

"Mr. White, what can you tell us about the progress being made toward a peace agreement?" one reporter asks the distinguished diplomat.

Henry White, a republican established himself as the United States' most gifted diplomat under Theodore Roosevelt and William Howard Taft. Working with Roosevelt, White has experience dealing with an overinflated ego. Yet nothing has prepared him to work with the likes of Woodrow Wilson. White agrees with Wilson's post-war plans and he will work tirelessly to promote those plans with fellow republicans back home. But in Paris, he has never felt so excluded from the decisions needing to be made. When Wilson decides to go it alone, he does so all by himself.

Looking at the reporter, "We are all working very hard to pursue the president's goals while here in Paris. I believe it is going well" White responds.

"What about particulars, what agreements have been reached at this time?" the reporters in the room are begging for anything newsworthy.

"Most nations here at the conference find most of the president's positions on peace to their liking, but there are a few things which will take time to find common ground," the commissioner responds knowing the vagueness of his response.

"What about boundaries, what will the new map of Europe look like?" comes another inquiry.

"It can be said with a degree of certainty that when the conference is concluded, the map of Europe will not look the same as before the war," came another vague response.

As with his fellow commissioners, White knows he can offer the press little more than vague generalities. On too many occasions, the commissioners have brokered deals within their committees only to have the president broker something different. While embarrassing to be so vague with the press, it is even more embarrassing to be specific only to later have it undone by the president.

Even Col. House finds it difficult to communicate with Wilson. Sitting in the Presidential suite alone with the president, House decides to speak up. "Mr. President, may I speak with candor?"

"My dear Col. House, you have always had my undivided attention. What is on your mind?"

"You brought four commissioners with you to Paris. Each one of these commissioners brings a great deal of intelligence, experience, and skill to the negotiating table in pursuit of your fourteen points. And yet Mr. President, you fail to seek their advice or consent on matters of importance. You frequently circumvent their positions as U.S. representatives on conference committees by negotiating and brokering deals of your own even after they reach a different agreement in committee."

"What are you trying to say, Col. House?"

"Mr. President, your representatives cannot work in this kind of environment. You give them responsibility, but you offer them no authority. Commissioners from other countries are beginning to doubt their credibility at the negotiating table."

"Just what is it you would have me do Col. House?"

"Let them do their job, Mr. President. Meet with them for advice and consent. Find out what they are doing, give them direction, and stand behind their efforts. Combine their responsibility with the authority to act. To do otherwise is to subvert the very process."

"So, Col. House, after insisting I head this delegation, you are now telling me I should be a rubber stamp."

"No, I am not telling you to be a rubber stamp, I am asking you to let your commissioners do their job."

"And I should not do mine? I am not only the head of this delegation I am the President of the United States. I do not believe I need permission to speak with the leaders of foreign nations, and I do not believe I need permission to reach an agreement with them on any and all issues.

"No, you don't but you should follow a process, and you should keep your negotiating team in the loop. Every commissioner is responsible for meeting with the press, and yet, no one knows what to say. As a result, the press is fed vague generalities on a daily basis in order to avoid unnecessary faux pas."

"All you need to tell the press is that the president is in charge and we are progressing on a steady course toward a successful agreement. If anyone has a problem with that, I can arrange their return home," the president says his arms crossed and a stern look on his face as if it were chiseled in granite. "Is there anything else Col. House?"

"No sir, I have heard quite enough," House says as he turns to exit the room.

"Col. House," the President calls out.

"Yes sir!"

"We have been friends for a long time."

"Yes, we have sir!"

"Well Colonel, you are either with me or you are against me," President Wilson says with finality.

"Thank you, sir!" House says as he opens the door and departs.

Woodrow Wilson does not realize it, but he is committing a huge error in leadership. No one can go it alone. Humility rather than egotism is critical to creating a loyal team. Wilson wants the spotlight, and yet he fails to realize that the spotlight shines brightest on a leader when the leader allows it to reflect off someone else. Wilson's messianic complex is driving a wedge between himself and some of his most ardent supporters.

Chapter 24

RECKLESS REBUKE

While Wilson moves forcefully ahead in France, his not-so-loyal opposition is solidifying forces at home in anticipation of his return from what is his second journey to Paris. The Irreconcilables are a group of 12-18 U.S. Senators led by Senator Henry Cabot Lodge. Other Republican members included George Norris of Nebraska, Robert La Follette of Wisconsin, Hiram Johnson of California, and Philander Knox of Pennsylvania.

In early May 1919, the Irreconcilables hold a meeting in the ornate senate office of Henry Cabot Lodge, the unofficial majority leader.

"Esteemed colleagues, in the very near future, President Wilson will return from Europe in all his glory to present the United States Senate with an ill-conceived treaty which compromises the security and sovereignty of this nation," Lodge proclaims to the gathering.

"I opposed this war from the very beginning," asserts Norris. "George Washington warned us against foreign entanglements in his farewell address, and this war and now peace treaty threatens to entangle this nation in the web of European politics. We must protect this nation from a treaty which may be good for Wilson but an Albatross around the neck of the country."

"My friends," says Philander Knox, "The economic stability of our country required our involvement in this war on the part of the Allies. Many of our wealthiest citizens, largest corporations, and financial institutions had millions to lose should the Allies fall victim to the central powers. In such a situation, our entire economic system could have been brought to its knees."

"Senator Knox, everyone knows you have long been in the pocket of big money. The wealthy put this nation at risk by playing fast and loose with their investment in the Allied cause. They did all this based on self-interest, and to your shame, you sir helped lead this nation into war. As far as I am concerned Senator Knox, your corporate and financial cronies are guilty of treason against the people of the United States of America," declares Senator La Follette.

"Senator La Follette, we are here today because we have a common enemy in Woodrow Wilson," reminds Senator Knox. "We may not agree on why he is our common enemy, but we do agree he has put the United States at risk with the treaty he is pursuing. If we do not defeat this treaty, not only our country, but the world will never be the same."

"Senator Knox, you have never been true to a progressive Republican Party. As Attorney General, your greatest contribution to the progressive cause was to advise President Roosevelt not to let great achievement suffer from any taint of legality while serving the cause of big steel and high finance. As Secretary of State, you spent your time encouraging and protecting American investments abroad. So now, why would it be surprising that you oppose a treaty of little benefit to your money-bag cronies?" Senator La Follette accuses.

"I'll have you know Senator that I served the United States honorably as Attorney General and Secretary of State. Just because I recognize the importance of industry, corporations, and high finance to the future of this great country is no reason to impugn my integrity," Knox says in his defense.

"Democracy is not for sale you scoundrel," La Follette protests with the passion of Christ clearing the money changers from the temple.

"Enough, we are not here to argue the future of progressivism in the Republican Party. I stand before you as an isolationist, but also a realist. The first casualty when war comes is truth. Now, we are confronted with a treaty necessitated by a big lie. And yet, the reality of it all is we are here at this point in history. We cannot turn back the clock, and so we must move forward into what is truly a new day. There are many admirable points in the peace treaty pursued by the president, but the League of Nations is not one of them. As a member of such an international organization, we would be surrendering aspects of sovereignty that should never be compromised. As a nation, we must always remain the masters of our own fate," Senator Hiram Johnson pleads while standing beneath a portrait of Henry Clay.

"We are united by our opposition to the League of Nations. We all know that should the United States join this organization all other arguments are moot. We must stay focused lest we give Wilson the opportunity to prevail. Unless Wilson is willing to compromise, we must succeed in defeating the treaty on the Senate floor. Once this battle is beyond us, we can return to the struggles so important to the future of this nation," the majority leader insists.

Looking at each person present at this meeting, Senator Norris speaks in a solemn tone that reflects the seriousness and importance of the moment, "Senators, our task will not be easy. We control only a small majority in the Senate. Among our members are several idealists who believe a democratic league can be the basis for peace and justice in the world. We must pull this faction into our group of irreconcilables by convincing them that their ideas are not found in the proposed League of Nations. We must help them see that while Wilson extols the virtues of the League, it is really a tool of Britain and its nefarious empire. If we can do this, and hold our ranks together, we will defeat this treaty."

As the meeting closes, each Senator feels the urgency of the task at hand. La Follette doesn't like Knox, and most of them disdain Lodge, but none of them trust Wilson. Each of them knows what needs to be done and departs with the determination to get it done.

Back in Paris, two young men who studied under Professor Wilson at Princeton earn the trust and confidence of the president. Even before arriving in Paris, Wilson created an irreparable rift between himself and his Secretary of State. And now, he finds himself two protégées eager to serve. Unbeknownst to Wilson, his two confidants are loyal to their Uncle Bert. John Foster and Allen Dulles provide the president with the very thing he desires while positioning themselves for future service and personal gain.

"My young charges," Wilson liked to call the Dulles boys. John Foster Dulles at 31 and Allen Dulles at 26 were young by any standards to be enjoying such kinship with the president on what are the most significant questions to ever confront the world. "We are on a mission ordained by God and blessed by the living Christ," Wilson tells John Foster and Allen.

Like Wilson, the Dulles are devout Presbyterians with a missionary view of the world. The old professor and the young students share a missionary zeal and view their work as an instrument of divine will. Like Woodrow Wilson's father, the Dulles boy's father served as a Presbyterian minister.

"Mr. President, your terms for peace are well received by all of the nations represented at this conference," John Foster assures the president.

"I am concerned that the demand to exact a pound of flesh in reparations from Germany is the wrong spirit upon which to base this peace," the president shares with an air of gravity.

"Someone must pay for this war, Mr. President. Without due reparations, the Allies will go bankrupt, as will those who have come to their aid in good faith. I have spoken with many of the delegates, and they are unwavering in their demand that Germany bears the brunt of financial responsibility for this war," John Foster shares as if a student in the first row of a class on international treaties.

"This is true Mr. President, Germany should not be let off the hook in the payment of war reparations, and this is a unifying sentiment among the nations attending this peace conference," Allen Dulles adds.

"What is most important Mr. President is the ascendancy of the United States as a world power of the first order. Your leadership has extended Manifest Destiny across the ocean. You said it best when you proclaimed our industrial fortunes are tied up with the industrial fortunes of the rest of the world. Well, this war has turned the tables, and now it is the industrial fortunes of the rest of the world that rely on the United States by God!" John Foster emphasizes.

"You seem very sure of yourself young man," the President observes.

"Our time has come, it is the role of the United States by divine right to intervene abroad to bring civilization to the uncivilized, democracy to the downtrodden, and progress through American industry, business, and high finance to all nations of the world," John Foster touts.

"Mr. President, you spoke to the conference about the poison of Bolshevism, and our Uncle Bert has described Communism as the most hideous and monstrous thing that the human mind has ever conceived supported by the criminal, the depraved, and the mentally unfit. This is a new evil which calls for our eternal vigilance," Allen observes now sounding like the student hoping to gain the good graces of the professor.

"It is true," Wilson observes, "Communism is the greatest enemy of capitalism. When we return home, we must act to protect our nation from an insurgence of subversives, anarchists, and socialists."

"Never before has there been a need for an organized agency dedicated to espionage at home and around the globe. We cannot defend ourselves against that which we do not know. We must make the protection of the homeland and our national interests around the globe our number one priority. We must consecrate the marriage between democracy and capitalism if we are to truly master the world," Allen says pounding his youthful fist on a nearby table for emphasis.

"The League of Nations is the key boys," President Wilson says with the assurance of a grandfather with years of experience. "Through the League of Nations, all things are possible. Most importantly, the League will provide Shakespeare's stage upon which the United States can act as the leader of the world."

The Dulles Brothers provide Woodrow Wilson with the positive stokes he needs to support his Messianic Complex. Wilson provides the brothers with the opportunity to make connections, gain experience, and develop a worldview that will drive them well into the 20th century.

As the Peace Conference nears a conclusion, and President Wilson makes plans to return to the United States from his second foray to Paris, he has little notion of the difficulties which lay ahead. His fourteen points provide a framework for peace, but he remains dissatisfied with the reparation demands placed on Germany as well as many of the territorial settlements of the treaty. Yet, his dream of a League of Nations remains alive. He doesn't seek all the concessions on the League that several Senators requested. He knows such requests will be rebuked in Europe. He will return home fully prepared to do whatever might be necessary to win Senate approval of the treaty which includes United States membership in the League of Nations.

As for the Dulles Brothers, they will continue their pursuit of what they consider public service for personal gain. They have been to the mountaintop with the president, and they thoroughly enjoyed the view.

Allen does not return to the United States, but rather remains in Europe enjoying his life in Espionage. Allen loves the intrigue, but most importantly he loves the women associated with a life of intrigue. Despite getting married to Clover Todd in 1920, Allen Dulles lives a life of infidelity. He views his lust for carnal pleasure as an asset in the espionage business. European women are devoid of inhibitions which makes them great lovers. They understand all the ways of pleasure and seek to please as well as be pleased. European women know how to use intoxicating perfumes in all the right places to attract a man's lips as a flower attracts a bee. Allen spends hours in bed with one and if lucky two women allowing him to enter and enjoy a world of physical pleasure. In time his wife learns of his frequent infidelities. While she doesn't like them, she endures them because that is the role of a wife. In some strange and twisted manner, she never considers leaving Allen, and always considers herself fortunate to be Mrs. Allen Dulles.

John Foster Dulles does not waste a minute putting his experience in business, politics, and diplomacy to work for personal gain. He is a young man with a puritanical bent who believes the more fortunate people in life are also clearly favored by God. John Foster Dulles is confident beyond a doubt that he is ordained by God to be a diplomatic messenger for Christ. There is and can be no inconsistency in his belief and his actions on behalf of the nation, corporations, and his personal interest, because they are all directed from above. Early in his career, John Foster Dulles helped organize the Amoco Oil Company. As an attorney at Sullivan and Cromwell, Dulles' clients' own mines in Chile and Peru, sugar plantations in Cuba, utilities in Panama, Oil wells in Columbia, banks in France, and paint factories in Italy and Russia. Two of his specialties are organizing overseas-loan syndicates for New York banks and helping utility companies take control of utilities in foreign countries. All of this fit into John Foster Dulles' worldview of Pax Americana and missionary work.

John Foster Dulles never shares his brother's lust for women, and frequently criticizes Allen for his conduct. But the brothers share the same worldview. They are joined at the hip when it comes to the lessons, they had been taught by Grandfather Foster and Uncle Bert. For the next forty years, John Foster Dulles and Allen Dulles will be two of the most powerful and dangerous men in the world.

In mid-May, 1919, Andrew Mellon, John D. Rockefeller, and Pierre DuPont, meet with J.P. Morgan Jr. in his 5th Avenue New York City office.

"What is the news from Paris?" Rockefeller inquires.

"I have received a confidential cable from John Foster Dulles. He has managed to make himself a valuable asset to the president. He says that the Peace Talks are going well with one exception," Andrew Mellon says a bit mysteriously.

"Well, what is it, Andrew? Don't delay in sharing the news with your fellow collaborators," Rockefeller insists.

"John Foster is fearful the League of Nations will undo all prospects of an American Empire. The charter for the league encroaches on the sovereignty of member nations. This means should the United States join this international organization; we will become subject to the decisions of the league in critical areas of trade and the military. John Foster Dulles says President Wilson is hell-bent on seeing the United States as a League member," Mellon offers his dismal account.

"Why in the hell would that bastard Wilson want to tie the United States to something so heinous as the League of Nations?" asks DuPont knowing he could answer his own question.

"Woodrow Wilson puts one thing above all else, himself," blurts Morgan. "The son-of-a-bitch would put one hand on the Bible while using the other to sell his mother down the river if it brought glory to himself. He sees himself as the savior of Europe. The League is his invention, and he will be the champion of the world. As a member, the world would turn to the United States for leadership, and there would stand Woodrow "Fucking" Wilson ready to command the world at the nation's expense. Hell, Wilson's second term will be up in less than two years, and he is counting on the world turning to him to lead."

"What about reparations? What is the treaty going to say about reparations?" Rockefeller wants to know.

"This is another area where Wilson will cut the throat of his countrymen in order to assure himself a place in the pantheon of heroes," Mellon snidely attests. "However, we have an ace in the hole gentlemen and things will work out to our benefit."

"What is it you speak of Andrew?" Morgan inquires.

"John Foster Dulles is our man and he is keeping an eye on our interests. Dulles serves on the treaty committee dealing with war reparations and he has been asked to draft what is called a "War Guilt Clause". Young Dulles will draft this clause, but our friend Benard Barach will submit it for adoption as his own."

"Can we trust Dulles?" asks DuPont.

"John Foster Dulles comes from a long line of diplomats well versed in using diplomacy as a means of protecting friends and feathering their own nest. His Grandfather John Foster, Ben Harrison's Secretary of State virtually created the process in the early days of U.S. foreign policy," Rockefeller offers as a testimonial. "Besides, Barach will make sure our interests are well protected."

"John Foster sent me a telegraph message several days ago. He said the European nations involved in drafting the treaty are hell bend on reparations," Mellon reveals. "The message further revealed the president wants a benevolent approach to the settlement. He asked me for some advice."

"So, tell us your advice Andrew," Morgan insists.

"I told him the president was a fool. You don't fight a war at such a cost and then let the perpetrator off lightly. I told him to ignore the president and place the entire blame on Germany for starting the war and require Germany to pay every penny in reparations," Mellon declares as the final word on the subject.

"Do we know the end result? Which master did young Dulles decide to serve?" DuPont asks a bit tongue in cheek, expecting Mellon to be without an answer.

"The cable came through this morning Pierre, the "War Guilt Clause" holding Germany completely responsible to pay war reparations is an official part of the treaty document. The Europeans will not allow this part of the treaty to be altered or removed under any circumstances. Gentlemen, our investment in the war is soon to pay dividends," Mellon announces.

"Well, I'll be damned, who would have ever thought we would owe any gratitude to those helpless, penniless Europeans? Perhaps they will stand behind their loans, and we shall have the goose who laid the golden egg. I will certainly drink to that," Morgan proclaims.

"Yes gentlemen, the situation with reparations will certainly feather our nest, but if membership in the League is approved by the Senate, our cash cow will be short-lived. We must contact Senator Knox and Senator Lodge to convey our feelings about such an entanglement. This war has laid the world at our doorstep and given time we can build a world economic order which will sustain our financial interests and legacies for centuries. On that, gentlemen, we can truly drink!" proclaims J.D. Rockefeller.

"Just a minute," DuPont cautions the group. "We cannot go about this haphazardly. We need to contact all those industrialists, businessmen, and financial titans who are part of the Bohemian Club and enlist their services in lobbying their respective Senators about this issue. They need to know that their jobs as well as the economic well-being of their states and this nation are on the line with the league. We need to do this in no uncertain terms. When Wilson returns from Europe, he must find a formidable opposition to the League of Nations."

"Pierre speaks wisely, there is perhaps no threat greater to our economic future upon which lies the economic future of this nation than the League of Nations. This insidious idea must be defeated!" Morgan announces while standing asking the others to clasp hands in a sign of agreement and unity. "Good, let us be about our business."

Woodrow Wilson prepares to depart Paris and the Peace Conference feeling rather self-assured that he has been the architect of a new world order. A Divine presence has guided him on this mission to save the world. His words and actions will be long preserved as perhaps greater than those of Washington, Jefferson, Lincoln, or Roosevelt. He is tired, but it is satisfying tired. He feels confident that the welcome awaiting him upon his return home will be glorious. He can see the great flotillas that will await his arrival. He can hear the cannons and fanfare which will announce his return. He has done something no other human being has ever attempted or accomplished, he has brought the world back from the brink of devastation and offered a new beginning for the community of nations. It is as satisfying as Woodrow Wilson will ever be again.

While President Wilson returns with a group of diplomats, he is returning mostly alone. During his time in Paris, he successfully alienated just about everyone around him. Even his lifelong friend Colonel House is disenfranchised by the President's lack of interest and appreciation of his thinking. Departing Europe on a different ship, Edwin "Col." House will never see or speak to Woodrow Wilson again. Despite all of this, Wilson knows from frequent cables that he is greatly admired by the American public, and his idea for a League of Nations enjoys vast popular support.

As the USS George Washington approaches New York Harbor, President Wilson can hardly believe his eyes. The harbor swells with ships and boats of all sizes. The sails of boats tall and small dance joyfully in the water celebrating their hero's return home. At first sight of the USS George Washington, the cannons begin their endless salute to the man who has carried the mantel of peace and freedom across the seas. Slicing through the throng of boats in the harbor, Wilson standing on deck can hear the shouts and cheers, he can see the passionate waving of hands and banners welcoming him home. Wilson wonders if such a feeling is what Christ may have felt on Palm Sunday as he entered Jerusalem. It does not occur to him that the same crowd which welcomed Jesus, one week later demanded his crucifixion.

Chapter 25

DIRTY DEEDS NOT SO CHEAP

Returning to the United States, President Wilson has no idea of the treachery lying in wait. In the fourth round of Dante's Ninth Circle, the traitors are the most wretched and decrepit of all who betray a man, ideal, or nation. The pungent odor of decay emanating from their lost souls hints at the demonic disposition of their plan. These are the men who conspire against the very nation which gives them life. These are the men consumed by money, power, and prestige. These are the men who will forsake their countrymen to perpetuate their own self-interest. Wilson doesn't see them looming in the shadows, he doesn't comprehend the depths to which the wealthy will go to undo what he considers the work of God.

Senator Henry Cabot Lodge of Massachusetts reigns as the Chairman of the Senate Foreign Relations Committee. Coming from a family of wealth and privilege, Lodge's loyalties are only to himself and his powerful and privileged friends. Lodge has been a friend and close confidante of Theodore Roosevelt. As a visionary and internationalist, Roosevelt very much supports the idea of a League of Nations. However, Roosevelt died in January 1919 putting an end to his ever-present political influence. Once cut loose from the mooring of Roosevelt, Lodge's already inflated ego had no restraints.

Senator Philander Knox also owed a great deal to Theodore Roosevelt. Serving as Roosevelt's Attorney General having been appointed by William McKinley in 1901 until his resignation in 1904, Knox functioned as a double agent between President Roosevelt and the Robber Barons during the president's first four years of trust-busting. Despite his oath of allegiance to the people of the United States, Knox can never sever his stronger ties with men like Henry Frick and Andrew Mellon.

Meeting in Lodge's palatial senate office, Knox shares concerns entrusted to him by the wealthy cabal he recently met with.

"Mr. Chairman, I have been asked to speak with you about the process which will be followed in the Senate's consideration of the Versailles Treaty."

"Proceed, Senator, time is of the essence."

"In speaking with such powerful men as DuPont, Rockefeller, Morgan, and Mellon, they are adamantly opposed to the League of Nations and need assurances that you as Chairman of the Foreign Relations Committee have a plan of action to assure its defeat."

"Senator Knox, I am not a proponent of the League of Nations. I do not believe the United States should relinquish any of its sovereign powers to an international body. So why are these distinguished men so concerned?"

"These men, representative of the industrial and financial power of this country are relieved to know the leaders of the European nations of the Allied Powers actually had some balls to stand firm on the issue of reparations. They are confident the war will now reap them the financial benefits they so richly deserve."

"So, what has their ass in a bind now? Don't they know I have no intentions of allowing the treaty to gain Senate approval under the current conditions?" Senator Lodge is definitive.

"Their concern Mr. Chairman is that you might not see the full ramifications should the League provisions in the treaty prevail."

"I understand the League provisions perfectly well Senator Knox. I am opposed to the League and I will fight to see it defeated. I will fight to defeat anything which might engulf the United States in future wars."

"I believe you do understand it Mr. Chairman, but bear with me while I explain the perspective of our friends."

"Get to it Senator Knox, and keep to the point."

"Article X says League members will respect and preserve against external aggression the territorial and existing political independence of all members. This article Mr. Chairman is a huge impediment to world capitalism. What if we need to be the aggressors? What if member nations act in a manner counter to the best interest of these financial giants? What if the actions of member nations negatively impact the economy of the United States? Would not such a situation threaten national security and justify aggression if necessary?"

"I see your point, Senator Knox."

"Mr. Chairman, we stand on the threshold of empire. I am not talking about a military or governmental empire. I am talking about a financial empire built on world capitalism. An empire of unimagined wealth, an empire of unlimited influence, an empire of power based on the purse strings of the world. Such an empire requires the ability to use all of its resources to maintain and protect its vital interests."

"Senator Knox, go back to this group and assure them that I have a plan. As Chairman of the Foreign Relations Committee, I can control the pace of treaty consideration by the Senate. I will make this ship move so slow it will not see the harbor for a long time. I along with you and several other Senators will use this time to discredit the treaty and the League of Nations. By the time we are done, the public will demand the treaty be rejected."

"Thank you and good day Mr. Chairman."

Settled back in at the White House, President Wilson learns of the deliberately laborious pace Senator Lodge plans to take in dealing with the treaty. On the opening day of the hearings before the Senate Foreign Relations Committee, Henry Cabot Lodge takes time to read aloud the entire text of the treaty. The president knows what he must do.

Despite the opposition of his wife and cabinet, President Woodrow Wilson decides to go on an extended tour of the nation to personally garner public support for the treaty which the Senate will be unable to ignore. Traveling to the Western states, President Wilson's journey covered 8,000 miles and 37 speeches in 21 days. Toward the end of this journey, the president suffers a series of minor strokes and one major stroke on September 25, 1919, in Pueblo, Colorado. Rushed back to the White House, the trauma and stress cause his collapse on October 2, 1919.

Reduced to an invalid, First Lady Edith Wilson keeps the president secluded from public view and only available to his personal physician Dr. Cary Grayson. While not dead, the president's poor health serves as a death warrant for the treaty and the League of Nations. Never relinquishing power and keeping the public at bay, the First Lady takes control of the situation and the Presidency counter to the dictates of the Constitution of the United States.

Despite efforts by the Senate to find a compromise on the treaty, President Wilson, or more than likely his wife, refused to give any ground. On March 19, 1920, a little over six months after President Wilson's collapse, the United States Senate votes 49 to 35 for the treaty as revised by the Senate but still falls 7 votes short of the required 2/3 majority for treaty approval. President Wilson's most crowning achievement fails, and along with it hopes for world peace.

In Europe, the formation of a League of Nations moves forward without the United States, Germans, and Bolshevik Russia. The shadow of these three nations looms largely over the rest of the world for the next two decades. With Europe lying in ruin, capitalism carries the day and seals the deal for the horrors yet to come. The demand for reparations is a crushing blow to Germany and in time devastates much of Europe.

The truth of Woodrow Wilson's illness and incapacity will probably never be fully known. Most of history either skirts these seventeen months or adheres to the myth that Wilson recovered enough to competently complete his term. More than likely the suspicion that his wife Edith and a close circle of physicians and servants acted as guardians of the presidency is accurate. It is said no one ever really saw the president. If someone had business to conduct, Edith took the issue, visited the president's room, and returned with a response.

These final months of the Wilson Presidency lived in the shadows. In the 21st Century, it is hard to believe that a president could be incapacitated for a short time let alone seventeen months and the whole time hides from the public. If it is true that the president could not perform the functions of the presidency on his own, and his wife acted as the chief executive in his place, this was an act of high treason. There are no provisions in the Constitution of the United States for a president's spouse to take over in the event of the president's inability to perform the duties of the president. However, there are provisions in the Constitution for the transfer of power should the president become unable to fulfill the duties of the president.

Woodrow Wilson, Edith Wilson, and several advisors to the president did not like Vice President Thomas R. Marshall, and they did not want to see him ascend to the presidency under any circumstances. At one point during this crisis, no one saw Woodrow Wilson for over sixty days. When a congressional committee gains access to see the president, it occurs under very controlled conditions and for a very short period of time when the president appears to be alert and in control of his faculties.

The problem in Wilson's case is no one of proper authority will sign off regarding his incapacity. We can only imagine the personality of Edith Wilson in shielding her husband from anyone other than his doctor. It is a matter of record that the president lay paralyzed unable to write his signature. Surely any public official who personally witnessed the president's condition and did not pursue the route of incapacitation would be guilty of conspiring against the Constitution of the United States and in essence, be contributing to the overthrow of the government. Regardless, Woodrow Wilson remains sequestered from the outside world for the remainder of his term.

The roadside of history is littered with evidence that suggests Democracy is nothing more than a ruse imposed on the public which allows the elite to rule. The road of history is paved with movements big and small to enfranchise those otherwise excluded from the democratic process. And yet, the question must be "Who controls the forces of power that influence and dictate the course of a nation?"

Nothing seems more powerful than money. If power corrupts, then total power corrupts totally. At every twist and turn of Wilson's presidency, the industrialists and financiers leveraged the power necessary to serve their best interests. Just as with Roosevelt and Taft before him, whenever Wilson gained congressional approval of some anti-corporate legislation, the men of big money with their team of lawyers and bags of cash found ways to turn it into windfall profits. These men of money and power were not satisfied with their control of the United States, they were now internationalists with a hunger for the bounty awaiting them around the world, especially in underdeveloped countries.

American imperialism would look nothing like the imperialism of the Old World. To the Robber Barons, imperialism has less to do with the control of land, and more to do with access to the world's resources one corporation at a time. The new imperialism has less to do with the planting of a flag, and everything to do with the establishment of a worldwide capitalistic system based on a free enterprise system that would allow them to engage in predatory practices at the expense of the people of other nations. The plan is flawless, paying off despotic leaders to gain access to their resources and cheap labor. Make a world capitalistic system critical to a stable economy at home and around the world. Create a fabric in which the best interest of the multinational corporation and national security were synonymous. Leverage the military might of the United States to protect and maintain corporate/national interests abroad.

All of these concepts for gaining control of the world economy slowly evolved from the heyday of the industrial revolution following the Civil War. Year after year, decade after decade, the Robber Barons conspired and leveraged their power and influence to manipulate and control the decision-making apparatus of the United States Government. Now, following World War I, these wealthy industrialists and financiers feel they are in an ideal position to control the reins of power.

Chapter 26

MARKETING IS THE THING

The Presidential Election of 1920 finds two natives of Ohio, Senator Warren G. Harding a Republican facing off against the Democratic candidate James M. Cox, Governor of the state of Ohio. Harding, a handsome man of loose morals, hires an advertising company to sell his image to the American public. Running on the slogan, "Return to Normalcy", Harding plays to the American public weary of war and internationalism. He promised to defeat the League of Nations, restore a strong economy, and maintain the independence of the United States from European intrigues. As a result of his campaign, Harding defeated Cox by the largest popular vote 60% to 34% in presidential history.

The captains of Wall Street and the titans of industry are elated at the demise of Woodrow Wilson and the rise of Warren Harding. Harding has no interest in being a leader. To Harding, the presidency represents a new status and ceremonial position from which he can quench his incredible social and sexual appetite. From the very beginning, Harding plans to fill government offices with friends and cronies who helped him obtain the highest office in the land.

Warren Harding's first action is to pay off the rich and wealthy who silently funded his campaign. Appointing the titular head of the Bohemian Club Andrew Mellon as his Secretary of the Treasury, Harding alleviates any concerns that his administration will do anything to obstruct a return of business to the pinnacle of national life to which it feels so entitled. At the helm of the treasury, Mellon can protect the best interests of his friends.

The Spoils System brought to prominence under the presidency of Andrew Jackson, serves as a rewards system presidential candidates can use to gain the favor, support, and financial help of office seekers. After years of corruption, the Pendleton Act of 1883 was passed by Congress in an attempt to drive the proverbial stake through the heart of this blood-sucking system of spoils.

Despite the best efforts of true public servants, the beast of spoils seemed to have nine lives. Legislation is only as good as those willing to enforce it. Too often, elected officials, intent on using politics and government for their own personal interests find ways to circumvent the law. No one discovers how to do this better than Warren G. Harding.

Harding appointed so many friends and campaign contributors to a position of power that many others, especially from his home state, moved to Washington D.C. anticipating their anointment. These people gaining privilege don't lurk in the shadows, quite the opposite. They proudly wear the moniker of a member of the Ohio Gang. With the aid of President Harding, the Ohio Gang claims dominion over government money and resources.

In an act of guile, Harding appoints his campaign manager as the Attorney General of the United States. Harry Daugherty does possess a law degree. He is primarily a political handler. As Attorney General, Daugherty's primary interest is finding ways around the law. Upholding the law doesn't even occur to him. In 1921, Attorney General Daugherty seeks a heavy-handed injunction against the railroad union to break up a strike harmful to his fat cat railroad friends. Throughout his three years as the nation's chief law enforcement officer, Daugherty manipulates insider dealing for government contracts and lucrative profits for his friends. In a two-million-three-hundred-thousand-dollar war contract swindle involving Wright-Martin Aircraft Corp, Daugherty himself is a company shareholder. The Attorney General's hypocrisy knows no bounds. From the very beginning of Prohibition, Harry Daugherty, and his lieutenant Jess Smith accept bribes from bootleggers, sell contraband, and are complicit with organized crime.

Only a disinterested Chief Executive remains ignorant of such conduct. But then again, it is plausible that Warren Harding knows and just doesn't care. In a conversation with an administration official, Harding said, "I do not worry about my enemies, it is my friends that have me walking the halls at night."

One of Harding's friends Albert Fall becomes the Interior Secretary in March 1921. Fall recognizes the naval oil reserves at Elk Hills, California, and Teapot Dome, Wyoming as potential cash cows for whoever controls the lease to these rich oil deposits.

In one of his first days at the Interior Department, Secretary Fall entertains a visit from close friends Edward L. Doheny and Harry F. Sinclair.

"Congratulations Mr. Secretary, you have landed yourself a very important position in the Harding Cabinet," proclaims Harry Sinclair as he enters the secretary's office with a hand of congratulations extended to Secretary Fall.

"I agree Albert, this indeed puts you in a very lucrative position," adds Edward Doheny.

Sinclair and Doheny are oilmen. Sinclair is the head of Mammoth Oil Corporation, and Doheny is the chairman of Pan-American Petroleum and Transport Company. These two oil titans are not making a social visit.

"What can I do for you gentlemen, I know you are far too busy to be making a social call," Secretary Fall reveals standing with his hands firmly planted on the huge walnut desk behind which he stands.

"Mr. Secretary have you considered the benefits of having the naval oil reserves under the auspices of the Interior Department rather than the Secretary of the Navy?" asks Doheny.

"I have not had time to consider much of anything. I have only held this office three days," Fall responds. "Perhaps you might enlighten me more."

"Here is the deal Albert, may I call you Albert? The naval oil reserves are on public land which deserves the oversight of the Interior Department. This Albert is your arguing point for getting these reserves under your control," Sinclair suggests.

"Once the oil reserves are under your control Mr. Secretary, you are in control of who receives drilling rights. This is where we step in and could be very helpful," Doheny asserts. "If you know what I mean Mr. Secretary."

"Gentlemen, even if I controlled these oil reserves, the awarding of drilling rights requires an open bidding process," Fall informs his guests as he lowers himself into the big leather chair often called the throne of power at the Interior Department.

"Albert," Sinclair says placing his closed right fist into his cupped left hand, "You gain control of the oil reserves, and we will find a way to make this a lucrative proposition."

"Let us know when this is accomplished," declares Doheny as he and Sinclair turn to depart.

Leaving the newly minted Interior Secretary, Sinclair and Doheny feel successful in greasing the skids for a lucrative deal. They both know Albert Fall. He is an accomplished person, but Albert has struggled with health issues all his life. He does not have a very strong constitution, and he is easily manipulated. His dubious involvement in some rather controversial murder cases makes him vulnerable to men of money, power, and influence. Sinclair and Doheny feel strongly that a lucrative deal will appeal to Fall's self-interest.

Left alone in his office, Secretary Fall leans back in his chair and contemplates what has just transpired. Holding the office for less than a week, he is confronted with a proposition that appeals to his self-interest. When accepting Harding's appointment, he never envisioned such a grand deal. He knows that what Doheny and Sinclair are suggesting is illegal, but he also knows these two men possess the legal counsel necessary to find ways around the law.

"Mr. President, Secretary Fall is here to see you," informs George B. Christian, Jr. the president's personal secretary.

"Send him in George!" the president directs as he lays his pen across the page upon which he is writing a plea to his former lover Carrie Phillips for reconciliation. For ten years, Carrie has been one of Harding's most treasured sexual partners, and then but a year ago, they had a falling out. The separation has been ugly involving threats and cash, but Harding still yearns for the nasty, kinky sex Carrie enjoys every bit as he.

"Mr. Secretary, how are things at the Department of Interior? I trust you are getting settled into your new role," the president greets as he moves from behind the desk to a nearby chair. "Sit Albert, and tell me what is on your mind?"

"Mr. President, it has come to my attention that the oil reserves at Elk Hills, California, and Tea Pot Dome, Wyoming are under the control of the Department of the Navy. This does not make any sense Mr. President. These two oil reserves are on public land and as such should be under the oversight of the Interior Department. I am here seeking executive action to make it so," Fall states bluntly. "I cannot be responsible or held accountable for public lands when critical aspects are under the control of another department."

"My you have been working hard Albert. I thought you might find the leisurely pace of Interior to your liking," Harding lets loose with a good laugh. "Sit back and relax a bit, Albert. Focus more on improving your poker game. Can I offer you a glass of whiskey?"

"I don't want to take up any of your valuable time Mr. President," Albert says as he rises from his chair. "Please tell me you will give some thought to my concern."

"I will Albert, I will. Now will we see you at the weekly poker game tomorrow night?" the president asks as he places his left hand on Fall's shoulder to emphasize sincerity.

President Harding likes to please people. He wants to be popular far more than effective. His friend Albert Fall has sought out a favor. A good politician knows that one good turn deserves another. If he can get this done for Secretary Fall, the secretary will be indebted to the president. In politics and government, you can never have too many favors in the bank.

"Secretary Denby, thank you for responding promptly to my request for a visit."

"You are welcome Mr. President how can I be of assistance?" the Secretary of the Navy responds.

"Edwin, I would like you to sign off on transferring authority over the naval oil reserves at Elk Hills and Tea Pot Dome to the Department of Interior," the president informs him.

"What has brought this about Mr. President?" asks Denby as he scratches his balding head inquisitively.

"I want to consolidate the authority of our public lands under the auspices of one department. I believe Interior is the proper place for such oversight," Harding offers as an explanation.

"I serve at your pleasure Mr. President," the Navy Secretary proclaims rising to attention and awaiting dismissal.

"Good, I will see that the paperwork is ready within a couple of days," Harding informs Secretary Denby as they walk to the office door.

Leaving the White House, Denby mulls over the president's request. Harding's rationale seems disingenuous, there must be more to it than meets the eye. The Naval Secretary heads directly to the Interior Department for a conversation with Secretary Fall.

Albert Fall immediately picks up on Denby's fishing expedition. He is not going to give the Naval Secretary any satisfaction.

"Secretary Denby, your news of the president's request catches me by surprise," Fall announces putting his best quizzical look on his face. "I would need to ask him myself."

Denby can't believe he is getting the old smoke and mirrors from the president and the Interior Secretary. What are they up to?

"Let me be clear Secretary Fall. If I sign Elk Hills and Teapot Dome over to the Interior Department, you better not forget me should any deals be cut," the Naval Secretary insists slapping his right hand down firmly on Fall's desk.

With the transferring of the Elk Hills and Teapot Dome Oil Reserves to the Department of Interior, one of the most corrupt deals in U.S. history is set in motion. Once in control of the oil reserves, Fall quickly leases these lands to Doheny, Sinclair, and other oilmen in exchange for over $400,000.00 in personal loans or more accurately bribes. When this scandal breaks, Doheny the culprit behind the scheme finds a way to not only get himself acquitted on bribery charges but foreclose on Fall's Tularosa Basin home recouping over $100,000.00 of his bribery money. On the other hand, the not-so-lucky Harry Sinclair receives a fine and serves six months for contempt of court. Still, his fortune and oil company remain intact. The rich have very little to lose in the course of shady dealings. Even if caught with their hand in the till they can afford the best representation and use their influence to weasel their way to a soft landing.

Fall on the other hand takes the fall. The Senate Committee on Lands and Public Surveys doing the investigation of this scandal holds Secretary Fall and Navy Secretary Denby responsible for fraud and corruption. Denby loses his job. Fall loses his job and earns the distinction of being the first cabinet officer sentenced to prison.

President Harding doesn't experience the embarrassment of the Tea Pot Dome Scandal. Harding died before the beginning of the investigation in October 1923. The investigating committee exonerates Harding of all knowledge or blame in the scandal. However, a reasonable consideration suggests that while Harding may not have actively participated in the scandal, he surely had a notion that something was afoul. But then again, Harding seems to have little interest in what was going on within his administration.

Chapter 27

THE POWER OF LUST

As a young man, Warren Harding attends Central College in Iberia, Ohio. Harding shows little interest in anything other than music, women, and poker. At nineteen, as an accomplished cornet player, Harding joins a band that went on to win several honors. What Warren enjoys about the band more than the music was the attention he receives from young women.

Warren Harding possesses the features of a Greek God. His cornet playing may have attracted attention, but his handsome good looks attract female interest. Harding quickly earns a reputation as someone who can sweep any pretty gal right off her feet. He also has the reputation of someone who gets what he wants. He doesn't like the word "no".

Rumors are often just rumors, but if you hear them several times, you begin to believe there may be more to them than just rumors. On this one occasion, Harding met this beautiful brunette named Rachel. At nineteen years old, many young women see Harding as a man of the world. He woos young women back to his apartment with his charm and what he proudly refers to as bloviating. He can spin a story and make just about any girl feel as if she is in the presence of someone worldly and accomplished. For Rachel, at fifteen years old, Warren Harding seems enchanting.

On this occasion, Warren has Rachel on his couch. His nose inhales the fragrance at the nape of her neck and his lips gently caress the highly excitable region just below the ear as his hands explore just above her knee on the inside of her thigh. In 1891, women, and in this case, girls wear several layers of clothing. Rachel has on a lovely blueprint long-sleeve dress tight at the waist, shoulders, and wrists. Under her dress, she wears an ankle-length petticoat, and under the petticoat a brassiere and panties. Rachel's father is a local banker, so she has access to modern perfumes which only makes Warren a more determined pursuer. As young Harding reaches beneath her dress, Rachel makes a horrid mistake by informing Harding she is indeed a virgin.

"Please Warren, be gentle I have never done this before," Rachel says in a soft breathy tone.

As Rachel speaks, Warren turns his head to catch the warm pungent odor of her breath. There is something about a woman's breath in the heat of passion that attracts a man's nose like bees to honey. Harding interprets Rachel's comment to mean she is offering herself to him.

"I will be ever so gentle my sweet Rachel. Just relax and enjoy the closeness we share," Harding says with assurance.

Moving his lips from her neck to her mouth, Warren unfastens the buttons on the back of her dress and slips it down over her shoulders revealing the white petticoat which is buttoned down the front. Rachel lifts her slender body and small tight ass to allow the dress to fall to the floor. Her body tingles as Warren kisses her shoulders and massages the back of her thighs just before they converge to form her incredibly beautiful butt.

Harding has not yet seen the magnificence of this young woman, but he has an incredible erection yearning for the promised land. His heart is pounding inside his chest like someone hammering on a bass drum. He has positioned his body between her legs and has her laid out against the couch. His lips and hands become increasingly hurried which causes Rachel to be alarmed.

"I don't know Warren," she says with hesitancy in her voice, "Things are moving terribly fast. Perhaps this is not the time."

"Don't worry Rachel, you want this as much as I do," he pronounces.

"But I have never done this before, I fear it is too soon," Rachel expresses while struggling just a bit to change her position.

As Rachel attempts to free herself from Harding's passion, he reaches with his hands and tears open her petticoat all the way to her knees revealing small succulent breasts and what must be the tightest and most glorious pussy just beneath her large panties. Rachel is now frightened and struggles to get free. But Harding is too strong and forcibly keeps her on the couch where he can enjoy every inch of her wondrous body as a lion lies enjoying its prey.

"Warren please stop," Rachel pleads.

All that Harding can hear is the revelation of Rachel's virginity, and her plea to be gentle. Now, with Rachel's change of heart, she is no longer relaxed, and Harding can no longer be gentle.

"Stop struggling Rachel," Warren demands "You will enjoy this as much as I."

Harding now forcibly lowers Rachel's bra below her small tits with large plump pink nipples awaiting his lips and tongue. Laying on Rachel with all the weight of his body, Harding begins to caress Rachel's nipples with his tongue. As her nipples harden and elongate, he latches onto them with his lips. Rachel has never felt anything so amazing in her life. The more Harding sucks and laps at her tits and nipples, the more the blood flows to her vagina causing her to want something she has never experienced before.

Rachel feels conflicted. She told Warren "No," but her body now says "Yes". She becomes emotional and begins to cry. Harding pays this no heed as he feels her body yield to his demands. Pulling her panties down over her legs to the floor, Harding takes a moment to admire this gorgeous specimen of a woman spread before him like some sacred sacrifice demanding his worship. Taking his hands, Harding uses Rachel's knees to spread open the gateway to glory. Rachel is weeping and makes no effort to resist.

Pulling her down so her pussy and ass are suspended from the edge of the couch and supported by her legs, Harding drives his erection deep into this uncharted territory. Rachel gives out a painful moan as Harding aggressively drives deeper and deeper until he has arrived at full penetration. What seems like an eternity to Rachel is only a moment for Harding. The tight young untouched pussy encapsulates his cock in such tight glory he cannot hold off ejaculation for long.

Harding makes no effort to pull before ejaculation. Why would he, if Rachel gets pregnant, it is not his problem. This is a day and age when women are scorned should they allow themselves to fall into this situation. Harding knows Rachel cannot and will not say anything about their liaison because it would tarnish her reputation, not his.

Pulling from Rachel, Harding uses her petticoat to wipe himself off and begins to get dressed.

Rachel now lowered to the floor leaning against the couch continues to weep. "You are an animal," Rachel mutters from beneath the tears.

"And you are the most magnificent of all my young conquests," Harding responds. "Now get dressed and get out of here, and don't you dare say a word about this, or I will make sure everyone knows you as the tramp you appear to be."

Rachel continues to cry as she raises herself up like some young deer just learning to walk. She is a bit unstable, but she manages to put her clothes back on even though her petticoat hangs loosely from all the missing buttons. She then experiences the indignity of asking Harding to help her button her dress in the back.

Placing his hands on her shoulders from the back, Harding pulls Rachel close and whispers, "You were magnificent my dear. I should like to see you again."

Rachel says nothing and leaves the apartment never to see or think of Warren Harding again until he begins to rise in political prominence.

Such an incident as this one is not uncommon for Harding. His reputation as a womanizer grows as does his reputation as a journalist, editor, and politician. These are the days when such indiscretions are off-limits to the press and regulated to the realm of common gossip. As such, Harding and eventually his handlers can deny and discredit such behavior. Harding's good looks, personal charm, and way with words make him likable and popular. He is a Teflon politician.

On the other hand, it is improper for women of the day to speak of their sexual conduct. If they are to reveal their sexual dalliances they will be seen as a harlot. If they are to suggest a man has taken advantage of them or forced himself upon them, they will be seen as foolish and weak for allowing such a thing to happen. If a woman allows herself to be in a position for a man to take advantage of her, it is her fault.

At a young age, Warren Harding developed an appetite for women, poker, whiskey, and a fine cigar. Early on he discovers that poker provides an avenue to fulfill all of his vices. Poker along with his success in publishing puts Warren in contact with men of influence, prestige, and power. It is through these poker games that Warren Harding becomes acquainted with Ohio Republican Party Boss Mark Hanna and Harry M. Daugherty a friend and ally of William McKinley.

Hanna and Daugherty recognize in Harding a person with real political possibilities. They see a man whom they can control. Knowing Harding's vices, these early influences convince him he should take a wife. This will give Harding the appearance of stability and solid morals so important to business and political success. Warren Harding possesses little interest in politics, but he does covet success and the acquisition of prestige.

As the owner of the Marion Daily Star, Harding makes the newspaper the most popular in the county. His chief rival, the Independent, is owned by Amos Kling. Kling and Harding are bitter enemies, but Kling has a daughter, Florence Kling DeWolfe, a divorcee five years Harding's senior. Harding needs a wife, and he needs someone stable and competent, not sexual. Florence Kling DeWolfe fits the bill perfectly. A rather homely woman, DeWolfe is smart, cunning, and serious.

Florence's father disowns her after her first marriage to a man totally unacceptable to Amos Kling. Now as a divorcee, Florence has taken an interest in the handsome Warren Harding. Part of her motive is admiration and the other part is she sees Harding as a way to further insult her father. Whatever the reason, Harding sees Florence as an opportunity to take a wife without changing his lifestyle. Florence has a son, Marshall, from her first marriage, and the young lad will keep her busy while Harding goes about his business. Warren Harding also sees Florence as a way to get to Amos Kling.

Warren Harding finds his wife to be a good business partner, conversationalist, and socialite, but he considers her too ugly for intimacy. They have no children which suggests they never consummated their marriage. For Harding, that is just fine. His infidelities provide more than adequate opportunities for sexual release, and to taste the fine nectar of many young beautiful women.

In 1910, Dr. Britton a friend of Harding's asks him to speak with his daughter Nan who has become smitten with Harding. The young girl of fourteen arrives at Harding's office alone. Warren quickly becomes intrigued by the sexuality of this young girl. Although fourteen, she has long flowing hair, beautiful eyes, full lips, small breasts, and well-defined hips.

"Nan, your father wants me to talk with you about what he says is your interest in me," Harding begins.

Nan, who is sitting on the couch in Harding's office across from Harding who is sitting in a chair, giggles at the comment saying "You are very handsome Mr. Harding."

"Nan, you are very young, and you cannot possibly know what you want in life let alone a man," Harding suggests.

"Mr. Harding, I am a woman in every way, and I do know what I want," she insists.

"Nan, I am thirty-one years, your senior, you cannot possibly be interested in a man of forty-five," Harding asserts somewhat hoping perhaps this young nymph is indeed interested.

"What does age have to do with it?" Nan asks. "I am a woman and you are a man."

"But I am a married man," Harding reminds her.

"I have heard the rumors, Mr. Harding. You enjoy the company of young beautiful women despite being married. Is this not true?" Nan says with a smile on her face and a lustful twinkle in her eyes.

Not responding to Nan's comment, Harding extols "Nan, as a young woman, your entire life lay before you. There are lots of men, handsome and successful men with whom you can fall in love."

Standing up, Nan looks at Harding "I am not interested in other men, I am interested in you. Now look at me," she says as she pulls her dress down around her shoulders. "Am I not the kind of woman you want?"

"You are," Harding admits.

"Then come and take me for I am ripe and ready to be taken," she implores as she walks over and places herself directly in front of Harding.

Unlike the young fifteen-year-old of those many years before, this fourteen-year-old girl who calls herself a woman offers Harding no resistance or regret. Dropping her dress to reveal beautifully soft white skin only covered with a bra and panties, Harding can no longer resist. Rising from his chair he takes the young girl and begins to discover all of the qualities which make her one of the most delightful women he has ever encountered.

When she kisses, she kisses deeply and passionately. When he fondles, kisses, and sucks on her breasts, she moans with pleasure which demands more. She lays herself on his couch like some sexual smorgasbord demanding he taste and experience every entrée she has to offer. And when it comes to consummating the encounter, she cries with joy and the desire for more.

Little did Harding know that this initial encounter with Nan Britton would not be one of his one-and-done affairs. While he reports back to Dr. Britton that all things are well with Nan, he has simply ignited a fire that will burn for the remainder of her lifetime. Nan agrees to not see Warren Harding again until she graduates from High School. In 1914, Warren Harding is elected to the United States Senate, and Nan Britton graduates from High School. From that time forward, they maintain an affair until Harding's death.

One account tells of Britton and Harding making love in a White House closet. Despite the cramped quarters, Britton tells of Harding's passion and strength as he braces her nude body against the closet wall and holds her firmly against his thighs as he pierces her pussy with deep thrusts which bring delight to them both. Nothing can detract from Nan's love for Warren Harding even though she knows he is a sexual beast. Years later, President John F. Kennedy is said to have replicated Harding's sexual passion in the same White House closet.

In 1919, Nan Britton gives birth to a daughter Elizabeth Ann. Harding never meets the girl or acknowledges her as his daughter, but he provides Nan with significant child support up until his death.

In the White House, Florence Harding, always suspicious of her husband's philandering employs the services of Private Detective Gaston Means to unearth the truth. In one of their meetings, Mrs. Harding reveals her suspicion and concern for Warren Harding's relationship with Nan Britton.

"I became suspicious of this girl, Nan Britton when she was but a child in Marion. She was a greatly over-developed child and wore extremely short dresses above the knees. It was not considered quite decent. And she was always doing everything on Earth to attract Warren's attention. And I could see from Warren's eyes and manner that this young girl affected him by her very presence. Mr. Means, it is said that Nan Britton has a daughter with Warren."

At this time, Florence Harding reveals her assignment for Gaston Means. "I need you to do anything possible to unearth the truth. I do not believe these rumors, but I want to know the truth. Please get me the proof I need."

In 1910 when Nan Britton is swearing and displaying her love for Warren Harding, she has no clue regarding Harding's affair with Carrie Fulton Phillips the wife of Harding's friend, James Phillips, the owner of a Marion Department Store. Carrie Phillips happens to be a friend and confidant of Florence Harding.

In 1901 when Phillip's toddler son James Jr. passes away, Warren Harding takes advantage of the young and beautiful Carrie's grief to get close to her. In the years following the boy's death, the Phillips and the Hardings take several trips together which afford Warren and Carrie the opportunity to initiate an affair.

Carelessness in their dalliances leads Florence and James to discover their spouses are lovers. Florence not only feels betrayed by her husband but also by her friend. This is not a first-time experience for Florence. By the early nineteen hundreds, she has discovered several of Warren's indiscretions of which a number are with her so-called friends. James too is devastated by the revelation involving his wife and friend. James immediately takes steps to separate the lovers by moving his family to Germany for a number of years.

When her husband and daughter return to the United States from Germany, Carrie Phillips remains behind. Then, as United States entry into World War I becomes a possibility, Carrie returns to the United States to lobby for isolation. At this time, Warren Harding is a United States Senator, and the two former lovers reignite the flame of passion and their affair.

Upon nomination as the Republican Party candidate for President of the United States, Warren Harding reveals to party leaders his affair with Carrie Phillips and the hundreds of love letters in her possession written on Senate stationery. In an act that has become all too common in modern politics, the party bosses seek to squelch the issue and keep the matter quiet. Being a shrewd operator, Carrie demands something in return for her silence. Quid Pro Quo is a powerful force in politics even if it so often smacks of just plain bribery. In return for a slow and long tour of Asia and the Pacific along with twenty thousand dollars, Carrie Phillips and her husband leave the United States and remain silent.

Over the years, Florence Harding becomes weary of her husband's infidelity. Despite all of her efforts, Warren continues to seek out young and beautiful women for his conquest. Finally, in August of 1923 while on a Western Tour of the United States, Florence Harding's wits are at an end. Confident no autopsy will be performed without her consent, Florence Harding poisons her husband. On August 2, 1923, Warren Harding slumps over dead at the Palace Hotel in San Francisco, California.

Despite suspicions of foul play, Florence Harding will not allow an autopsy. Warren Harding's doctors explain his death as prolonged ptomaine poisoning and a heart attack. The fact is that Harding has not eaten anything which has not been eaten by many others.

Back in Washington D.C., Col. Miller and Gaston D. Means, a private detective hired by Florence Harding are aghast at the news of the president's death. After contacting a reporter friend of his in San Francisco, Col. Miller receives the following word: "Circumstances of his death appear shrouded in mystery."

Gaston Means' mind turns to a conversation with Mrs. Harding in which she said, "I am determined. I will not be thwarted!"

Means asked himself over and over "What happened?" and each time he is confronted with the face of a determined Mrs. Harding.

During the same conversation, Means remembers Mrs. Harding asking him, "No matter what news you might hear my dear Gaston, will you be my friend and protector?"

"I will always stand by your side, Mrs. Harding," Gaston responds.

Upon returning to Washington with her husband's body, Florence Harding calls for Gaston Means to come to her side. Arriving at the

White House, Means finds Mrs. Harding sitting alone. Entering the room, he notices her demeanor to be calm and composed. Mrs. Harding pours them both a drink.

"Mr. Means, where is Nan Britton," Mrs. Harding asks.

"She is in Europe," Means responds.

"Who controls the president's body?" Mrs. Harding inquires.

"You do," Means says.

"Am I able to prevent an autopsy?" she asks in a matter-of-fact manner.

"Yes, you can," Gaston assures.

"Mr. Means, I was alone with the president when it was time for his medicine. I gave his medicine to him and he drank it. He lay comfortable for a minute with his eyes closed. Then suddenly he opened his eyes wide, moved his head, and looked straight into my face. I was standing by his bedside," she explains still composed and in control.

"Do you think he knew?" Gaston asked assuming Mrs. Harding was taking him into her closest confidence.

"Yes, I think he knew. Then, he sighed and turned his head away over on the pillow," she said, "and I waited for some time before calling for assistance."

Mrs. Harding went on to explain to Gaston Means that the president's death came in time to protect his legacy. She emphasizes the notoriously corrupt nature of the Ohio Gang which had grown to control the president. She claims his impeachment is imminent should he continue to live. She said over and over, "I have no regrets."

Then, Mrs. Harding's conversation quickly turns to concern about Nan Britton and her daughter.

As the First Lady of the United States, Florence Harding assassinated her husband.

Following Harding's death, Nan Britton turns to Florence Harding for the support of her daughter. Harding will have nothing to do with Britton's request and leaves the president's former lover and daughter to drift alone absent the president's support. A few years later, Nan Britton, desperate for income and support for her daughter becomes the first mistress of a president to write a tell-all book. In the book, Britton very explicitly portrays her affair with Warren Harding and the depth of his sexual desires.

Nero may have fiddled while Rome burned, but it was Harding who diddled while the wealthy ran the country.

Chapter 28

FELLOW TRAVELER

Warren Harding didn't cause the Industrialists and Financiers any concern. His policy of isolationism did nothing to curtail the advances of private adventurism, imperialism, and international business which found fertile ground in the wake of the First World War. The peace settlement dictated by the Treaty of Versailles lays responsibility for all war reparations on Germany. The treaty ensures a great profit will be reaped by American businesses and financiers for their investment in the war. The treaty breaks up old empires leaving vulnerable emerging third-world states. The repudiation of the treaty and the League of Nations by the United States Senate ensures there are no foreign entanglements to hamper international business and the expansion of U.S. economic power around the globe.

In the small town of Plymouth Notch, nestled in the back hills of Vermont, Vice President Calvin Coolidge receives late-night news of the president's death. Surrounded by his family, Coolidge's father, a notary gives his son the oath of office as prescribed by the Constitution of the United States. Using a family Bible, Calvin Coolidge, a man with deep regard for God and the nation becomes President of the United States.

With the nation in mourning, Coolidge's ascendency to the Presidency received little attention from the common man. However, in the towers of power, men take notice that an unknown quantity now ascends to the highest office in the land. Senator Henry Cabot Lodge shakes his head in disbelief that Coolidge, a man who very well would have been replaced on the ticket by Harding for the 1924 Presidential Election, now holds an office where he never belonged. Upon learning of Harding's death, Senator Lodge exclaimed, "My God, this means Coolidge is president."

On another front, Dwight Morrow and his wife Betty dining with Robert Frost welcome the news of Morrow's old Amherst College classmate and friend's ascension to the highest office in the land. Morrow, a wealthy financier associated with J.P. Morgan and Co. played an instrumental role in securing a huge loan for the Allied powers during World War I. Morrow knows that Coolidge adheres to the Amherst commitment to learning over thinking promoted by college president Alexander Meiklejohn. This means Coolidge can be counted on to adhere to conservative principles important to a laissez-faire approach to business.

Alice Longworth, Theodore Roosevelt's daughter proclaimed, "Calvin Coolidge is a great threat to the activist wing of the Republican Party and the legacy of my father. Coolidge will allow the wealthy to run roughshod over the country. We are all in deep trouble."

Calvin Coolidge believes in small government. He believes in the United States as a union of states. He believes these states, as he feels the founders intended, need to be free to function with little intrusion from the federal government. He also believes in the spirit of the individual and feels that each individual has a right to whatever they may attain including great wealth. This philosophy brings great comfort to the wealthy power elite across the United States.

In an address, Coolidge proclaims, "The only hope of perfecting human relationships is in accordance with the law of service under which men are not so solicitous about what they shall get as they are about what they shall give. Yet people are entitled to the rewards of their industry. What they earn is theirs, no matter how small or how great. But the possession of property carries the obligation to use it in a larger service."

Interestingly, Coolidge believes in a sense of Noblesse Oblige, and yet he doesn't believe the government should enact legislation or put in place regulations that mandate such behavior. His naïve philosophy places in business and the wealthy a trust that given the opportunity, they will do the right thing out of a sense of service. Coolidge backs his belief in a hands-off approach to business by placing the nation's industrial policy in the hands of Secretary of Commerce Hebert Hoover who aggressively uses governmental authority to promote business. Coolidge appoints commissioners to the Federal Trade Commission and the Interstate Commerce Commission who do nothing to ensure the conduct of business under their authority remains true to the general welfare of the nation. Government regulation and oversight so important to the relationship between business and the common people of the United States becomes non-existent under President Coolidge.

Many of the reforms which Coolidge supported as the governor of a state, he pays no concern about as president. This all emerges from his belief in a limited federal system and the power and authority which belong to the states. Unleashing such a hands-off philosophy on a nation that just acquired such incredible influence around the world brings with it grave danger.

In Geneva on vacation, John Foster Dulles meets with his brother Allen to discuss the state of government in the United States, and the opportunities available throughout a world still reeling from the impact of a World War. Meeting in the back room of a small pub, the brothers speak frankly without concern for unwanted ears.

"By God Allen, I believe we were born just for this time," John Foster proclaims to his brother. "World War I provided you and me the opportunity to befriend influential leaders around the globe. Our star is ascending, and we must position ourselves to take advantage of every opportunity to advance our personal interests."

"I agree, John, we cannot allow the opportunity to promote U.S. economic interests to escape our ability for self-promotion. If we fail to advance our own prestige, as well as the financial benefits to be gained, the ghost of our grandfather will forever haunt our sleep," Allen emphasizes crossing his arms.

"There is no better time, Allen. We have a weak do-nothing man in the White House with an isolationist Congress. We have a world torn asunder by the ravages of war with nations groping for help from wherever it might come. It is the perfect setting to take advantage of the situation," John asserts.

Taking a long draw from his cigar, Allen pauses to consider it all. Following a sip from his brandy, "The world is comprised of world powers that are no longer powerful. Empires are shattered with new nations emerging in their place. Developing nations in the Middle East, Africa, South America, and Asia control rich natural resources but are too weak and undeveloped to turn them into an economic base. Time is of the essence, and we must act quickly before someone else does."

"Secretary of Commerce Hoover is a good friend of the industrialist and financier. His experience as a mining engineer allows him to make many friends across the continents. He will not stand in our way, but rather help open doors with his influence. Hoover is a wealthy man and he admires men of wealth. He too believes this should be the first of many American centuries. He also believes it can best be accomplished with the federal government taking a back seat to private enterprise," John Foster proclaims as he leans across the table to emphasize the seriousness of the matter.

"What about our old professor Woodrow Wilson's proclamation to make the world safe for Democracy? Where does this fit into the equation of what we do?" Allen asks while leaning back in his chair and pulling hard on his cigar.

"Democracy is a ruse brother. It is a great smokescreen. You and I know most cultures and people have little ability for self-government. Hell, look at the United States. Democracy is nothing but a sales job to make people believe they control their own destiny. The United States never has been and never will be ruled by the people. From the very beginning, it has been the wealthy and educated who have run the country. Sure, there are changes which occur to the social and even at times economic order, but they are changes which do not jeopardize the power of the wealthy and ruling class," John Foster Dulles firmly reminds his younger brother.

"There is a certain Darwinist nature to the social and economic evolution of the United States," injects Allen. "People do not remain loyal to their culture, but rather their socio-economic class. The rich remain loyal to the need to stay rich and increase their wealth whenever possible. It does not matter race or religion, if you are rich, you share the same self-interest."

"Exactly Allen, we are positioned to help the wealthy including ourselves gain dominion throughout the world," John Foster Dulles proclaims like some preface to his manifesto.

"So, what is the grand design, John? How do you suggest we move forward from here?" Allen asks.

"We cannot afford to be short-sighted on this Allen. It is the 1920s, and you and I are young with nothing to lose and everything to gain if we play our cards right," John says.

"Ah cards, now there is a game I like very much. Give me a good card game, cigar, brandy, and a woman, and I will show you a happy man," Allen says with a big smile.

"Damn it, Allen, be serious. If we play things right, you will have plenty of time for all the luxuries of life you can imagine," John reminds his brother.

"Why John, I did not think you approved of my lifestyle. I thought you frowned on my proclivity for smoking, drinking, and bedding women. You do know John, if you weren't so righteous, you might like it if you tried it," Allen says with a laugh. "If you like, I know a couple of beautiful young sisters who would be happy to join us later. A good blow job might be just what the doctor ordered," Allen adds.

"Knock it off Allen, keep your frivolity to your own time. We have important business at hand, and I need you to stay focused," John Foster demands with a stern look of disapproval for his brother's digression into the deviant.

"Okay John, get with it I might want to contact those sisters myself," Allen notes with a big smile.

"Allen, I can be of most service to our personal interests by working with United States Companies to secure holdings in third world countries. I will use my influence to mine the sugar resources of the Caribbean and Central America. I'll do what I can to develop inroads into the oil fields of the Middle East. I will seek to make deals with emerging nations in Africa to gain access to their rich mineral deposits. I can best do this as an agent of Sullivan and Cromwell. My position as an international attorney gives me access to the men in power which is lucrative for the law firm, American corporations, and us. The current hands-off policy of the United States government allows us the freedom to make these things happen," John declares.

"So where do I come into the picture?" Allen asks.

"Espionage my dear brother, the art of espionage. As a partner with Sullivan and Cromwell, you can use this as a cover for the real work of espionage. You work the back channels to gain me the inside information I need to make and seal deals. You help create the environment for these things to happen. There are greedy men everywhere, and I need to know who they are and their weaknesses. Your undercover work can give me the advantage needed to get powerful men in these countries to do business with me," John shares with his brother.

"I like my role John, it is perfect for my interests, and it will give me excitement and access to beautiful, rich, and powerful women. What if I discover the powerful men of a particular country are not interested in doing business with you?" Allen asks.

"Brother we are just scratching the surface of a new world. A world in which the United States rules supreme by virtue of our economic, technological, and military power. We are not there yet, but in the near future, we must position ourselves to create situations where people willing to do business with us are put in power around the world. This is where your job of espionage becomes interesting. If we play things right, the day will come when we actively engage in regime change for the purpose of economic influence and dominion. If we can create a world in which the vital interests of the United States are directly linked to the economic interests we have in a particular country, we can create a Pax Americana," John Foster Dulles reveals.

Both men sit in silence contemplating the depth and breadth of their conversation. It is not too difficult for them to see themselves as the two most powerful men in the world. Perhaps not now, but if they played things right, the inevitability seems certain.

Allen sits for a moment sipping his brandy and drawing frequently from his cigar. The smoke circles his head as he contemplates the extent to which espionage and subversive activity can work to create a new world order. As he sits there, he hardly noticed his brother get up to leave simply saying, "Talk to you later little brother."

Realizing he sits alone Allen's thoughts turn to the two beautiful

Chapter 29

SIMPLETON AT THE HELM

Coolidge's indifference to business and finance can't have come at a more critical time. World War I created a boom. Through mass production, new consumerism emerges in which ordinary citizens can purchase homes, cars, and modern appliances on time. This access to modern conveniences seems like a bargain to the common man who yearns to enjoy the spoils of a prosperous society. You name it, people can buy it. Yet the devil is in the details, and the details reveal a system in which the wealthy use modernization as bait to hook unsuspecting men and women into financial commitments in which they pay a heavy price in interest for participation. The economy is based on fake money and speculation which supports a dangerous and irresponsible process.

Coolidge says, "The business of America is business! The government needs to get out of the way and let corporations and financial institutions build prosperity." Coolidge is not a crooked man, but rather a naïve man with an unsubstantiated faith in the wealthy to build more wealth, and use that wealth to lift up the less fortunate.

In the years following World War I, industrial production increased by forty percent. The stock markets built on this false economy soar as everyone wants a piece of the economic pie. People with limited means are living well above their ability to pay because of the new economic strategy called "buying on time". Repossession once considered a crooked man's scheme becomes an integral part of the new economy.

So, the nation partied thinking the time has come for a great economic surge that will finally uplift everyone to a decent standard of living. While European nations are turning to socialism as a means of sharing wealth, the United States touts capitalism as the pathway to a better life. The money changers aren't the bulls of Wall Street, but rather wolves in sheep's clothing pretending to have the best interest of the people and the country at heart. During this time called the Roaring Twenties, President Coolidge enjoys the accolades of a grateful nation when in fact his only action is inaction.

In 1923, a group of the world's most successful financiers gathered at the Edgewater Beach Hotel in Chicago. These tycoons are extremely rich and altogether they control more wealth than there is in the United States Treasury. As part of the process of indoctrinating the masses, these individuals publish their success stories everywhere suggesting what they have is available to anyone. There is nothing like a good sales job, and these individuals know the importance of successfully duping the public.

These giants of high finance include Arthur Cutten, the greatest wheat speculator of the time. Samual Insull is the president of the nation's largest utility company. Howard Hopson is president of the country's largest gas company. Ivar Kreuger is head of the world's greatest monopoly. Jesse Livermore is considered the greatest bear on Wall Street. Charles Schwab is the president of the largest independent steel company. Richard Whitney is the president of the New York Stock Exchange. A cabal of nastier and more wicked men has never been contrived.

Schwab rose to prominence by working his way up the ladder at Carnegie Steel, U.S. Steel, and Bethlehem Steel. A staunch anti-union man, Schwab used the Pennsylvania State Police to bust up the 1910 Bethlehem Steel strike. During World War I, Schwab ignored U.S. neutrality laws and shipped munitions to the Allies via the Canadian underground. Despite his illegal adventurism, Schwab became Director General of the Emergency Fleet Corporation with authority over all U.S. shipbuilding. Using this position to his advantage, Charles Schwab profited greatly from the war. Thomas Edison once called Schwab the "master hustler". By 1923, Schwab is a millionaire many times over. It is

Schwab who requests these titans of American finance and industry to join him for this meeting.

In 1907, Howard C. Hopson obtained a position with the Interstate Commerce Commission, and in 1908 he joined the Public Service Commission of New York. As a New York utility regulator, Howard Hopson used insider knowledge to buy up a conglomeration of electric and gas companies in New York, Ohio, and Pennsylvania in the early 1920s. In 1921, Hopson purchased the Associated Gas and Electric Company (AGECO) and turned it into one of the country's largest utility holding companies. As a huge pyramid scheme, AGECO is always one step ahead of its lenders and stockholders. Throughout the 1920s, Hopson makes hundreds of acquisitions through the selling of new securities paper and manipulating the market and speculation.

Richard Whitney came from an established banking family, his father George was president of North National Union Bank in Boston, Massachusetts. At age 23, Richard established his own brokerage firm in New York City and used money borrowed from his uncle, a partner in J.P. Morgan & Co., and a brother, an official at the Morgan Bank, to purchase himself a seat on the New York Stock Exchange. With his inside position on the Stock Exchange, Whitney becomes a principal broker for J.P. Morgan & Co. and is eventually elected to the governing board and president of the New York Stock Exchange. During the 1920s and 30s, Whitney gets involved in speculative investments which led to embezzlement and an eventual prison sentence.

Arthur Cutten grew up in Ontario, Canada, and moved to Chicago at the age of 18. As an employee for a commodity broker, Cutten studied the rudiments of grain trading and speculated on commodity prices through the purchase of advanced contracts. Capitalizing on the rising prices for Midwest wheat, Cutten manages to save up a small fortune and buy himself a seat on the Chicago Board of Trade. With his information gained from the Board of Trade, Cutten becomes one of America's most successful commodity speculators and richest citizens. Cutten is known to have been the ringleader of several insider consortiums formed as trading pools to manipulate market prices.

Samual Insull, a British-born innovator, and investor emigrated to the U.S. to work for Thomas Edison. Along with other Edison Pioneers,

Insull founded Edison General Electric with the help of Vanderbilt, J.P. Morgan, and others. He left Edison General Electric to become president of Chicago Edison. With his new position and wealth, Insull purchases portions of utility companies, railroads, and broadcasting companies to amass a small empire.

Jesse Livermore also known as the "Boy Plunger," the "Great Bear," the "Wall Street Wonder," and the "Cotton King," is one of the most flamboyant and successful market speculators in the history of Wall Street. Livermore made and lost several multi-million-dollar fortunes as he uses fraud and speculation to manipulate the market and bamboozle investors.

Ivar Kreuger isn't even a U.S. citizen. Kreuger is a Swedish businessman who uses Kreuger & Tool a multi-billion-dollar match conglomerate to run a huge Ponzi scheme through a complex structure of hundreds of subsidiary shell companies. Hiding his manipulation by cooking the books, he insists that financial statements not be audited. One of Kreuger's biographers calls him a "genius and swindler". The renowned economist John Kenneth Galbraith called Kreuger the "Leonardo of larcenists".

The Edgewater Beach Hotel located in the far-north neighborhood of Edgewater in Chicago; Illinois opened in 1916. The Edgewater is a Spanish Colonial Revival style stucco in the form of a Maltese Cross. This group of America's wealthiest like to surround themselves with the very best of everything. The Edgewater offers the most modern of facilities and accommodations. The elegant Marine Dining Room provides the finest cuisine anywhere. The boys particularly enjoy the music of Ray Miller's Band, and on this occasion, they specifically request his band be present for their listening pleasure. They also enjoy the company of professional baseball players, and at the Edgewater, you might see Babe Ruth, Rogers Hornsby, Edd Roush, George Sisler, Ty Cobb, and other greats when their teams are in town. These men are also smitten by the starlets of the day. Wealth meant access to beautiful women, and nothing is more pleasing than a flirty starlet like Lillian Gish, Lil Dagover, Gloria Swanson, or Mary Pickford.

On this date in 1923, there couldn't have been a gathering of more notorious characters had it been Al Capone, Dutch Schultz, and

Lucky Luciano. Calvin Coolidge ascended to the Presidency following Harding's death, and now it looks as if Coolidge will win the office in his own right. Sitting in one of the hotel's plush suites, these men snack on the finest seafood brought in from the Great Lakes, drink the most expensive Whiskey, and smoke fine Cuban cigars.

"It is great to be in Chicago, a city which completely ignores the trappings of the federal government and allows people to live the good life," Charles Schwab begins.

"Yea it's great Charlie, but hell it's great to be anywhere when you can buy whatever you want. There isn't a damn thing in Chicago I couldn't get tenfold in New York," Richard Whitney says.

"Being rich is a bitch," chimes in Howard Hopson, "So why are we here, it is certainly not because we enjoy each other's company."

"Did you hear Will Rogers the other day, he said there are ten men who could buy the world, and ten million can't get enough to eat," notes Samual Insull. "I suggest we are here to discuss how we might fulfill Roger's prophesy.

"Rogers is a funny man, but there are hidden truths to what he has to say," adds Schwab.

"Consider this Rogers gem, we don't have to worry about anything. No nation in the history of the world was ever sitting so pretty. If we want anything, all we have to do is go and buy it on credit," Insull adds. "I believe we are here to see that all Americans line our pockets with their desire to buy things on credit."

"Look," says Cutten, "Not one of us is rich because of what we can do, but rather what we can get an unsuspecting public to do. The public is so hungry for a piece of the prosperity pie that they don't even notice the pie has no filling."

"That is why we are here gentlemen," asserts Schwab, "Now is not the time to back off. With a president like Coolidge for four more years, we have a free pass to continue our creation and manipulation of a false sense of prosperity to the American people."

"My friends, I would like to raise a toast to the Secretary of Treasury Andrew Mellon for his creative leadership in shepherding the Revenue Act through Congress two years ago. Thanks to Secretary Mellon, we will see our taxes reduced from the 78% we once paid to the current 50%

and lower. Gentlemen, Andrew Mellon has put a great deal more cash in our pockets. To Andrew Mellon!" chimes Howard Hopson.

"It is so important we take full advantage of a president who has no interest in meddling with business. The man is a dullard and a coward. He hates conflict and will do just about anything to avoid confrontation. We must take advantage of this hands-off environment to solidify our position at home and around the world. The iron is hot and it is time to strike," Injects Ivar Kreuger.

"I certainly agree with the accolades heaped on Andrew Mellon by this group, but I don't think we should overlook the service John Foster Dulles has provided at Sullivan and Cromwell. While a young man, Dulles is an insider. His influential roots run deep, and he is truly a friend to the ruling class. His international work is opening opportunities for us everywhere, and with a hands-off president, there are fortunes to be gained," Leon Fraser makes note of the possibilities.

"John Foster Dulles is a self-righteous bastard, who absolutely hates the masses. He believes that the wealthy are blessed by God and all those of the lower class have been deemed unworthy by the Almighty. He is an easy target to do our work, especially if there is something in it for him," says Richard Whitney.

"What are you trying to say Whitney that you love the masses? Get real, you are no different than the rest of us, you see the masses as a means by which we can all get filthy rich," responds Jesse Livermore.

"Let there be no doubt, I value the masses to the degree to which they can elevate my personal wealth, position, and power. My point is John Foster Dulles loves God but hates common people. He sees our work as God's work because it perpetuates his belief that we are God's chosen people. With his knowledge, skill, and connections, he is a valuable resource," defends Whitney.

"Gentlemen, we are riding a wave of great prosperity. We are fortunate to have men in high places as our allies. We are being provided the tools and opportunities to create and make piles of money. The masses are fascinated with the modernization of society. They can't get enough and they want it now," emphasizes Jesse Livermore.

"This is a time of great consumerism," says Arthur Cutten. "The more we can get the masses to purchase things on credit, the more we make by doing nothing. Increased consumerism drives up the market which fills our coffers like an ever-expanding balloon."

"Three cheers to President Coolidge, Secretary Mellon, and young Foster Dulles," says Richard Whitney.

There can be no doubt, that the Roaring Twenties just keep roaring along. People feel like they have the world on a string. Who needs money when there is credit? The common man feels he has found his cloud with a silver lining.

In the midst of prohibition, Americans party like there will be no tomorrow. Regardless of the law, booze flows freely due to the power of the wealthy, mobs, and a thirsty nation. Women gain the vote in 1921, and they demonstrate their newfound freedom by joining the party. Known as flappers, liberated women dress more liberally, dance the jitterbug, smoke, drink, and frequent the entertainment clubs called Speakeasies.

While the nation celebrates prosperity, something different occurs at the labor level of society. The very people sustaining consumerism are not being duly compensated in the workplace. Despite knowledge of the growing contradiction, President Coolidge adopts a posture of indifference to the growing unrest of workers over low pay, poor working conditions, and safety.

When finally determined to act, Coolidge stands by the owners (wealthy) who impose restrictive contracts barring union membership. When urged to do so, Coolidge brings in armed thugs to attack strikers and staged lockouts. The president quickly intervenes against the miner's strike as well as the steel strike of 300,000 workers where union leaders are arrested on dubious charges.

Union leaders and members define the situation in the correct terms. The prosperous economy serves as a smokescreen for a class struggle in which those with all the chips are not going to willingly relinquish a dime, and they will fight and conspire to keep it that way.

The 1920s are not that far removed from President Lincoln to forget that the Great Emancipator once proclaimed Labor superior to Capital. Without labor, there can be no capital. The Union Leaders and members understand that the only hope of labor, the middle class, or the poor is to stand together against the wealthy in achieving fair treatment in the workplace.

In June 1923, two old warriors and a young upstart in the Union movement meet at the home of Eugene V. Debs at 451 N. 8th St., Terre Haute, Indiana. Debs' home is a large two-story house with a wrap-around porch and a small garden. In comparison to the mansions of the great industrialists and financiers, Debs' home is modest in design, structure, and furnishings. However, Debs' wife, Kate, inherited a great deal of money from a wealthy aunt and wants to have the pleasure of nice things. As Debs gives his guests a tour of his home, they marvel at the porcelain tile fireplace, mahogany dining, and parlor furniture, and the Haviland China gracing the dining room table.

Debs invites his guests Samuel Gompers and John L. Lewis to join him on the front porch where they can enjoy a warm sunny June Indiana afternoon. As the men settle into their chairs, Kate brings a plate of sandwiches and bottles of cold Pablo Near Beer made by Pabst. While each man enjoys a good beer, prohibition is in effect, and near beer is the best Debs can do.

This is not a normal gathering of powerful men. Gompers and Debs are between twenty-five and thirty years older than Lewis and nearing the end of their lives. Gompers fell ill in February but recovered enough to travel to Terre Haute to enjoy the warm fresh mid-western air. Gompers and Debs have much in common, but they are not close friends or allies. Gompers abhors socialism as something which detracts from the union movement, and Debs is a devoted Democratic Socialist. Lewis is a rookie as a union leader with only three years at the helm of the United Mine Workers of America.

Yet these three men now sit together to discuss their common cause. Debs knows how important the upcoming Presidential election of 1924 is to hardworking Americans. Having been a presidential candidate for the Socialist Party on several occasions the last time in 1920, Debs understands how critical it is for people of labor to work together.

"Samuel, I know you and I do not necessarily see eye to eye, but I appreciate you taking the time to travel this far to meet. I do hope you are feeling better, and wish you good health," Debs begins.

"I have made this trip because I feel it is important Eugene. I have not and never will join the socialist party because I believe when men become enthusiastic about socialism, they usually lose their interest in the union. On the other hand, I regularly attend socialist meetings because of the fine speakers, inspiration, and new ideas. I am here because I respect you as a speaker, thinker, and leader," as Gompers introduces himself.

Feeling a bit out of place with these lions of labor, John L. Lewis begins to speak, "I appreciate the opportunity to meet with the two of you. I have admired your courage and leadership for years, and I only hope I can live up to such high standards."

"Tell, us about yourself Mr. Lewis. In such a short time you have made quite a name for yourself. Being the president of the United Mine Workers is no small accomplishment, and your boldness is renown," notes Samuel Gompers.

"I am a southern Iowa boy from the small town of Cleveland in Lucas County, Iowa. Cleveland is a company town built around a coal mine. I was raised in faith as my mother and grandparents were members of the Reorganized Church of Jesus Christ of Latter-Day Saints. My devotion to a fair social order and looking after the poor comes from my faith. For a number of years, I worked at the Big Hill Mine at Lucas before moving to Panama, Illinois where I was elected president of the UMW local. You know the rest, Mr. Gompers."

"Of course, I know the rest son, but Mr. Debs does not. When he invited me here to meet, I requested he also invite you. So, complete your introduction," directs Gompers.

"In 1911, Mr. Gompers as the head of the American Federation of Labor hired me as a full-time union organizer. Over the years I have worked my way up the ladder of union leadership until I found myself at the top three years ago," Lewis finishes.

"Perhaps not the top John, if I recall two years ago you unsuccessfully challenged me for the Presidency of the AFL. You must have seen one more rung on that ladder to the top," Gompers reveals with a hearty laugh.

"With no disrespect Mr. Gompers, leadership needs to be challenged once in a while or it becomes lethargic and ineffective. I saw my challenge to your leadership as a service to the union," Lewis retorts with an unusual smile.

"Thank you for your introduction, John. What Samuel does not know is I have been following your rise for a number of years, and I am inspired by your leadership, and grateful for the sympathy that mineworkers show for our socialist movement," Debs responds.

"Mineworkers are sympathetic to the socialist movement, but we are very suspicious of the communist movement which tries to infiltrate our union," Lewis says.

"I am not a communist, Mr. Lewis, I am a Democratic Socialist. I believe in a socialist economic system under a democratic system of government. Let us be clear in our discussion that no one sitting here today is a communist or a communist sympathizer," Debs asserts.

"While I am not a communist," chimes in Gompers, "I do admire the militant economic program promoted by Marx. Nothing changes unless it is forced to change. You know this John and it is this belief which makes you such a strong and effective leader," testifies Gompers.

"We are indeed an assorted lot," says Debs. "We have all been united in our cause to improve the lives of hard-working people and their families while being frequently at odds with each other. Well today, I request that we put our philosophical differences aside, and discuss what we might be able to accomplish together as our nation and people face a Republican Party hell-bent on destroying labor and working people through their hands-off approach to dealing with the wealthy."

"So, I take it you are not considering another run for the presidency in 1924 Mr. Debs," suggests Samuel Gompers.

"I have run my races Mr. Gompers and the horse can run no more. It is time to look elsewhere for someone who can carry the torch for the common people of this nation," stresses Debs.

"We certainly can all agree that Coolidge is not the man for us. So, what are our options?" asks Lewis.

"It is difficult to determine what the Democrats might do. They are in shambles, and it could take them multiple ballots to select a candidate. I suggest we position ourselves to support "Fighting Bob" LaFollette for President," maintains Debs.

"Why LaFollette?" solicits Gompers.

"Senator Robert LaFollette has been a stalwart progressive throughout his career. He has championed many unpopular causes because it was the right thing to do. He opposed entrance into World War I, supported Women's Suffrage, and has always stood by workers. Besides, he stood by me in opposing my imprisonment for opposing the war. I owe Robert LaFollette more than my gratitude," declares Debs.

"I remember your speech at your sentencing, Mr. Debs. A truly inspirational bit of oratory which certainly impacted my resolve as a leader of the working class," claims Lewis. "If you don't mind, I would like to recite a bit from memory."

"Please indulge us," urges Gompers.

Continuing, Lewis shares, "I am thinking this morning of the men in the mills and factories; I am thinking of the women who, for a paltry wage, are compelled to work out their lives; of the little children who, in this system, are robbed of their childhood, and in their early, tender years, are seized in the remorseless grasp of Mammon, and forced into the industrial dungeons, there to feed the machines while they are being starved body and soul . . ."

"Very good Mr. Lewis, your memory is strong," admires Debs.

"Oh, I am not done Mr. Debs, let me continue," says Lewis. "Your honor, I ask no mercy, I plead for no immunity. I realize that finally, the right must prevail. I never more fully comprehend than now the great struggle between the powers of greed on the one hand and on the other the rising hosts of freedom. I can see the dawn of a better day for humanity. The people are awakening. In due course of time, they will come into their own."

"What a marvelous bit of oratory Mr. Debs, simply brilliant!" conveys Gompers. "So, you believe LaFollette is the man to carry this torch forward in our struggle?"

"I do, and if we can put aside some of our philosophical differences and unite under the banner of a better world for working people, we can be a powerful force for a LaFollette candidacy," avows Debs.

"This is where I find it difficult to compromise. Socialism seems to forget the importance of unions to working men and their families," Gompers attests.

"Unionism is an important cause and it has done much to advance the best interest of working people. However, socialism is a system, a system based on the idea that all people should share in the wealth of a nation. Under a socialist system, there no longer exists the need for unions. The system ensures that all people benefit from capital and labor in a fair and judicious manner. Workers now earn a living wage with full benefits and safe working conditions. Socialism accomplishes all those things which the union struggles to advance year after year. Socialism removes the obstacles a capitalistic system uses to prevent the advancement of labor. How do you fail to see this Mr. Gompers?" Eugene Debs asserts in frustration.

"Oh, I see it, Mr. Debs. I see a redistribution of wealth that will lift all men, women, and children out of poverty and create for them a life of dignity. I see a time when labor enjoys an equal place at the table with capital. I do not see it now or anytime too soon. For that reason, I shall devote my time and energy to the union cause," Gompers declares.

"I understand such a pragmatic approach Samuel, and for this very reason, I believe we should pledge our faith and support to Fighting Bob. Of all those in the fray for president, LaFollette is most likely to advance the cause of working men and their families," Debs reasserts.

"Then let it be done," declares Gompers. "What say ye, Mr. Lewis?"

"Let it be done," Lewis echoes.

Unfortunately, labor finds sympathy in no quarters of influence. A majority of the United States Supreme Court are either outright pro-business or take a laissez-faire approach to economic issues. Justice McKenna a long-term member of the court wrote the majority opinion on the Lochner Decision. Justice Van Devanter from Ohio is an elitist and has deep ties to the Union Pacific Railroad. Justice McReynolds adheres to laissez-faire economic theory. In 1922, Justice Pitney was replaced by Pierce Butler a conservative leader who opposes any regulation of business. These four stalwart pro-business justices only need one swing vote to keep the Supreme Court an advocate for business and finance.

Government is not of or by the people. Those who claim positions to the highest offices in the nation are more often than not from the wealthy class. Presidents tend to appoint wealthy men or women to the office of influence and decision-making because they are felt to be better equipped and prepared to handle the responsibilities of such an office.

It is class discrimination at its best. Even in these times, the people who run for federal office and win are often those possessing the most cash or backed by the most cash. There are exceptions, but for some reason, even the best and brightest of this group of people are discredited should they step beyond the unwritten code that the wealthy rule.

Even when a minority group successfully gains inclusion in the ruling club, it is the wealthy of that minority who gain admission. This is because, within the wealthy, there are no minority groups, only the wealthy group. There is a prevailing characteristic of the wealthy class which is to maintain and increase their wealth. Once wealth is attained, no one wants to give it up. There is a grand conspiracy at work to ensure the wealthy remain at the top of the economic food chain.

The wealthy taking what they want is a story as old as man's existence on Earth. To hide this fact behind a façade of rhetoric about democracy, freedom, and self-rule is the greatest smoke and mirrors trick of all time. The fact is we have created a new royalty out of the ashes of the old colonial system. Just as in medieval times, the wealthy reign supreme in every shape and form, through every publication and production. They own the world and they have made it their playground while others struggle to survive.

Unlike the past when the ruling class used brute force to enforce their desire, modern rulers have mastered the art of deception to achieve their goals. All of this emerges following World War I in the rich and fertile ground of a people wanting normalcy. Materialism and consumerism became indispensable tools in the quest to influence the American people and control the economy.

The indignities suffered by the poor and struggling classes cross all peoples and designations of people but not equally. It is critical to acknowledge that all differences in people pale in relation to the class struggle they all have in common. And yet, certain minorities face an economic mountain much steeper and more rugged than others.

This may all seem like a lot to lay at the feet of the Coolidge Administration, but the complicity cannot be denied. The sacred God is money. The national basis of that money is critical to the nation's makers. Like the rich doing whatever is necessary to stay rich, a nation particularly this nation of the rich must do whatever is necessary to maintain dominion. Following World War I, the rich in the United States recognized the opportunity to take advantage of vulnerable nations around the world.

In the 1924 Presidential Election, Calvin Coolidge runs for re-election against John Davis of the Democratic Party and Robert LaFollette of the Progressive Party. Coolidge carries thirty-five states winning three hundred and eighty-two electoral votes with fifty-four percent of the popular vote. Robert LaFollette won one state (his home state of Wisconsin) with thirteen electoral votes and seventeen percent of the popular vote. Most notably, LaFollette comes in second in eleven Western States. With the support of the railroad workers, AFL, the Socialist Party, and many other progressives, he garners nearly five million popular votes. Nonetheless, the culture of big money still carries the day for Coolidge.

In 1925, the League of Nations adopts the Geneva Protocol which outlaws the use of chemical and biological weapons in war. President Coolidge immediately came out in support of this protocol. Coolidge doesn't consider the opposition which might arise from Veteran groups, the American Chemical Society, and chemical manufacturers such as DuPont.

In a bit of chutzpah, the American Chemical Society (ACS) opposes the Geneva Protocol as a counter to National Security and the best interest of humanity. Trying to make the argument that chemical weapons are more humane than other conventional weapons, the ACS plays the trump card by saying joining the Geneva Protocol will place the U.S. Chemical industry under the authority of the League of Nations.

The real issue of money trumps any consideration regarding the ghoulish nature of chemical warfare. Pierre du Pont and his cronies leverage their influence by strong-arming enough members of Congress to assure the defeat of any resolution which might tie the United States to the Geneva Protocol.

Rich people do not like taking any chances when it comes to their wealth, so the major players in America's chemical companies decide to hold a meeting of the minds. Taking the lead, Pierre S. du Pont requests the presence of John Francis Queeny, Eugene Meyer, William Ripley Nichols, and Frederick Rowland Hazard Jr. to meet at his Longwood

Garden Estate near Kennett Square, Pennsylvania. Pierre takes great pride in his Longwood Garden Estate creating beautiful gardens of flowers as well as those to resemble the great gardens of England, France, and Italy. He enjoys showing off the estate his money made possible to create.

All of the men invited to this meeting have a vested interest in keeping America's chemical interests in their hands and away from any foreign influence. Over the years their families have amassed great wealth by creating chemicals useful in the waging of war.

Fredrick Rowland Hazard Jr. actually came from a family with a longer history in chemical production than du Pont. After gaining great wealth and prestige, the Hazards purchased the Solvay Process.

John Francis Queeny created the Monsanto Corporation just outside of St. Louis, Missouri in 1901. As a relatively new member of the chemical club, Queeny doesn't want to see his hard work lost to any kind of international agreement.

Born in Los Angeles, Eugene Meyer set out as a young man to make a fortune in speculation and investment. In 1920, Meyer and William H. Nichols purchased five small chemical companies to form Allied Chemical and Dye Corporation. As an up-and-comer of influence, Meyer served on Wilson's War Finance Board, Coolidge's Federal Farm Loan Board, and later Hoover's Federal Reserve Board.

William H. Nichols is one of the founders of the American Chemical Society in 1876. He served as President of the Society of Chemical Industry in 1904, President of the Eighth International Congress of Applied Chemistry in 1912, Chairman of the Board for Polytechnic Institute, and Chairman of the Committee on Chemicals for the Council of National Defense in 1917.

"Friends, welcome to Longwood Gardens, I thought on such a beautiful day it would be nice to meet here in the garden setting. My servants will see to it that we are well provided for in drink and food," du Pont assures.

"Nice spread if I must say so myself," the pompous Fredrick Hazard Jr. asserts to his host, "It is amazing the wealth to be gained from war."

"I think we all know the spoils of war, Fredrick," du Pont responds, "But I think you will agree our business is about protecting this country.

It is a business of which I am very proud. The wealth I have gained as well as the rest of you have come as a result of our service to this country."

"Well said Pierre," interjects John Queeny, "I do not believe Fredrick intended any offense. As a relatively new member of this club, I am in pursuit of great wealth while providing a great service. I hope my descendants will be doing this for a long time to come."

"That is precisely why I asked you all to join me today," Pierre reveals, "It is our responsibility, if not duty, to see that the United States does not participate in the Geneva Protocol."

"I cannot believe that Silent Cal decided to speak out on this one. What the hell is he thinking that the United States take part in this international conspiracy to control the chemical industry?" Eugene Meyer proclaims. "I served on Wilson's War Finance Board, and I can tell you that Wilson for all his faults understood the importance of the chemical industry."

"I've been involved in the chemical business longer than any of you, and I can tell you without reservation that Wilson's favoritism shown Allied Chemical during the war allowed for some shady dealings," spouts Fredrick Hazard Jr. "I know, we all made a killing, no pun intended, from the war, but you guys, at Allied Chemical, walked away with the lions share."

"Give it a fucking rest Fredrick! Eugene and I have been involved in national and international leadership positions promoting the best interests of the chemical industry for many years. It only made sense that Wilson would select one of us to help with the war effort. We didn't do anything you would not have done in a similar position. So how about we stay focused on the issue at hand?" William Nichols pronounces with a great deal of anger and frustration in his voice.

Standing before the group, Pierre du Pont attempts to establish civility and return the group to the topic for which he invited them to his estate, "No one can deny the importance and contributions of the Hazard Family, and Fredrick Hazard Jr. to the chemical industry. Without the Hazard Family, we might all be doing something else. On the other hand, Fredrick, your family has been the beneficiary of dealings with many past presidents which has had great financial benefit. So, can we get down to discussing the topic at hand before it threatens to undo us all?"

"We can Pierre, and thank you for recognizing the importance of my family and myself to the world of chemistry," Fredrick says as he stands and bows to the group.

"So, what is it we must do?" asks John Queeny.

"The first thing we must do is tell Silent Cal to shut the fuck up, and return to his position as an obedient lap dog," proclaims William Nichols.

"How do we tell the President of the United States to do that? asks Queeny somewhat perplexed by the idea.

"I will visit the White House and have a come to Jesus with the Coolidge boy," Fredrick says with a chuckle.

"Don't you need to be invited?" Queeny inquires.

"Young man, you need to understand the ways of the world. When you have the money, you have the power. My family contributed a great deal of cash to Mr. Coolidge to help assure his election in '24. Calvin Coolidge owes me, and asking him to shut his trap is only a small favor. I think he will follow suit," Fredrick declares with supreme confidence.

"Good," responds du Pont. "With the President behaving himself, we only need to make certain congress does likewise."

"Look, we have all invested thousands of dollars in the election of U.S. Senators, so it is time we call in the chips," says Meyer.

"What if they don't want to play?" asks Queeny.

"Mr. Queeny, I have no doubt that in time you will be one powerful and ruthless son-of-a-bitch, but for now, you need to listen and learn. When you contribute money to a candidate, they know that you expect something in return. When you tell them what you need and want, they are expected to act in accordance with your wishes. If they do not do so, they need to understand that their time in office is in jeopardy," instructs Fredrick Hazard Jr. "Did you contribute to anyone's campaign who got elected John?"

"I did, I helped several Senatorial candidates across the mid-west," Queeny responds.

"So, you now have a mission," directs Pierre. "You are to contact each one of the Senators whom you helped get elected and tell them they are not to vote for the United States' participation in the Geneva Protocol."

"What is my rationale other than self-interest for telling them this?" inquires Queeny.

"You, tell them that it is not in the best interest of national security to have the chemical industries of the United States bound to some foreign control. You tell them that the United States has far more to lose than to gain from this international agreement. You tell them that it is an issue of national sovereignty," William Nichols proclaims.

"What if they do not agree?" asks Queeny.

"If they do not agree, you look them straight in the eye and say, "With all due respect you bastard, you are nothing more than a pimple on a dead goat's ass, so if you want to continue to be a U.S. Senator, it would be in your best interest to do as I suggest," says Hazard Jr. raising his voice to near shouting level. You then say, "Good day Senator," as you turn and walk out.

"Won't that just piss them off and make them more determined to vote for the Protocol?" Queeny asks with a quizzical look on his face.

"Look, John, we are all going to do just as Fredrick has said. We have done this before, and we will do it again," asserts Pierre. "In most cases, the Senator will come to his senses and vote as we have instructed. Should the Senator not follow our instructions, we make an all-out effort to end his career the next time he comes up for reelection."

"By God, I believe we will make a man out of this boy yet," declares Hazard Jr.

"Politicians, regardless the office, serve at the pleasure of the ruling class which is us. Sometimes there may be a conflict within the ruling class, and we try to negotiate our differences within our own class. When the differences can't be negotiated, the politician may have to make a choice. In these cases, the unwritten rule is to respect the politician's choice. The politician cannot be expected to follow two masters who disagree. We do not want war within our own class. We must all work to protect our wealth and our power," informs William Nichols.

"As for this issue, the Geneva Protocol, there is no conflict within our class. This is an issue that impacts the chemical industry the most, but rest assured, it also impacts the oil industry, steel industry, and high finance in a way that will prompt their actions as well as ours. Furthermore, through the Veterans groups, we will have the poor and middle-class veterans fighting for our cause in the name of national security. In my mind participation of the United States in the Geneva Protocol is dead in the water, but we must not leave things to chance. Therefore, it is time for us to act," declares Pierre du Pont. "Now gentlemen, let's enjoy some drinks, a good cigar, and a fine meal."

With the plan laid out, these five captains of the chemical industry set forth to undermine the Geneva Protocol and assure that the United States be one of the only nations in the world to not be a part of an international agreement putting restrictions on the use of chemical warfare. This theme of U.S. non-participation in international agreements becomes all too common over the next 90 years. When the best interest of the United States is defined as synonymous with the best interest of the wealthy class, the United States often chooses to go it alone.

Labor has never been more forceful than in the fifty years between 1890 and 1940. During the Coolidge Presidency, labor sought to level the playing field by demanding fair wages, better working conditions, shorter hours, and other benefits. Calvin Coolidge remained indifferent to the plight of labor and the growing unrest on wages, working conditions, and safety.

In 1922, with Warren Harding as President, coal miners who endured the worst in wages and working conditions went on strike demanding things change. The Harding Administration's pro-business approach allowed the mining companies to hire strike busters who used strong-arm tactics to intimidate, bully, and harass striking workers. Because the mining company owned the town, workers had to seek refuge outside of town in order to organize. Using their control over all town commerce, the mining company used fear and starvation as tools in bringing striking workers to their knees. All this time, the federal government stood idly by washing its hands of such matters.

President Coolidge who believed in a hands-off approach to business took the exact opposite approach to dealing with labor. Time and time again, Coolidge would dispense federal agents to deal with unruly workers.

From the beginning, Coolidge believed the business of America was business. He believed the government should get out of the way and allow corporations to build prosperity. During the roaring twenties, industrial production increased 40% as did the gold and silver flowing into the coffers of the rich. The Stock Market soared as everyone wanted a piece of the economic pie. Unfortunately, the economic pie was filled with speculation and fake money.

As the poor and middle class fought to get their fair share of prosperity, the Coolidge Administration stood by the wealthy as employers as they imposed yellow dog contracts, barred union membership, staged lockouts, and brought in armed thugs to deal with unruly workers.

Working as a pawn for the privileged class, President Coolidge ushered in an economic recipe for disaster. The rich would get richer and the poor would get poorer while the middle class used the new consumer-based economy to borrow money and speculate to create an economic bubble destined to bust and wreak havoc on the social order of the United States.

A nation is not just a group of people sharing a common geographical area; a nation is a group of people under a government. World history is filled with nations ruled by men who issued decrees to meet their every need. The people of such nations suffered greatly at the hands of greedy, unscrupulous men and women.

The United States was formed to be something different. In the United States, the nation was formed under a set of laws to govern the actions of leaders as well as protect the interest of its people. However, when those elected to govern refuse to use the law to protect the people, a vacuum occurs which enables individuals to act as their own private despot in business, industry, finance, and power. When this occurs, the rule of law gives way to new abuse, profiteering, and corruption.

Such is the environment in 1926 when John Foster Dulles becomes one of four controlling partners at Sullivan and Cromwell the leading international law firm in the world. John Foster Dulles, a conniving fox has already been let into the proverbial henhouse of international politics by President Wilson and his Secretary of State Robert Lansing who is Dulles's uncle. Now, John Foster Dulles has his claws sunk in deep as a legal representative for international giants such as Brown

Brothers, Lazard Freres, Goldman Sachs, First National Bank, and J.P. Morgan. As a purveyor of international financial entanglements, Dulles is in a perfect position to set the stage for Pax Americana. Dulles is not of altruistic motive he comes from a family of opportunists. He has one thing in mind, and that is the promotion of international dominance by American corporations and businesses for personal gain.

Nothing displays John Foster Dulles' penchant for self-gain like the rebuke of William O. Douglas as an employee of Sullivan and Cromwell for his brother Allen. Douglas is a highly capable attorney who believes the United States has a duty to lead by example and forge a world based on fairness and peace. J.F. Dulles does not see things this way and shuns Douglas who would one day become a great jurist on the U.S Supreme Court.

John Foster Dulles believes in manifest destiny, American exceptionalism, and imperialism as key tenets in establishing an American Empire. As an insider, Dulles is determined to do everything and anything possible to advance the power and prestige of American corporations and businesses around the world. Passing up on William O. Douglas allows John Foster Dulles to bring his espionage-loving and womanizing brother into the fold. By adding Allen to the firm's roster, John Foster Dulles strengthens the firm's international position by making espionage a part of the firm's calling card.

Only in a hands-off environment can people of great wealth and power wield such influence. American corporations expanding overseas to play opportunistic games with developing countries and nations with despotic rulers creates entanglements impacting the nature of the United States and the lives of its people. In time, due to economic factors, the well-being of these international corporations will be inseparably linked to national security. In time, the people of the United States will pay through treasure and life for the protection of these huge financial conglomerates.

Chapter 30

HYPOCRISY KNOWS NO BOUNDS

It is hard to imagine that before the people of the United States struggled with the idea of a Catholic President or a Morman President, they embraced the administration of a Quaker President. A review of the Quaker religion reveals a devotion to the common good, an acceptance of all men as they are, and a desire to share the bounty of one for the good of all. In modern days, this notion would lead to such condemnation that any person seeking high office would suffer a character assassination from which there would be no rebound.

Herbert Hoover exists as a Republican anomaly in that he doesn't adhere to a laissez-fair approach to big business. Hoover represents the liberal wing of the party, and while he serves honorably under Harding and Coolidge, he doesn't ascribe to their belief that the interest of big business corresponds with the interest of the nation.

Upon his nomination for president by the Republican Party, Hoover said the following which even to this date are words of wisdom to live by: "In this land, dedicated to tolerance, we still find outbreaks of intolerance. I come of Quaker stock. My ancestors were persecuted for their beliefs. Here they sought and found religious freedom. By blood and conviction, I stand for religious tolerance both in act and in spirit.

The glory of our American ideals is the right of every man to worship God according to his own conscience."

The people know Hoover as a great humanitarian, and he draws his support from labor and the middle class. With Samuel Gompers and Eugene Debs gone, John L. Lewis emerges as the most influential union leader in the country. Lewis knows Hoover and believes him to be a man of courage, integrity, and action. He believes that Hoover will indeed support the cause of working people and fight to break the chains of despotic rule corporations hold over workers. With all this in mind, Lewis throws his support behind Hoover to become President of the United States in 1928.

Meanwhile in Chicago, Jane Addams invited Florence Kelley and Charlotte Perkins Gilman to Hull House for a meeting regarding the presidential election of 1928. Each one of these women is proclaimed a socialist dedicated to improving the lives of the poor, working families, women, and children. Each one works tirelessly to achieve the ratification of the 19th Amendment on August 18, 1920, which gives all women the right to vote.

In the election of 1920, Warren Harding won with 60.3 percent of the popular vote. While the United States enjoyed a prosperous age during the Roaring Twenties, Addams, Kelley, and Gilman are concerned women voted for the handsome Harding rather than consider the issues. As president, Harding failed miserably in addressing issues important to these three social activists. Wanting a president dedicated to improving the lot of all people, these three women meet hoping to avoid the disaster of Harding and Coolidge.

"Come in ladies, let's meet here in the study where we will be left alone," Addams invites her guests. "Have a seat and I shall see if I can round up some tea."

Returning with three cups and a teapot, Addams offers her guests something to drink. "Please take as much sugar as you like," she implores Kelley and Gilman.

As she takes a seat around a small coffee table, Jane Addams begins, "Eight years ago, we brought a long and hard fight to a conclusion with the 19th Amendment. I, like you, thought this would usher in a new day for our nation. After decades of men making the decision regarding the president, I thought the participation of women would ensure better results. Instead, we have suffered the blight of two presidents owing service to the wealthy class. Harding and Coolidge have made our life more difficult, and impeded the pursuit of our cause. Thank God Harding is dead, and Coolidge is heading for the pasture."

"Amen to that sister Addams," chimes in Charlotte Perkins Gilman, "To swallow and follow, whether old doctrine or new propaganda, is a weakness still dominating the human mind. In order to break free from old dominion, we must create a new point of view."

"Oh Charlotte, you are ever so perceptive. I have loved your work and lectures ever since reading "Similar Cases" as a young adult. Now, in my old age having traveled these many miles in search of a better world, I all too well know the reality of people's resistance to change," says Florence Kelley fighting back tears.

"Capitalism is so consuming. The very nature of the system preys on self-indulgence and personal gain. If only we could find among our nation's leaders a champion willing to end capitalism's greed and distinctions between classes while promoting a peaceful, ethical, and truly progressive human race," Gilman invokes.

"How hard it is to break the bonds of the wealthy and their indifference to the plight of the masses? Each one of us has dedicated our lives to the less fortunate. We have fought for children, women, work safety, and fair wages. Yet, in all our effort, we have made but a dent," reminds Addams.

"We must remember what we have accomplished over the past many years by hammering away at the political fabric of this nation. We made one dent and then another until we knocked down the wall of gender oppression. We accomplished the vote, but let that be the first step in our struggle knowing the struggle will be long and hard," implores Gilman.

"I am in full agreement, there can be no pause in the agitation for full political power and responsibility until our voices and influence can neutralize the hold the wealthy have on this country and change the course of public policy for the good of all people," declares Kelley.

"Unless our conception of patriotism is progressive, it cannot hope to embody the real affection and the real interest of the nation, "pronounces Addams. "The good we secure for ourselves is precarious and uncertain until it is secured for all of us and incorporated into our common life."

"Truer words have not been spoken, Jane. Your wisdom is profound but we must have a champion at the top to lead the fight," asserts Gilman.

"In three months, the people of this nation will be asked to choose between Herbert Hoover and Al Smith for president. We must decide with whom we stand if we are going to make a difference," inserts Kelley.

"Unless he is a wolf in sheep's clothing, Herbert Hoover cuts a broader swath than other Republicans. Hoover's humanitarian work has been exemplary. His Quaker roots give reason to believe he will act for the good of all people," proclaims Addams.

"As someone raised in the Quaker religion, I can attest to a religious belief based on humility and humanity. In all his previous activities, Hoover has demonstrated an adherence to his Quaker roots. However, Hoover is himself a rich fat cat. So, what will dictate his decisions as President, his Quaker roots, or his wealth?" questions Kelley.

"The issue is who will dictate to the President? I am greatly concerned by Al Smith's Catholicism. The Catholic religion is highly patriarchic, and I do not want a President under the thumb of Rome," warns Gilman.

"This is very unusual for us sisters. We are progressives, and the Democratic Party is the party of progressivism. Al Smith is the Democratic candidate, and yet we sit here speaking out for Herbert Hoover. My concern with Smith goes back to his 1919 decision to not reduce the cost of milk in New York which led to starving children. How can a man like this be trusted to act on behalf of ordinary people?" shares Addams.

"Smith has baggage," warns Gilman. "While there is no proof of corruption, he is too closely aligned with the Tammany Hall machine. So often where there is smoke, there is fire. I do not feel he can be trusted with a progressive agenda."

"How ironic, after eight years of Republicans Harding and Coolidge, we find ourselves favoring Republican Hoover for President. I sure hope he will not disappoint us by continuing along the lines of his predecessors," Kelley concludes while shaking her head in disbelief.

"Thank you for joining me today sisters. I know our support can help Herbert Hoover," Jane Addams notes rising from her chair indicating an end to the meeting. "I must now return to the responsibilities of trying to help one person at a time."

In the campaign of 1928, Herbert Hoover offered a humble leadership aimed at uplifting all people in a nation where all things are possible. He seems like the ideal candidate, the ideal person to lead a nation devoted to liberty and justice for all. In November, 1928, the people of the United States elect Herbert Hoover, a Quaker and humanist to the presidency of the United States.

We all know what it is like to unwittingly inherit the curse of someone else even if it is of a minor degree. As for Herbert Hoover, he is about to inherit the curse brought about by the unrestricted greed of America's leading class. Incubated in the heyday of the Industrial Revolution and nurtured by an unrestricted financial system, the bubble of American wealth has outgrown its elasticity.

Adding to the greed of the American Aristocracy can be found the unbridled commercialism of the rising middle class. During the Roaring Twenties, money (real and phantom) become available to working-class people for the purpose of improving the quality of their lives. People are rushing to take advantage of modern marvels and being able to purchase these things on credit. Banks are overextending their capacity to remain solvent by making credit available to people who over-extend their personal capacity to pay. With no restraints on this abusive financial practice, the bubble grows to dangerous proportions. If anyone notices, no one seems concerned.

At the turn of the century, President Roosevelt and Taft saw the dangers of unrestricted wealth and acted to bring it into balance with the best interest of the nation. Wilson too emerged as a champion for the common man, but war and international glory brought about his demise. As for Harding and Coolidge, these two men as well as the Republican Party had no desire to challenge the power of the wealthy. In fact, they adopted a philosophy based on the idea that the wealthy are the gateway to prosperity for all. So, for eight tumultuous years, the wealthy enjoyed a free-for-all in which they preyed upon those of lesser means through gimmicks of consumerism, phantom investments, and market manipulation only to line their own pockets.

So, when the bubble bursts, it is not the industrialists or the financiers who suffer. It is those who bought things on time, but now can't pay. It is those who invested but find their investments worthless that suffer the loss. Small businesses operating off of credit fold as consumers can't honor their debt. Farmers who managed from one year to the next on credit can't pay their debts upon notice and therefore over 400,000 farmers lose their farms. Individuals with investments find their investments worthless, and those with money in banks receive nothing because their bank doesn't have the cash.

The phony economy that grew out of the do-nothing management of the Harding and Coolidge Administrations lands squarely in the lap of the new president, Herbert Hoover. Hoover, a man who has rescued Europe from the devastation of the First World War is caught off guard by the onset of the Great Depression. Hoover the engineering genius, feels helpless as the do-nothing approach of his predecessors buries him in an economic disaster of unequaled proportions. Hoover, the humanitarian flounders to find his humanity during a time of his nation's greatest peril.

Great Depression mythology suggests that the Great Depression hit the wealthy the hardest. This is depression mythology. In most cases the wealthy were well insulated from the devastation of the Great Depression. No one from Wall Street jumped out windows or committed suicide. This impression only dilutes the reality of this great economic disaster. The Great Depression hit the consumers hardest who were lured into believing they too could have it all. The middle class disappeared as unemployment and destitution left people grasping for hope that someone would come to their rescue.

For all the promise Herbert Hoover represents it doesn't manifest itself in action or results. In actuality, Hoover believes government should not meddle in business. He believes that business will take the appropriate action to correct existing problems and restore the economy. So, he sits, and he waits, and he waits, while millions of people across the nation are homeless and struggle just to feed and clothe their families.

With each passing day, week, month, and year, the Great Depression eats away at the fabric of the United States. Shantytowns (called Hoovervilles) made of cardboard spring up across the country. Soup kitchens provide some sustenance to long lines of men, women, and children. But the worst of it involves the loss of hope and the fear that no one cares.

In the upper echelons of society, you cannot tell anything is wrong. The wealthy go about their business of counting money and making it safe and secure. They are not threatened because they don't suffer. They simply close plants or downsize employees to address any issue of increased expenses or reduced revenue. By taking such action, they can maintain a healthy profit margin. No one begrudges a profit margin. Profits are important to the success of a business. However, with millions of men, women, and children suffering from the depression, the wealthy did not do their part to alleviate the suffering.

As the Great Depression settled in like a dark cloud over the nation, the mood of the common people changed. People began to question the viability of democracy and capitalism. It was one thing for a political and economic system to give way to such a fall, but it was another thing for the government to sit back and allow it to persist.

Desperate people in desperate times will turn to whatever hope they might find in any corner of a dark room. People became angry and impatient while Hoover went camping and fishing with his high society friends. Hoover the humanitarian, the genius, the savior of Europe, is Hoover the inept, the indifferent, a president incapable or unwilling to restore a broken nation.

As Hoover's first and only term as president progressed, people become increasingly despondent and disenchanted with their country. Across the nation, socialism and communism which recently took root in Eastern Europe under the Marxist philosophy begins to find fertile ground in the United States. The people who nurtured a new system of government created but one hundred and forty years earlier are having second thoughts about their democratic system of government. Millions of people would welcome a despot if such leadership could bring an end to their misery.

Despite all this, Hoover does nothing. Thousands of people marched on Washington demanding action, and Hoover did nothing. Veterans denied their benefits for service to the nation march on Washington only to be met by the United States Army in which they had served.

Army General Douglas McArthur meets the marching veterans and turns them away as if they are some invading army.

If any charismatic leader arrives on the scene determined to overthrow the existing government, the time and conditions are right to mobilize a disheartened people. It is by the grace of God and the looming hope provided by a presidential election that such a thing doesn't occur.

As Hoover's term nears a close, he finally recognizes that business will not right the economy on its own. He begins to acknowledge the severity of the depression and the calamities which loom ahead should nothing be done. Facing a disgraceful defeat for re-election, Hoover reaches out to his Democratic opponent Franklin Roosevelt asking him to depoliticize the depression, and join with Hoover in supporting a number of executive moves aimed at providing relief and preventing future deterioration of the economic system. Roosevelt, knowing Hoover has the authority but lacks the political and moral will to act on his own refuses to join Hoover in any collaboration which might return Hoover to office.

Chapter 31

MEET THE NEW BOSS

Many of the things Hoover requests are ideas Roosevelt plans to do himself once in office. The dilemma involves the sentencing of millions of people to continued desperation until after the election and the inauguration of a new president. It shall always be debatable whether Roosevelt's refusal of Hoover's request is self-serving, or visionary in understanding the short-term sacrifice which must be made to ensure the long-term gains.

What is visible is the miraculous rescue of a nation on the brink! Since the end of the Civil War and the full onslaught of the Industrial Revolution, the wealthy and the ruling class had been one and the same. Despite the Herculean efforts of Teddy Roosevelt and William Howard Taft, the Robber Barons, the Wolves of Wall Street, the industrial and financial giants ruled the day. Democracy was successfully turned into a plutocracy through the conspiring and conniving of those who controlled the reins of production.

Greed is an all-consuming and eventually destructive thing. There is no satisfaction for those who seek to possess and control it all. Using every lever at their disposal, the ruling class takes advantage of war with no concern for loyalty, life, or limb, but only profit. They use their money, position, and power to manipulate markets at the expense of consumers, who are their fellow countrymen. They buy politicians and corrupt elections to secure the favor of those who live in the halls of power. By the time Herbert Hoover becomes president, the wealthy, and the ruling class laid the foundation for the greatest economic disaster in the nation's history. In many ways, Hoover is a victim. And yet, there is no excuse for his lack of leadership during this most perilous time.

During the first part of the 20th Century, the United States emerged as a world power. The industrial revolution along with an enviable Navy accelerated the spreading of U.S. influence and power. The great industrialists could not operate their growing enterprises and continue to amass their dominant wealth without access to much-needed resources found in third world nations. Through the idea of Pax American, American Exceptionalism, opportunistic, and outright imperialistic practices, the world economy slowly became inseparably linked to the United States. So, when the Great Depression hit the United States, it is no surprise depression struck a heavy blow around the world.

It was the industrialists and financiers who invested heavily in the Allies during World War I. It was the industrialists and financiers who insisted that Germany bear the brunt of reparations following the war. So, when depression struck Germany, it is no wonder that the German people looked for a leader to pull them from the abyss. Not so much unlike the United States, the German people found a leader who they were ready to follow without question. This fact has profound consequences for the years to come and inexplicably impacts the direction of world history.

It is the industrialists and financiers bankrolling United States Senators, who defeat the membership of the United States in the League of Nations. Without the United States, the League is a three-legged stool with one leg missing. It is only a matter of time before this international organization gives way to world turmoil.

In the United States, the people are about to elect a president who hails from the wealthy ruling class but possesses the wisdom of a truly compassionate and democratic leader. On November 8, 1932, Franklin Delano Roosevelt defeats Herbert Hoover in a landslide victory. With a nearly 18% popular vote margin and 472 electoral votes, Roosevelt's mandate is clear. Furthermore, both chambers of the United States Congress turned Democratic.

On Saturday, March 4, 1933, Roosevelt delivered his Inaugural speech. The opening to his speech speaks directly to the American people, "So, first of all, let me assert my firm belief that the only thing we have to fear is. . . fear itself – nameless, unreasoning, unjustified terror which paralyzes needed effort to convert retreat into advance. In every dark hour of our national life, a leadership of frankness and of vigor has met with that understanding and support of the people themselves which is essential to victory. And I am convinced that you will again give that support to leadership in these critical days."

Roosevelt used his speech to outline his plan, the New Deal aimed at healing the wounds of the Great Depression. He is determined to put people to work. He is determined to help American farmers. Before real action can occur, 400,000 farmers are forced off their land. He is determined to protect the people from the financial abuses that led to the Great Depression.

In the last element of his plan, Roosevelt recognizes the evils of his own social class. In his speech, he says, "Finally, in our progress toward a resumption of work we require two safeguards against a return to the evils of the old order: there must be a strict supervision of all banking and credits and investments so that there will be an end to speculation with other people's money, and there must be provision for an adequate but sound currency."

Franklin Roosevelt was immediately deemed a traitor to the wealthy and ruling class. He cannot be bought, and his wife also a patrician is as strong-willed as he is and a steady influence on the rudder of the state.

As the Roosevelt era begins, it looks as if the stranglehold the wealthy have on ruling the United States is truly coming to an end. There is good reason to believe that Franklin D. Roosevelt can take this nation in an entirely different direction if he chooses to do so. The people, so desperate for a strong and decisive leader would consider a Roosevelt dictatorship if it means a return to prosperity. There is little doubt such a move on Roosevelt's part would be met with strong opposition, but as President of the United States, he has the cards of power and public opinion in his favor. Roosevelt could move this country toward a truly socialistic economic system if he so desires. His power and influence combined with public opinion could make this so.

The miraculous news is that Franklin D. Roosevelt, a man of great intelligence who has faced and overcome great personal adversity chose to save the nation of Washington, Adams, and Jefferson rather than create something in his own image. In most cases, Roosevelt honors the democratic restraints put upon the executive branch of the government. He does what he feels is necessary for the time and situation he faces, but he does so by recognizing the constitutional checks and balance system which exists to keep one branch of the government from becoming too powerful. Roosevelt possesses the wisdom to see that the people need relief from the Great Depression and that the government must play an active role in seeking and providing that relief. His programs and initiatives move a truly capitalistic system in a socialistic direction without capitulating to the tenets of socialism. For the better part of the Roosevelt era, F.D.R. makes the titans of industry and finance take a back seat to the interests of the American people. His presidency is truly a profile of courage and an illustration of great leadership.

The lessons of the first four decades of the 20th Century teach the American people and those involved in good government that restraints are necessary to ensure business serves the people and the nation, and not vice versa. What time reveals is that restraints are not enough in a system prone to manipulation. One safeguard becomes just another obstacle to overcome in the quest for economic domination.

What never seems to be learned is if you allow the fox into the hen house, the results will not be good. Time and time again, the American people and their elected officials allow those with ulterior motives to gain access to the citadel of power and influence. Time and time again, the people of the United States are victimized, and the entire notion of democracy is undermined.

Power corrupts, and total power corrupts totally. In our capitalistic society, money is power. We see this throughout our history, but it becomes prevalent during the 20th century. It is important to learn the lessons of history in an effort to prevent reoccurring problems. If you fool me once, shame on you, but if you fool me twice, shame on me. The American people have not learned the lesson of allowing the wealthy class to become the ruling class. Some will say the accumulation of great wealth is part of the American dream available to all. History doesn't support such a notion. The number of people with great wealth compared to the number of people struggling to live from day to day suggests the direct opposite.

Throughout history, those in power have oppressed those out of power. In the old world, men ruled. In the beginning, the United States became a nation of laws, not men, to undo this historical trend. While the history of the United States supports the idea that freedom and liberty are expanding entities due to increased enfranchisement over the years, this same notion does not apply to social and economic enfranchisement.

The prevailing economic rule is that those who control wealth strive to increase their holdings while keeping in their place those of limited means. This predatory approach when unchecked leads to an economic environment that leads to disasters such as the Great Depression.

But the worst is the subjugation of people to the economic whims of the upper class. Whether the subjugation is overt or covert, it is the essence of the great heist. Deep inside such a system, corruption emanates from predatory capitalism. Freedom does not exist where the subjugation of any type is allowed to prevail. This is the great struggle for democracy in pursuit of life, liberty, and justice for all.

increase in the number of people struggling to live from day to day suggests the direct opposite.

Throughout history, those in power have oppressed those out of power. In the old world, monarchs ruled. In the beginning, the United States became a nation of laws, not men, to avoid this historical trend. While the history of the United States supports the idea that freedom and liberty are expanding entities due to increased enfranchisement over the years, this same tradition does not apply to social and economic enfranchisement.

The prevailing economic rule is that those in control will always strive to increase their position while keeping in their place those of limited means. This [illegible] position, which [illegible] leads to an economic environment that leads to disasters such as the Great Depression [illegible]

[illegible] the world [illegible] the subjugation of people to the economic whims of the upper class. Whether the subjugation is overt or covert, it is the essence [illegible]. Decadence and systemic corruption [illegible] freedom [illegible] does not exist where the subjugation [illegible] allowed to flourish. This is the great struggle for democracy [illegible] life, liberty [illegible] for all.

ABOUT THE AUTHOR

The author of this book has loved history since his days as a junior high student at Peterson Community School in Peterson, Iowa. In 1975, Bill graduated from Buena Vista College with a B.A. Degree including a minor in history and political science. From 1975 to 1977, He was an educator and coach at the American School in Tehran, Iran. After returning to the United States, Bill taught high school history, government, economics, sociology, and psychology until 1982. From 1982 to 1983, He earned 27 credits toward an M.A. Degree in history from Northeast Missouri State University. Bill possesses an M.A. Degree in Educational Administration from the University of Northern Iowa, and a Specialist Degree in Educational Administration from Drake University. After 35 years in education, Bill spent eighteen months campaigning as the Democratic candidate for the United States House of Representatives from Iowa's 4th Congressional District.

The author has written extensively about education for local publications. In 2020, Bill published his first novel entitled "*2039*". The book "*2039*" as well as "*The Great Heist*" are available through Amazon, Barnes and Noble, Target, and a full range of book outlets. "*2039*" and "*The Great Heist*" are also available as eBooks.

ABOUT THE ART

The cover art for "The Great Heist – Democracy's Corrupt Underbelly" is brilliantly created to exemplify the evil that emanated from the Industrial Revolution and the rise of the American Aristocracy. Grounded in a relentless pillaging of natural resources, and the perverse abuse of labor, the Robber Barons amassed a wealth that allowed them to control the course of a nation. The cover art depicts a nation in distress with an upside-down flag. The smoke stacks soil the capital as the use of money soils the democratic process. The sinister nature of the Robber Barons exacts the lifeblood of those with little means to power their use of graft for personal gain. The art screams out there is something rotten in the United States. The evil nature of predatory capitalism is consuming the potential greatness of a nation at the expense of its people.

ABOUT THE ARTIST

Justin Pritchard spent his youth in the beautiful rolling hills of northeast Iowa. Following graduation from Valley High School in Clermont, Elgin, and Wadena, Iowa, Justin pursued a degree in art at Iowa Central Community College in Fort Dodge. Justin earned an associate's degree in art.

Justin has always been a creative soul. For Justin, art is a passion. With a flair for abstract art, Justin created his first album cover for Brutal Republic, a rock group out of Fort Dodge, Iowa. Justin formed the company Abstract Entity Art as a means of promoting his art career. In 2021, Justin did the cover for the novel *2039* by Bill Maske.

He creates a style that speaks to the intellectuals and fits between rock and rollers, country, hip-hop, bluesy, young or old. Other works of Abstract Entity Art by Justin Pritchard can be viewed via Facebook at Facebook.com/JamosMolokai